TO THE ARCTIC BY CANOE
1819-1821

To the Arctic by Canoe 1819-1821

The Journal and Paintings of
Robert Hood
Midshipman with Franklin

Edited by
C. STUART HOUSTON

THE ARCTIC INSTITUTE OF NORTH AMERICA
McGILL-QUEEN'S UNIVERSITY PRESS
MONTREAL AND LONDON   1974

© McGill-Queen's University Press 1974
International Standard Book Number 0 7735 0192 4
Library of Congress Catalog Card Number 74 77504
Legal Deposit third quarter 1974
Bibliothèque nationale du Québec

Design by Anthony Crouch
Composition in Trump Medieval by Mono Lino Typesetting Co. Ltd.
Printed in Canada by Bryant Press Ltd.
Illustrations between pages 188 and 189 printed by Herzig Somerville Ltd.
Paper: Suede Coated Book

Contents

Illustrations

Maps

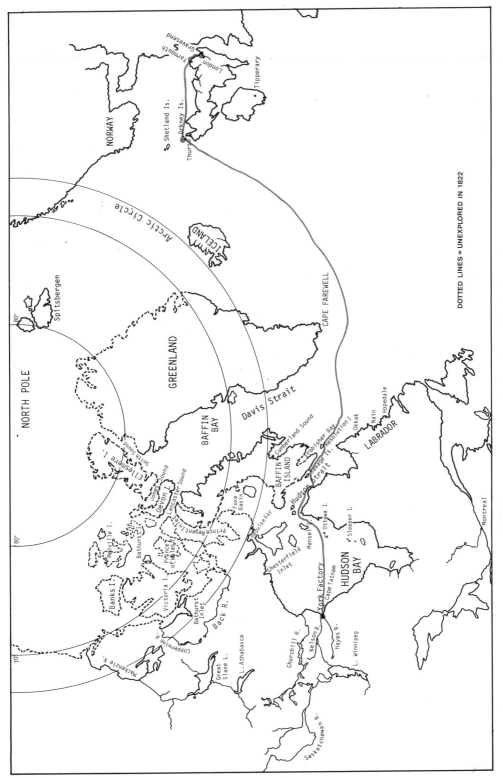

The Atlantic Ocean and Northern North America

DOTTED LINES = UNEXPLORED IN 1822

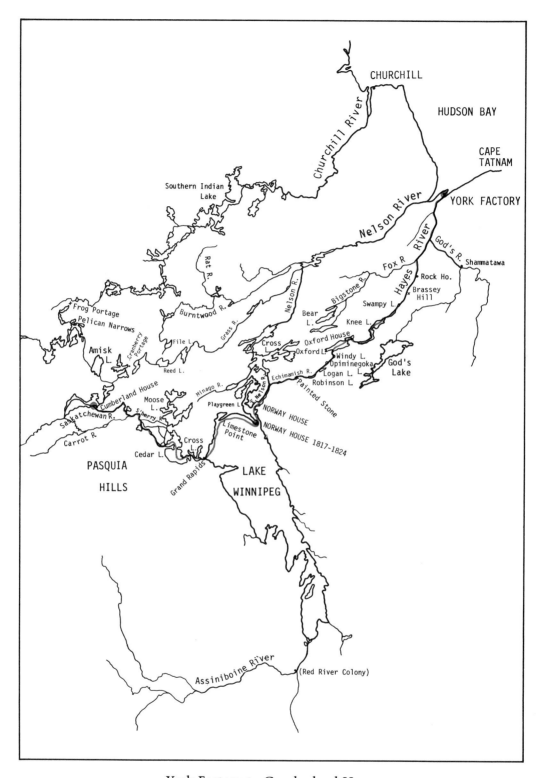

York Factory to Cumberland House

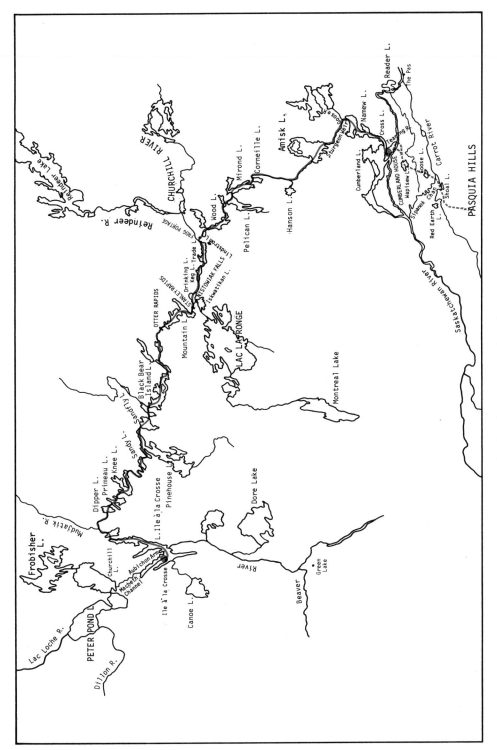

Cumberland House to Ile-à-la-Crosse

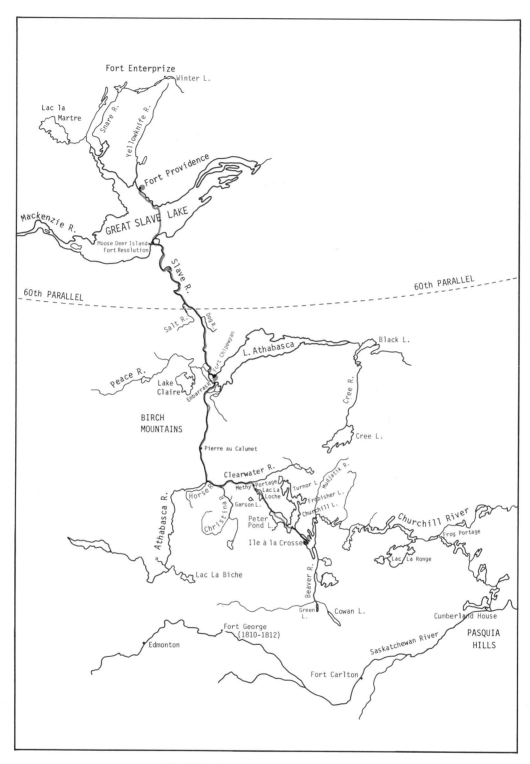

Ile-à-la-Crosse to Fort Enterprize

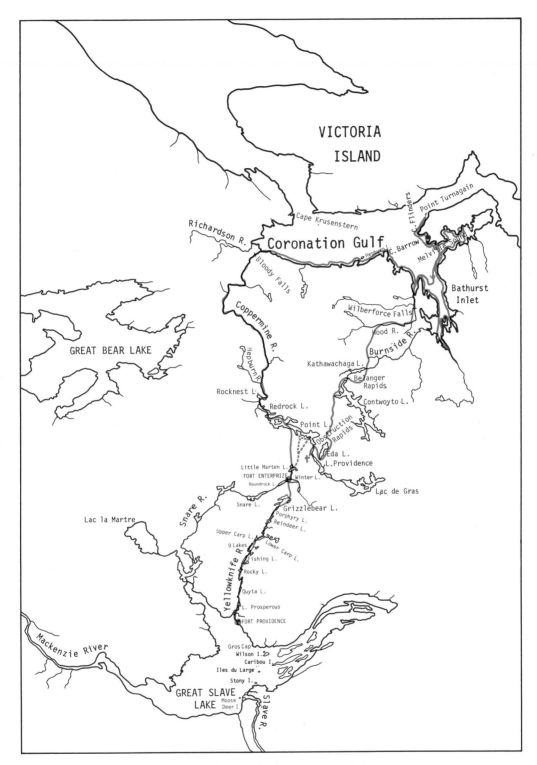

Great Slave Lake to Bathurst Inlet

Foreword

A REVIVAL OF GEOGRAPHICAL EXPLORATION FOLLOWED THE CESSATION
of the Napoleonic wars in the early nineteenth century, when there
were still some large unmapped regions in Africa and the Arctic,
both lands of extreme though opposite climates. The stories of the
many discoveries during that time are more often than not those of
Great Britain and its distant colonial lands. The fruits of this
second blooming of discovery were to be gathered not only by
geography, but by the sciences, literature, and the arts as well.

Samuel Hearne, in July 1771, was the first European to descend to the mouth of the Coppermine River and thus to reach the
Arctic Ocean after having travelled with his Indian companions
through Rupert's Land. Alexander Mackenzie travelled to that
same ocean in 1789, down the river now named after him. Both had
well-defined commercial objectives for their exploits—they were
looking for metal and fur. More complex motives are behind the
travel through the Barren Lands by five British seafarers, the next
to reach the Arctic Ocean by an overland route.

The defeat of the French and Spanish fleets at Trafalgar in
1805, that most glorious action of the British navy, choked Napoleon's power on the sea, and the battle of Waterloo in 1815 completely removed any threat to Britain from a hostile France. Yet for
some mariners of England there was to be no retirement. John
Barrow, the powerful Secretary to the Admiralty, appears to have
been the right man in the right place at the right time. His plans,
drawn up in 1818, to renew the search for a Northwest Passage
received strong backing from the scientific community, a group
that before the nineteenth century had exerted little influence on
the policies of state. The early 1800s had seen the rapid ascent of
the natural sciences, and Barrow foresightedly enlisted the support
of the Royal Society to help him in organizing a series of scientific
expeditions.

The quest for the Northwest Passage in Barrow's time thus
became much more than a search for a cheaper route to the riches
of the Orient. It became a means to perpetuate the pride of a nation
in its navy, an outlet for the energies of its naturalists, and, for
some, a personal obsession. Because of these multiple human

facets of glory, curiosity, and folly, the narratives of arctic explorers fascinated the Victorians. That they still interest readers today is witnessed by the recent spate of reprints and of newly written books on nineteenth-century explorations.

Midshipman Robert Hood's account of the first Franklin expedition, that journey by five British sailors in canoes manned by French Canadians and half-breeds, was used extensively by Franklin when he wrote the *Narrative of a Journey to the Shores of the Polar Sea, 1819-22,* but it has never before been published in its entirety and in its original form.

Dr. C. Stuart Houston's profession and interests closely parallel those of Sir John Richardson, the surgeon and naturalist to the Franklin expeditions. Dr. Houston's medical studies demonstrated the relation of the practice of swaddling infants to the high incidence of congenital hip disease among Saskatchewan Indians; his bird studies led to a book centred around Richardson's ornithological contributions.

Robert Hood's narrative is a well-written, fascinating epic of true adventure 150 years ago. Produced in the far north under hardships difficult to imagine today, it is full of careful observations in natural history and ethnology. It is also a warmly human document revealing a sensitive person with an innate concern for his fellow man. It is not difficult to see why Hood was respected as a competent and trustworthy observer, esteemed as an artist, and loved by his companions. John Franklin expressed his and others' feelings when, upon hearing of Hood's death, he felt sorrow for the death of a friend blessed with 'excellent qualities of . . . heart'.

Director,   W. O. KUPSCH,
Institute for Northern Studies,
University of Saskatchewan.

Preface

SPRING IS THE MOST APPEALING SEASON ON THE CANADIAN PRAIRIES, AS the pulse of resurgent life marks the release from the long, cold winter. One of the first signs of spring is the emergence of the gophers or ground squirrels: Richardson's, Franklin's, and Hood's, each named for an officer of the first Franklin Arctic Exploring Expedition of 1819-22. And while the first flower to bloom on the warmed hilltops as the melting snow recedes is the crocus anemone, it is soon followed by a profusion of beautiful little white flowers, named *Phlox hoodii*, in honour of Robert Hood.

Each spring, then, one is naturally reminded of the officers of the Franklin expeditions who, en route to the Arctic, visited Cumberland House and Fort Carlton in the 1820s. Of the four capable and talented officers on the first expedition searching for the coveted Northwest Passage, Hood alone failed to return. It is evident that, like his three officer companions, all of whom achieved fame and knighthood, Robert Hood was a man of accomplishment and of great promise.

His journal and paintings, now published for the first time, ensure his place in the company of famous men who opened the Canadian North. It is tragic that he perished so early in his career.

C. STUART HOUSTON, M.D.

Acknowledgements

THIS BOOK IS A REALITY ONLY BECAUSE OF THE UNSTINTING HELP GIVEN by a great many people. The first acknowledgement must be to Mr. and Mrs. Richard Garnett Birch of Surrey, B.C., for the extended loan and use of Hood's original journal and many of the paintings. Mr. Birch's cousin, Mrs. Eileen Adkins of Seattle, Washington, kindly loaned two waterfowl habitat paintings, and his nephew, Rev. Arthur Birch of Saskatoon and his niece, Mrs. Miriam Thompson of Nanaimo, B.C., kindly loaned a number of the paintings. Six paintings from the Manoir Richelieu Collection are reproduced by permission of the Public Archives of Canada.

Douglas H. Bocking of the Saskatchewan Archives kindly provided a tape recorder to allow transcription and his secretary typed the first two drafts of Hood's journal. Dr. Walter O. Kupsch, Director of the Saskatchewan Institute for Northern Studies, offered criticism of the introduction and footnotes and kindly provided the foreword.

Those who read the entire manuscript at some stage and provided valuable suggestions and corrections were, in addition to Douglas H. Bocking and Walter O. Kupsch, the following: Margaret Belcher, Department of Modern Languages, Regina Campus, University of Saskatchewan; Dr. Balfour W. Currie, Vice-President (Research), University of Saskatchewan; Dr. Clarence J. Houston, my father; Dr. Leslie H. Neatby, retired Professor of Classics, historian, and author; Dr. Stanley D. Riome, optometrist and member of the Historical Trails Canoe Club; J. Frank Roy, English Department, City Park Collegiate, Saskatoon.

Particular recognition is due Dr. Balfour W. Currie, who provided the footnotes on aurora, magnetism, and climatology. A former Head, Department of Physics and former Dean, College of

ACKNOWLEDGEMENTS

Graduate Studies, University of Saskatchewan, he was physicist with the Second International Polar Year at Chesterfield Inlet in 1932-33 and has published about fifty papers on auroral and ionospheric phenomena.

Other special assistance was provided by John Black, whose studies of auroral phenomena gained him a Ph.D. degree, and Robert Gallernault, an L.I.P. grant researcher specializing in Saulteaux and Cree language and local history, Indian and Northern Curriculum Resources Center, University of Saskatchewan. Loren Teed, artist, teacher, and cartographer, prepared the maps.

Additional assistance was provided by many others, including M. Bell, Orest Buchko, Edward Dawson, Hans S. Dommasch, J. B. Gollop, John Hudson, J. Klaponski, J. Lockyer, Rev. B. Mathieu, O.M.I., Robert Olson, Dale Perry, J. G. Rempel, Betty Strutt, D. W. A. Whitfield, R. Williamson and Gary A. Wobeser. Gollop and Whitfield both read portions of the manuscript.

Mrs. Jean Friesen and Mrs. Joan Matlock patiently typed and retyped the manuscript. My wife, Mary, prepared the index and helped in innumerable ways. Stan and Marg offered constructive criticism, and Dave and Don were skilled and patient proofreaders.

Brigadier H. W. Love, Executive Director of the Arctic Institute of North America and Robin H. Strachan, Director, Beverly Johnston, Executive Editor, Margery Simpson, Senior Manuscript Editor, Anthony Crouch, Production Manager, and three anonymous readers at McGill-Queen's University Press, all deserve my sincere appreciation for their helpful criticism and encouragement.

This work has been published with the help of a grant from the Humanities Research Council of Canada using funds provided by the Canada Council and a grant from the Principal's Publication Fund, University of Saskatchewan, Saskatoon.

C. STUART HOUSTON, M.D.

Previous Use of Portions
of Hood's Journal

Considerable portions of Hood's journal were published in John Franklin's *A Journey to the Shores of the Polar Sea in the Years 1819, 1820, 1821 and 1822*. In his fourth chapter, Franklin used the account of Indian snowshoes from Hood's chapter 3. Franklin's fifth chapter is entirely derived from Hood's journal. It reproduces the remainder of Hood's chapter 3, omitting only thirty-eight paragraphs and some scattered sentences, and concludes with the first thirty-nine paragraphs of Hood's chapter 6, which describe the journey from Cumberland House to rejoin the others at Fort Chipewyan. Elsewhere in his account, particularly in his sixth chapter, Franklin used many of Hood's sentences verbatim. In the Appendix to Franklin's *Journey*, Hood's detailed notes on the aurora borealis and magnetic needle at Cumberland House occupy a seven-page section. Their date of 11 June 1820 indicates that copies of these portions were left behind at Cumberland House for transmission to England, when Hood and Richardson left for Fort Chipewyan on 13 June. As well as making use of these portions of Hood's journal, the Appendix contains other material supplied by Hood. A sixteen-page section on the aurora borealis at Fort Enterprize, ten pages of daily magnetic needle observations from 12 January to 9 May 1821, and a page of celestial observations made on 28 December 1820 and 1 and 15 January 1821 were all notes made by Hood and transmitted to England before the expedition left for the Arctic. He apparently did not have time to transcribe these into his formal journal.

Much of Hood's chapters 4 and 5 was printed in the Winter 1967 issue of the *Alberta Historical Review* (15: 6-17). The transcription was evidently from the microfilm copy made by the Glenbow Foundation and contains a few errors. Hood's observations on canoe-building were quoted in full by Judge F. W. Howay in an article, 'Building the Big Canoes', in *Beaver* (270: 38, 42).

ROBERT HOOD

Introduction

ROBERT HOOD, THE SECOND SON OF THE REVEREND RICHARD HOOD, LL.D., was born in 1797. He was educated in the town of Bury, Lancashire, eight miles north of Manchester.

At fourteen, Hood became a midshipman, the first step in the training of a naval officer. One of his duties on ship was to keep a log; two of these books are still in the possession of his family. The first records his service from 28 August 1811 to 23 August 1812 on the famed frigate, *H.M.S. Imperieuse*, then under command of Captain Henry Duncan, and the second, spanning the period from 7 October 1815 to 12 October 1816, is the log of *H.M.S. Spey*, under Captain John Lake.

It is probable that his education was continued on board ship and that he and his fellow midshipmen waited on the chaplain each morning for instruction in Latin, Euclid, navigation, and French, as did Edward Parry twelve years earlier.[1]

Perhaps the enormous reduction in naval establishment after the French wars left him unemployed, as we have no record of his naval service in 1817 and 1818. In 1819, he and George Back were chosen as the two midshipmen to accompany the overland arctic exploring expedition led by Sir John Franklin.

Franklin's first expedition sailed from Gravesend on 23 May 1819, following Ross's 1818 expedition in a determined resumption of Britain's search for the Northwest Passage. At that time, the northern coast of the North American continent was completely unknown, except at two restricted loca-

1. Ann Parry, *Parry of the Arctic* (London: Chatto & Windus, 1963), p. 15.

tions: the mouth of the Coppermine River, visited by Hearne on 17 July 1771, and the delta of the Mackenzie River, reached by Mackenzie on 12 July 1789.

Franklin's party was instructed to explore by land the northern shores of the continent, east from the mouth of the Coppermine, while at the same time Captain Edward Parry was to attempt the passage from the east by sea. They were instructed to keep exact records of latitude, longitude, magnetic variation, and weather at each locality, and to make observations of the aurora borealis, minerals, and all aspects of natural history.

At the start of the expedition, John Franklin was 33 years of age, Dr. John Richardson was 31, the midshipmen, George Back and Robert Hood, were both 22, and the seaman, John Hepburn, was 30.

The expedition got off to a bad start and continued to be plagued by many difficulties. Franklin had been told it would be easy to hire additional men when they stopped at the Orkney Islands, but a sudden increase in the herring fishery that year had provided employment nearer home for 1,200 men, and he was able to hire only four of the ten men required. The voyage was unusually long and arduous, and when the party arrived at York Factory, the Hudson's Bay Company headquarters, they could hire only one additional man. None of these five men was willing later to accompany the expedition beyond Lake Athabasca.

Bad luck seemed to dog the expedition at every turn. Many of their misfortunes were due simply to the escalating conflict between the Hudson's Bay Company and its rival in the fur trade, the Montreal-based North West Company. This situation is therefore worthy of some comment. The British Northwest was then nearing the climax of what A. S. Morton has termed its period of 'Violence, 1804-1821',[2] a period that began with the formation of a larger and stronger North West Company by the incorporation of Alexander Mackenzie's XY Company.

There was a marked difference in the administrative organization of the two rival companies and between the men employed by them. The Hudson's Bay Company had a somewhat rigid hierarchy and most of their employees were English-speaking, Protestant Orkneymen, cautious and pru-

2. Arthur S. Morton, *Sir George Simpson, Overseas Governor of the Hudson's Bay Company* (Toronto: J. M. Dent, 1944), pp. 19-32.

dent, and more at home keeping books than paddling canoes. These men were pitted against the reckless, venturesome, largely unschooled, Catholic, French-speaking voyageurs, under direction of a loose and changing association of Highland Scottish business partners.

In this far-flung, sparsely settled, and essentially lawless land, the rival companies had built their establishments side by side. At first they seemed to get along better than might have been anticipated. Yet the North West men at times were capable of violence, and did what they could to divert the Indians from the Hudson's Bay Company. In 1809, for example, they drove Peter Fidler from his established post at Ile-à-la-Crosse and then burned it to the ground.[3] The Orkneymen were jealous of the North West Company's monopoly of the rich Athabasca area and the Canadians in turn envied the Hudson's Bay Company's shorter, cheaper route for transporting goods.

It is seldom appreciated that the Hudson's Bay Company did a considerably smaller business than the North West Company. In 1795, the Hudson's Bay Company had an estimated two-fourteenths of the trade while the North West Company had eleven-fourteenths; in 1814 the ratio of fur value was £15,000 to £48,000 and in 1816, £8,000 to £29,000.[4] It is not surprising then that the North West Company, the larger of the two, was able to give more assistance to the Franklin expedition than was the Hudson's Bay Company, particularly at Ile-à-la-Crosse and beyond. Unfortunately, the conflict between the two companies reduced the capacity of either to give the help so desperately required.

Hood recorded his dismay at the extreme rivalry between the two fur companies: 'It may injure its opponent, though it cannot benefit itself, which is the first object of all other commercial bodies, but the second of the fur traders.'

When Lord Selkirk in 1811 received 116,000 square miles for a settlement in the Red River valley, his benevolent attempt to aid starving, dispossessed people in Scotland was viewed by the North West Company traders as a serious potential threat to the fur trade. They saw in the settlers a possible restriction of their freedom, and they were particularly antagonistic to Selkirk because he was a major shareholder in the Hudson's Bay Company.

To use Hood's words, the Northwesters did their best to

3. Earl of Selkirk. *A Sketch of the British Fur Trade in North America with Observations relative to the North-West Company of Montreal.* (London: J. Ridgway, 1816), pp. 73-75.

4. E. E. Rich, *The History of the Hudson's Bay Company 1670-1870.* (London: Hudson's Bay Record Society, 1959), II, 186 and 267.

'blast in the germ' the young Red River colony, as exemplified by the 'massacre of Seven Oaks' in 1816. In turn, Selkirk imported soldier-settlers from the de Meuron regiment. They made possible the seizure of the North West Company officers at Grand Rapids in 1819, including J. G. McTavish, who was visited by Franklin and his officers while he was in detention at York Factory awaiting passage to England for trial. In retaliation, the North West men lay in wait at the same place in 1820 to capture the Hudson's Bay officers.

Meanwhile, in 1815, the Hudson's Bay Company had begun a somewhat belated attempt to enter the rich Athabasca and Peace River regions. This venture, however, was marked by many reverses, largely due to deliberate obstruction by their rivals. Despite the charter of 1670, granting the Hudson's Bay Company exclusive trading rights to those lands draining into Hudson Bay, their territory was encroached on freely by the North West Company; the latter company considered the Athabasca area, over the height of land and in the arctic watershed, to be their own private preserve and resented the Hudson's Bay Company's intervention. The first winter, sixteen Hudson's Bay men perished; the second winter, their leader, John Clarke was 'arrested' by the opposition; the third winter, there was consequently no wintering party; the fourth winter, their new leader, Colin Robertson, was also arrested.

Thus it happened that the two companies were unable or unwilling to provide adequate supplies for Franklin's party. Beyond Ile-à-la-Crosse, the Hudson's Bay Company was not well enough established to be of major assistance. Both companies were weakened by their continuing interference with each other, and each wished to hoard supplies needed for their competition in trade. The expedition therefore gave up the original plans to winter at Great Bear Lake, a better base for arctic exploration (as the second Franklin expedition was to demonstrate in 1825-27). Winter Lake, north of Fort Providence, was chosen instead as a location for receipt of additional supplies—though as it happened, insufficient were obtained to justify the change. In fact, some of the goods sent for the expedition in 1820 failed to reach them—five pieces (about 400 pounds) delivered at Grand Rapids and three pieces (240 pounds) delivered at Cumberland House by the Hudson's Bay Company arrived only after the departure of the North West Company canoe assigned to carry them. Later canoes of each company left them to be carried by the other company so that they never did reach the expedition.[5]

George Simpson's arrival in the Athabasca district in September, 1820, was of great portent for the fur trade, but did not strengthen the prospects of the Franklin expedition. Simpson, lured from a counting-house in London as a potential governor, was in charge of the Athabasca district in his first winter, and he was anxious to compete successfully with the North West Company. Simpson rebuked his subordinate Robert McVicar at Great Slave Lake for being too generous with stores provided to the Franklin expedition. Later that winter, George Back walked from Fort Enterprize to Fort Chipewyan, a return trip of 1,104 miles, to intercede with Simpson for more supplies on behalf of John Franklin. Back got little satisfaction. Simpson wrote to McVicar: 'The Committee are anxious to render every facility and assistance to the "Discovery Expedition" consistent with the safety of their Trade, but that is not to be sacrificed on any consideration ... their necessities are a very secondary consideration to our own difficulties; ... we must not loose sight of our own Interests to promote their views.'[6]

Simpson, jealous of the partiality shown to the North West Company by members of the expedition and perhaps feeling a bit guilty concerning his stinting help to them, made the following entry on February 8, 1821:

'Mr. Back paid me a visit preparatory to his departure; from his remarks I infer there is little probability of the objects of the expedition being accomplished, not so much on account of any serious difficulties to be apprehended, but from a want of unanimity amongst themselves; indeed it appears to me that the mission was projected and entered into without mature consideration and the necessary previous arrangements totally neglected; moreover Lieut. Franklin, the Officer who commands the party has not the physical powers required for the labor of moderate Voyaging in this country; he must have three meals p diem, Tea is indispensible, and with the utmost exertion he cannot walk above *Eight* miles in one day, so that it does not follow if those Gentlemen are unsuccessfull that the difficulties are insurmountable.'[7]

Simpson was biased and unfair to Franklin. The previous

5. George Simpson, *Journal of Occurrences in the Athabasca Department,* ed. E. E. Rich (Toronto: Champlain Society, 1938), p. 208.

6. Ibid., p. 243.

7. Ibid., p. 261.

winter, Franklin, Back, and Hepburn had walked the 250 miles from Cumberland House to Carlton in thirteen and a half days through deep snow. Because the dog sleds were heavily loaded, the officers were forced to walk, and they averaged each day more than double the eight miles mentioned by Simpson.

In evaluating progress, one must remember that the expedition was under admiralty direction. Despite their fortitude and competence, the naval men at times proved inexperienced and helpless as they faced the problems of exploration by land. As George Simpson intimated, the planners in London had not fully appreciated the problems involved, including the shortness of the arctic summer. No one foresaw, for example, that the Coppermine River would not melt until the third of July. It was unwarranted optimism to expect that they might in one summer traverse 800 unexplored miles from the mouth of the Coppermine to Repulse Bay, 600 miles north of Churchill. No one knew that Bathurst Inlet, including Melville Sound, would require 460 miles of careful circumnavigation, even though the distance across its mouth from Cape Barrow to Cape Flinders is only 37 miles.

As Nanton has observed, things would have gone better if there had been several more seamen like John Hepburn.[8] The experience of later northern explorations indicates that the expedition would have fared better had they taken fewer men to the coast and left some behind at Fort Enterprize, where they could have supervised the collection of provisions for the next winter. But this is the wisdom of hindsight. It was some years before Dr. John Rae and Thomas Simpson demonstrated how a small party of skilled and experienced men could travel lightly and live off the land, and it was not until the next century that Vilhjalmur Stefansson proved this possible even in the dark arctic midwinter.

To their credit, the surviving officers and the Admiralty learned from their mistakes. Most men, after such horrendous experiences, would have retired from exploration. Yet Franklin, Richardson, and Back returned in 1825 on a well-organized, well-planned expedition, competently supported by a now-unified fur trading company. This time they surveyed 1,237 miles of arctic coastline without serious difficulty and, apart from an accident on the return journey to

8. Paul Nanton, *Arctic Breakthrough* (Toronto: Clarke Irwin, 1970), p. 3.

Montreal, without loss of life. Their natural-history observations alone occupied six volumes.

Robert Hood's journal, meticulously written in his own beautiful, legible script during the cold winter at Fort Enterprize, is evidently a compilation of his daily notes, supplemented by his memory. That he expected it to be published is obvious from his statement in reference to Hearne, 'I shall endeavour to spare the reader the trouble of referring to his work.' The journal, printed here in full for the first time, gives insight into one of the most important journeys in the exploration of the Northwest—truly the 'Arctic Breakthrough' as Nanton's title indicates. It provides on-the-spot comments on the state of the fur trade and the rivalry between the two fur companies. Chapter 4 provides one of the best accounts available of the life of the Cree Indians at that time.

Hood gives us a less formal and less rigid version of events than does Franklin's official account. Incidents such as that of the cowardly man who hid with the women and children and the rather explicit account of the sailors' intimacies with Eskimo women were not mentioned by Franklin. While Franklin merely speaks of 'discharging those men who were less willing to undertake the journey',[9] Hood more specifically states that the three Englishmen were 'deterred by the dread of famine and fatigue, which they thought we were doomed to encounter'. Other details are enlightening, such as Wentzel's information that by late September the ice was already strong enough to support Indians visiting Fort Providence; Franklin evidently did not wish to mention or accept this evidence concerning the early onset of winter. Hepburn's four-day absence when he became lost in a fog seems to have been more serious than Franklin indicated.

Hood was a careful surveyor and draughtsman. Franklin described how he assisted in surveying the Hayes River: 'The survey of the river was made by taking the bearings of every point with a pocket compass, estimating the distances, and making a connected eye-sketch of the whole. This part of the survey was allotted to Messrs. Back and Hood conjointly: Mr. Hood also protracted the route each evening on a ruled map, after the courses and distances had been corrected by observa-

9. John Franklin, *Narrative of a Journey to the Shores of the Polar Sea in the Years 1819, 20, 21 and 22.* (London: John Murray, 1823), p. 166.

10. Ibid., p. 28.

11. Ibid., Table VII, pp. 636-638.

12. R. G. Madill, 'The North Magnetic Pole', *Beaver*, 280 (1949), 8-11.

13. Franklin, *Narrative of a Journey 1819-22*, p. 539.

tions for latitude and longitude, taken by myself as often as the weather would allow. The extraordinary talent of this young officer in this line of service proved of the greatest advantage to the Expedition, and he continued to perform that duty until his lamented death, with a degree of zeal and accuracy that characterized all his pursuits.'[10]

The determination and talent displayed are as incredible as the wide variety of these pursuits. In the above instance, imagine making accurate maps, squinting by the light of a candle, sitting on the bare ground tormented by hordes of mosquitoes and blackflies at the end of an exhausting day!

The official Franklin journal credits Hood with ten observations of magnetic variation, latitude and longitude between York Factory and Cumberland House in 1819, thirteen observations between Cumberland and Fort Enterprize in 1820, and fifteen along the arctic coast in 1821, in all many more than were credited to Back; Franklin took fewer recordings of magnetic variation, but more of latitude and longitude alone.[11] Hood made an estimation of latitude at Fort Enterprize on December 28, bare-handed, when the thermometer registered 46 degrees below zero. The last of his observations, many of which were correct to the nearest minute, was made just below the Wilberforce Falls on 29 August 1821. The amazing accuracy of Franklin's maps therefore reflects much credit on this young midshipman. Furthermore, as Madill has indicated, Hood was the first to carry out a careful magnetic survey in Western Canada, measuring the dip as well as the magnetic declination.[12]

Franklin gave Hood great credit for this ingenuity in scientific matters: 'He also, by a skilful adaptation of a vernier to the graduated circle of a Kater's Compass, enabled himself to read off small deviations of the needle, and was the first who satisfactorily proved, by his observations at Cumberland-House, the important fact of the action of the Aurora upon the compass-needle. By his ingenious Electrometer invented at Fort Enterprise, he seems also to have proved the Aurora to be an electrical phenomenon, or at least that it induces a certain unusual state of electricity in the atmosphere.'[13]

Hood's journal gives us considerable insight into the personality of its author. His wry, sarcastic humour was evident from his descriptions of the Indians; after enumerating the typical articles of clothing of the hunter, he added that it was only 'the most prudent man...who possesses them at the same time'. The journal reflects a philosophic bent of mind, with a certain natural shrewdness in Hood's observations of human motivation. Commenting on the discomforts of travel, he noted that: 'no evil makes an impression so evanescent as pain.' His comments on the attraction of life in the fur trade country revealed a rare comprehension. But a very human quality of impatience shows through when he says 'if this undertaking can claim no other preeminence, it is at least distinguished by the most tedious and vexatious delays that have been incurred in the whole progress of discovery.' His modesty is revealed in his failure to mention his own bravery when he quickly jumped into a canoe and shot the Otter Rapids, in an unsuccessful attempt to save the life of Louis St. Jean, their Canadian foreman.

Hood never ceased to be impressed by the vastness of the 'fur countries' and the sparseness of the population. He noted with dismay what little attempt was made to cultivate arable land. He commented on additional possibilities for commerce, such as increased trade with Eskimos and the use of buffalo wool for cloth, and noted the benefits that would accrue from well-built roads, particularly at the major portages.

As a minister's son, Hood was probably the most formal of the four officers. All were devoted and earnest Christians; L. H. Neatby has described how both of Franklin's wives had to discourage him from being overly religious.[14] Penetrating the wild northwest, these men represented an aggressively professing section of Christian society, years before the first missionaries became established west of the Red River. Hood in fact died with *Bickersteth's Scripture Help* in his hand.

After the passage of 150 years, it should be permissible to tell the story of Hood's romance during the cold winter at Fort Enterprize. We know that Kescarrah, the Copper Indian guide, was 'too feeble to hunt' and 'almost entirely occupied in attendance upon his wife', who suffered from a large basal cell carcinoma which had destroyed much of her nose. Since the wife wanted to stay near Dr. Richardson in order to obtain daily medicine, and since she also required the services of her

14. Leslie H. Neatby, *Search for Franklin* (Edmonton: M. G. Hurtig, 1970) p. 57.

daughter, Green-stockings, this small family of three stayed at the fort after the other Copper Indians returned to their winter camp on 10 December 1820.

Green-stockings was nearly sixteen and, as Franklin said, 'considered by her tribe to be a great beauty'. Hood evidently agreed with this assessment, for she and her father posed as his models for a painting.[15] It seems that his fellow midshipman, George Back, shared his admiration and that the two would have fought a duel over her had Hepburn not overhead them and removed the charges from their pistols during the night. Although the expedition's dire shortage of supplies was reason enough to send George Back on his five-month, 1,104-mile walk to Fort Chipewyan, it did, as Leslie Neatby has indicated, separate Back and Hood and thereby relieve the problem of their rivalry.[16]

These details were printed in the journal of Joseph René Bellot who, when he was commissioned by Lady Franklin to search for her missing husband in the Arctic in 1851-52, took along the faithful but gossipy 62-year-old John Hepburn. Bellot was regaled with all sorts of tales of the first Franklin expedition of thirty years before; amongst other things he was informed that Hood had fathered a daughter at Fort Enterprize in 1820-21.[17] The tale was confirmed many years later by a letter written to a friend of the Birch family in 1953 by Clifford Wilson, then editor of The Beaver, asking if he knew that Hood had left a 'souvenir' in the north. Wilson said that the child was listed as the 'orphaned daughter of Lieutenant Hood' in the 1823 census at Fort Resolution.

L. H. Neatby has said of Hood, 'If the silhouette of him which survives is an index of his physique, his was not the stuff of which pioneers are made; the effeminate delicacy of his outline is in utter contrast with the massive, irregular profile of Franklin.'[18] After learning of his son's death, the Reverend Dr. Hood wrote to Dr. Richardson on 22 October 1822: 'Alas! I feared that his frame was not sufficiently robust to encounter the appalling hardships attending on Captain Franklin's expedition, but he would engage in it.'[19]

Though he was chosen chiefly for his artistic and scientific abilities, the selection of Hood for such a laborious expedition suggests that he had at least normal stamina. Nowhere is there mention of any symptoms to suggest that Hood might

15. Opposite p. 254 in Franklin, Narrative of a Journey 1819-22 and in Hurtig reprint.

16. Neatby, Search for Franklin, p. 47.

17. Joseph René Bellot. Memoirs (London: Hurst and Blackett, 1855), vol. I, p. 252.

18. Leslie H. Neatby, In Quest of the North West Passage (Toronto: Longmans Green, 1958), p. 57.

19. Rev. John McIlraith, The Life of Sir John Richardson (London: Longmans Green, 1868), p. 116.

have suffered from tuberculosis or other disease contributing to his eventual debility. As an officer, Hood was assigned to arduous and time-consuming intellectual and scientific activities, and therefore was relieved of the manual labour expected of the hired Canadian voyageurs, who did the paddling and portaging. In fact, his intensive industry in writing, drawing, and recording observations of aurora, magnetism, and meteorology may have contributed to his death. Franklin said of Hood after the winter at Fort Enterprize: 'Ever ardent in his pursuits, he had, through close attention to his drawings and other avocations, confined himself too much to the house in winter, and his health was impaired by his sedentary habits.'[20]

During the exploration along the arctic coast when rations were particularly short, it was Hood's task to distribute the provisions to the men. Franklin noted that Hood, to be scrupulously fair, 'always took the smallest portion for his own mess' [21] at the very time when all suffered from hunger. On the overland hike back from the Arctic Ocean, the voyageurs took turns leading the way, but Hood each day had the fatiguing position of second in line, to keep the compass bearings. After three weeks he became so weak he had to relinquish his place.

While the confinement of the previous winter, the ardours of the journey and the shortage of food contributed to Hood's physical deterioration, the most important factor seems to have been his sensitive gastro-intestinal tract. The lichen brew on which they depended for their meagre sustenance caused Hood painful cramps and diarrhea—very weakening for an already debilitated man. Two voyageurs, Credit and Vaillant, similarly affected, were the first to perish on 6 October.

Thus by the early days of October 1821, malnourished, dehydrated, and increasingly susceptible to the cold, Hood faced almost inevitable death. That death was hastened, however, by a bullet. After an argument with Michel Terohaute, an Iroquois suspected of having turned cannibal, Hood was found shot through the back of his head.

Richardson's journal comments as follows: 'The loss of a young officer, of such distinguished and varied talents and application, may be felt and duly appreciated by the eminent characters under whose command he had served; but the

20. John Franklin, *Narrative of a Journey 1819-22*, p. 309.

21. Ibid., p. 419.

calmness with which he contemplated the probable termination of a life of uncommon promise; and the patience and fortitude with which he sustained, I may venture to say, unparalleled bodily sufferings, can only be known to the companions of his distresses.'[22]

Not until 15 December did the survivors, who had narrowly escaped death themselves, learn of Hood's promotion to lieutenant. This was forty-seven days after his tragic demise.

Hood's journal covers only the period from 23 May, 1819 to 15 September, 1820. He died just over one year later, on 20 October, 1821.

Hood's journal was taken back to England by Franklin, who used portions of it in his published journal and then returned it to Hood's family. Robert Hood's sister Catherine (who married a young curate, William Roe, later to become an archdeacon), kept the journal and passed it on to her daughter Marion, who married George Birch. When Marion's eldest daughter died in 1933, Robert Hood's narrative was fortunately found in a box of old books in the attic of a coachhouse at the family home in Roscrea, Tipperary, Ireland. After its discovery there, the journal reverted to a younger son of Marion, Alfred Birch. In 1943 Alfred Birch passed it on to his son, Richard Garnett Birch, grandson of Marion and the great-grandson of Hood's sister Catherine.

In editing Hood's journal I have, for the most part, retained his punctuation and spelling of place names, but have corrected obvious slips of the pen and expanded those contractions (such as his lavish use of the ampersand) which can only distract and irritate the reader. Modern names have been added in square brackets. A typescript copy of the journal, which faithfully reproduces his original spelling and punctuation, was made in the early stages of preparing this book. Copies have been deposited in the Saskatchewan Archives, University of Saskatchewan, Saskatoon; the Library of the Arctic Institute of North America, Montreal; and the Library of the Scott Polar Research Institute, Cambridge.

Hood's memory is already perpetuated by a flower, the moss phlox, *Phlox hoodii*, a sedge, *Carex hoodii*, a small mammal, the thirteen-striped ground squirrel, *Citellus tridecemlineatus hoodii*, and by the mighty Hood River that plunges over Wilberforce Falls before entering the Arctic Ocean. Publication of his narrative and his previously unpublished paintings provides a further monument to the name and achievements of Robert Hood.

NARRATIVE OF THE PROCEEDINGS OF AN EXPEDITION ON DISCOVERY IN NORTH AMERICA

Under the Command of Lieut. Franklin, R. N.

by

ROBERT HOOD

Admiralty Midshipman attached to
the Expedition

Chapter 3d.

Proceedings at Cumberland house during the Winter. Departure of Messrs. Franklin and Back on the snow to Lake Athapescow. Final departure of the remaining part of the expedition in canoes.

The arrival of the Expedition having been wholly unexpected at Cumberland house, we were not accomodated without difficulty; but our men were immediately employed to prepare a house for our reception, within the stockades, which had been partly erected in the summer. It was built of wood, the interstices being choaked up with mud, and the roof boarded. The chimneys were made of stones, and the windows of moose skin parchment. Our tardy people were a month in completing it, and it proved rather too

A PAGE FROM HOOD'S JOURNAL

1

Gravesend to
York Factory

Departure from England; narrow escape from shipwreck; tedious passage, and arrival at York fort.

On the 23rd of May, 1819, the expedition embarked on board the Honourable Hudson's Bay Company's ship, *Prince of Wales*, and weighed in company with the *Eddystone* ship, and the *Wear*, brig.[1] We anchored with the flood tide having an easterly wind; and arriving on the 24th at the Great Nore were detained by a fresher gale than is usually experienced in England at this season.[2] After a delay of several days, we reached Yarmouth, where we landed, to provide ourselves with some necessaries, which had been overlooked in the hurry of our departure from Gravesend. While thus occupied, the reports of guns from the roads announced a change of wind, and hastening to the beach we found that the ships were already under sail. Our companion, Mr. Back, had unfortunately separated from us on particular business, and we were compelled to repair immediately on board the *Prince of Wales* without him. The ships, which had been for some time hove to, bore up with a strong gale, and we were soon carried out of sight of Yarmouth. We were however satisfied that Mr. Back would follow us to the Orkneys.

The winds compensated for their detention of us hitherto, so that on the 4th of June we were enabled to cast anchor at Stromness, in Mainland, the principal of the Orkney Islands. Having procured a house situated on a little eminence near Hoy Sound, we landed the instruments and books, and took up our residence there during our stay. We were fortunately in the neighbourhood of the manse, which was occupied by Mr. Clouston, the minister of Stromness. This venerable and hospitable man had received the visits of almost every northern dis-

1. The *Eddystone* and *Prince of Wales* were the main supply ships for the Hudson's Bay Company. In 1815, the *Eddystone* had been trapped in the lower part of Hudson Bay all winter, and in 1816 the *Prince of Wales* similarly had to winter at Moose Factory. A brig was a two-masted sailing vessel, but the *Prince of Wales* and *Eddystone* were full-rigged, three-masted ships of 342 and 245 tons respectively.

2. The Nore is a 'local deep' in the estuary at the mouth of the Thames.

coverer since the time of Cook,[3] and he conferred that honourable title upon us in advance, by the kindness of his reception.

Mr. Franklin with some difficulty engaged four men to accompany us in that part of the expedition which was to be performed by water. They had before wintered some years in Hudson's Bay, which is principally supplied with men from the Orkneys. We might possibly have obtained a greater number; but we had been informed by all the servants of the Company that we should meet with many persons at York Fort, about to return from the expiration of their engagements, who would be easily persuaded to accompany us.[4]

On the 9th to our great satisfaction Mr. Back made his appearance. His adventures were very remarkable. He had arrived on the beach at Yarmouth, as the ship was passing at the distance of 300 yards, and applied to some boatman to carry him on board, which might have been accomplished in a few minutes; but discovering the emergency of his case, they demanded 20 guineas as the price of his passage. As he was not provided with more than 15, they positively refused to assist him, and he threw himself immediately into the Northern Mail.[5] The east coast of England, and particularly the Downs, is infested by these wretches, who match their opportunity to second the strokes of misfortune, and prey upon the remnant, which perhaps the charity of the creditor has spared. Mr. Back arrived at Thurso after eight days of incessant travelling, and crossed the Pentland Firth in a passage boat. He experienced uncommon instances of liberality and benevolence on the road; where his fellow passengers, who knew nothing of him, except that he was destitute of necessaries, compelled him to receive supplies of linen, coats, etc., with no other security than his promise for their return.

These Islands have been so elaborately described by Dr. Barrie, whose long residence in them furnished him with all the necessary materials, that nothing is left to the casual visitor but the wonder how

3. Rev. William Clouston actually began his incumbency in 1794, 15 years after Cook's death. [Sir John Sinclair, *The Orkney Parishes* (Kirkwall: W.R. Mackintosh, 1927), p. 129.]

4. The small population of the Orkneys must be appreciated. In 1794, Stromness, the second largest town, had a population of only 1,344, with a disproportion of 851 females to 493 males, because so many men were employed elsewhere. [Sinclair, *The Orkney Parishes*, p. 112.] In 1819, Stromness had a population of about 2,000. [William Peace, *Peace's Hand-book to the Orkneys* (Kirkwall: William Peace, 1862), p. 81.]

5. There were 42 horsedrawn mail coach routes carrying passengers in Great Britain by 1797; this at eight days was probably the longest route.

he procured so much.[6] Stromness is a town which will appear to advantage in the eyes only of those who have been conveyed thither across an ocean, from a barbarous and desert country. It is a narrow defile between small huts built of stones, mud and plaster, with certain spaces occupied by heaps of dirt and the frames of boats. The way is frequented by numerous little gazing urchins, and an uncouth looking race of pigs, who are almost compelled to trip the passengers up for want of room. When pressing necessity has driven a stranger into a shop, its proprietor after much importunity, issues from the inner recesses, and regards his customer as if he was an intruder. He deals his goods like one who bestows a favour, which he generously refrains from enhancing. Yet some of these people are rich and could afford better habitations. The appearance of the church ranks it above the rest of the town; but one particular marks their connection. The door is covered with advertisements of the most offensive nature.[7]

[paragraph crossed out]

On the 16th [June], the Hudson's Bay ships had completed their stores, and the number of passengers for Hudson's Bay. We sailed at noon, and by 8 o'clock in the evening, succeeded in beating through Hoy Sound. The barren hills intersected by stone walls, the waving wreathes of smoke ascending over the low land from the burning kelp, and the mountains of Hoy intermingled with the clouds, had little to remind us that we were still among the British islands; but our parting with its inhabitants renewed those sensations which we flattered ourselves we had long before finally dismissed.

During our passage as far as Cape Farewell, the winds were very unfavourable, and the progress of the ships slower than it had been on any former occasion. The westerly winds brought clear, cold weather, and those from the south were accompanied by thick fogs and constant rain. The northwest gales were unusually violent and lasting.

The first novelty that engages the attention in these northern latitudes, is the continuance of daylight throughout the twenty-four hours. It occasions a contention between the desires of the mind and of the body, which produces a certain degree of restlessness, till custom has established a change of habits.

6. Barrie [sic]: The Rev. George Barry, D.D., author of *History of the Orkney Islands*, 2nd ed. (Edinburgh, 1808).

7. Including notices requesting volunteers for Franklin's expedition: 'the church-door...was the surest and most direct channel for the conveyance of information to the lower classes.' [Franklin, *Journey 1819-22*, p. 3.] The church was built in 1717.

On the 22nd of July, we had only advanced to the longitude of Cape Farewell. Our fellow passengers, going out in the service of the company or as settlers for Lord Selkirk's colony, had not prepared themselves for these preliminary difficulties; and early disappointment, however trivial, withers the fair flowers of expectation. For sea sickness there is no relief, except sleep, which was prevented by continual noise, and rest precluded by perpetual motion. This situation is truly miserable; but it is too common to excite any commiseration.

The Aurora Borealis was visible for the first time at 10 p.m. on the 19th, in the form of a bow, from WNW to NE. On the 25th we had opened the entrance of Davis's Straits and fell in with one of the Greenland whalers.[8] The master of this vessel informed us that he had only left the ice two days, that there was more of it this season in the straits than he had ever met with before, which had occasioned the loss of his bowsprit, and in consequence of it and his other damages he was returning to England. The Greenland fleet was fishing along the edge of the ice, in Lat. 74°30′ N., standing into the open sea to the northward.[9] We had hoped that the north-west wind which harrassed us, was driving the ice out of Hudson's Straits and clearing a passage for us; but it now appeared that we had been doing penance in vain. We rejoiced, however, to find that the open sea in Baffin's Bay had afforded such a good opportunity for the discovery ships under Lieut. Parry.[10]

The length of the twilight occasioned an infinite variety in the colours of the clouds, the outlines of which appeared very strongly marked in clear weather. This evening, from the surface of a dingy mass which overhung that part of the horizon where the sun had set, an army of fantastic shapes burst into existence, and crossed suddenly by a departing ray, which left its track on fire, they changed first to crimson and then to purple. The colours fading at the water's edge, they assumed so strikingly the forms of white icebergs, that we were much divided in our opinions, when an impervious dark blue cloud descended like a curtain, and veiled the most beautiful sky I ever saw.

On the 27th [July], in Lat. 57°46′, Long. 47°32′, we sounded with

8. The *Andrew Marvel*.
9. In Baffin Bay, 1000 miles farther north.
10. Parry's First Voyage of 1819-20. While Franklin attempted it by land, Parry was to explore the Northwest Passage by sea. Parry, in the most successful voyage ever made in the Arctic by a sailing vessel, reached 113° longitude and thus earned a £ 5,000 reward by being the first to penetrate beyond 110° longitude West. [William Edward Parry, *Journal of a Voyage for the Discovery of a North-west Passage from the Atlantic to the Pacific* (London: John Murray, 1821).]

650 fathoms but did not reach the bottom. The temperature of the water at the surface was 45°, and of the air 46°. A register thermometer, being attached to the lead, showed extremes of 40.5° and 52°, and a bottle which went down 450 fathoms brought up water of the temperature of 41°.[11] If these experiments were oftener made, many interesting questions might be decided with regard to the origin of some shores and the disappearance of others, which have left nothing to the enquiring navigator but a passage on the spaces which they once occupied. But commerce has ever been indifferent to the progress of that knowledge which does not produce immediate advantage.

On the 28th, we tacked to avoid a ledge of ice, which seemed to be composed of several detached pieces of field ice. Large finners [finback whales] were blowing, and ranging about with great rapidity in this frigid neighbourhood.

On the 29th, while running with a fair wind, in a thick fog, we passed a piece of ice and immediately afterwards found ourselves in the midst of such quantities of it that we forced our way with great difficulty. Retreat was impracticable, and we advanced, the hulls of the ships hid by the icebergs and their sails frequently disappearing in the fog. An incessant roar filled our ears on the left, proceeding from something which we could not discern. Above water, the ice was white and blue, and where seen through it, dark green, making a contrast with the grey sea and murky fog, almost too powerful for the eye. Every moment, a new form rose through the gloom, presenting the semblance of houses, leafy forests, or herds of deer on its ridge. After sailing 16 miles, and receiving some severe shocks, we entered the open sea, having left our consorts far behind. We soon, however, heard the reports of their guns, and they joined us in two hours. We saw neither birds nor fish near this ice, which was probably one of those masses that drift yearly through Davis's Straits down into the Atlantic, there to dissolve by the united powers of the water and sun. The temperature of the water was 34° and 35°, and though so little above the freezing point, its conducting power certainly enables it to dissolve the ice faster than the air; for some of these pieces, as also the larger icebergs which we saw afterwards, had evidently turned over, for their former water lines were perpendicular to the horizon. Indeed, we saw several small pieces perform this evolution. The temperature of the air was 44°, and that of

11. Fresh water is most dense at 39° F., but density of salt water depends on, and increases with, salinity.

the water five miles from the ice, 38°.

On the 3rd of August, we were encompassed by icebergs of great magnitude. One of them near us, measured by no other base-line than that which was afforded by the ship's run, was 62 feet high and 1154 feet long. On the 5th, in Lat. 61°20' N., Long. 61°12' W., the variation of the compass was 54°30' W. Another iceberg, of conical form, measured 149 feet in height. It could not have been less than 150 fathoms below the surface of the water. We were now almost daily compelled to change our course, to avoid the ice; but were not again completely enclosed.

On the morning of the 7th, we were rejoiced by the sight of land at the distance of four or five leagues. This, by our reckoning, was the Island of Resolution, at the entrance of Hudson's Straits. A fog, however, soon limited our view to our consorts and the ice about us. At 9 a.m., the wind failed, and the *Eddystone* became so entangled in ice that we sent a boat to her assistance, and the *Wear* followed our example. At 10, the land was visible for a few moments and again totally obscured. We could no longer distinguish our consorts, nor direct ourselves; but we concluded that we were driving towards the entrance of Hudson's Straits. Shortly after 12, the shore broke once more upon our view, at the distance of 50 yards. It consisted of two inaccessible rocks, of bare stone, with an iceberg between them. They rose almost perpendicularly, till their summits were lost in the fog. The tide, which was ebbing, forced us rapidly towards them, and destruction, apparently so inevitable, stupefied our people with dismay. We had no resource against it; our stern boat was absent, and the remaining boats were stowed in board, and so lumbered, that it required infinite labour to get them out. The strength that is supplied by terror effected this, after a fruitless effort to clear the anchors; but the confusion which always accompanies it had nearly rendered the labour unavailing. A boat was put out, between the ship and the rocks, at the instant that she struck in the midst of ice, over which it was lifted by the crew, and escaped being crushed, contrary to our expectations. The shock unhinged the ship's rudder, which was replaced by the next blow. She had fallen upon a point, across which the tide was drifting her into the bay occupied by the iceberg. The boat now took her in tow and, assisted by the swell and a light breeze, succeeded in dragging her off. The shore disappeared in a few minutes, and our deliverance from this imminent danger was scarcely more unexpected than our approach to it. We had, however, little cause for congratulation; large leaks having been found in the stern-post. Disaster had not yet done with us.

The current drove us against an iceberg, the projections of which threatened the masts, and tore away part of the chains. The iceberg was aground, and we were swept swiftly past it, with appalling noise, but less real danger than we had already incurred. Another light breeze favoured us, and we endeavoured to steer out, when a reef of rocks was providentially discovered so close, that we weathered it with the utmost difficulty.

We now perceived the *Eddystone* with three boats towing her from the rocks, and to them, her people were indebted for their preservation. On joining her, we made signals of distress, which she answered by sending her carpenter, with what other men she could spare, and taking us in tow. We judged the leaks to be near the stern-post, and from the closeness of the timbers in that direction, our endeavours to stop them were wholly ineffectual. As the night advanced, the wind increased to a heavy gale off the land, and being at about midnight embayed in ice, we let go the tow rope, as we were involving the *Eddystone* in difficulties from which we derived no advantage. The sails were split, but the people could not leave the pumps to furl them, and the stern boat was destroyed by the ice. Buffeted in every quarter, the leaks gaining upon us, and the people overcome by fatigue, many had already given themselves up to despair. To them death itself appeared less terrible than a continuation of such painful labour. At 6 o'clock on the morning of the 8th there was more than five feet of water in the hold. In these critical circumstances, the vigorous conduct of a few persons revived the hopes of the weak, and the energy of those whose strength remained. Mr. Franklin's profession secured attention to his advice, and the passengers ranged themselves indiscriminately at the pumps, a party employing themselves with buckets at the after and main holds. They worked perseveringly and were regularly relieved. Even the women would not be excluded, and they displayed surprising strength and alacrity in the execution of the tasks aliotted to them. By these means, we contrived for a long period to prevent the water from rising, though it did not appear to diminish. But we could not have maintained this equality for the night. At 3 p.m., the wind having moderated, it was determined to prepare for the worst, by sending the women and children on board the *Eddystone*. One man was dastard enough to conceal himself among them, and voluntarily class himself by his cowardice, with those whose natural timidity sometimes renders them useless. He was sent back to meet the execrations of his companions.[12]

At 6 p.m., we perceived that we were gaining on the leaks, and the carpenters stuffed all the crevices, with oakhum, that they could reach. A sail covered with every substance that could be carried into the leaks by the pressure of the water, was drawn under the quarter and secured by ropes on each side. Between 7 and 8 p.m., it was found necessary to pump only ten minutes, to keep the ship clear, and as a watch during the night was sufficient for that purpose, we enjoyed in reestablished security the repose which is always so grateful to the wearied, but never so sweet as after the execution of successful labour.

It may here be mentioned that the leaks continued in nearly the same state till our arrival at York Fort, when, on their again becoming alarming, the ship was hove down, and to the astonishment of her crew, a large hole was found near the keel, under the starboard fore chains. Her stern-post was uninjured; but the hole not having penetrated beyond the outside planks, the water had gushed into the afterhold, wherever the ceiling was cut. Many of the holes in the ceiling had not been filled up; so that the leak was stopped by means beyond our conjecture; nor could we conceive how the ship had received the blow, for we had perceived only the larboard side, and the stern-post, to touch the rocks.

We had still much cause for anxiety, not having seen the *Wear* since the morning of the 7th. She sailed badly, and we supposed that if she had not been wrecked, the westerly gales must have driven her down upon us. In the midst of our distress, we had not forgotten her, and she now absorbed the whole of our consideration. During the 9th and 10th, we beat to windward among ice islands, towards Resolution. On the 11th the wind changed, and we stood inshore, with the *Eddystone*. We sought with eager curiosity, the scene of our own calamity, which we judged to be six or seven miles to the southwest of a high remarkable point, called East Bluff.[13] The country was wild, craggy and barren, but contemplated in safety, its features lost half their horrors. No vestige of the *Wear* was visible. As the ships had been ordered to rendezvous off Cape Saddleback, in Hudson's Straits, and it was thought possible that she might be before us, we bore up with a fair wind, and entered the straits.

12. Franklin does not deign to mention this attempted desertion.

13. The tip of Meta Incognita peninsula at the southeastern extremity of Baffin Island. Less than a mile from shore it reaches an elevation of 1,010 feet.

At the entrance of these straits, a strong southerly current has been observed by most navigators. Near the Islands of Resolution, the ebb tide running out of the straits, meets that which issues from Frobisher's mistaken inlet, and the former being the strongest, carries the latter towards the northeast.[14] But the masses of ice, which are sometimes attached to the shore, and sometimes collected in particular positions by the influence of the wind, must so alter the course of every body of water coming in contact with them, and occasion such a variety of changeable eddies, that any prescribed course would probably conduct the seaman to the very perils which he wished to shun. His only plan is to be prepared for accidents, and in foggy weather, to anchor on an iceberg sufficiently large to touch the ground before his vessel. The primitive discoverers of these seas encountered and overcame difficulties which must be seen to be duly estimated. They were unprovided with all that can give security to a sea life; they had much to perform, and their means were exceedingly limited; little remains for us, and our resources are so many, that, if it was possible to equal them in success, we should never rival them in merit, till we penetrated regions in which danger was new, and science useless.

On the 12th [August], we saw Cape Saddleback,[15] but were disappointed in the chief object of our concern. We were now just so far short of certainty that the *Wear* was lost, as to leave room for hope.

The entrance of the straits had been much choked by ice, but here we found the sea quite clear. The last northwest gale and the current had carried it out, and after this period, we saw no more.

On the 13th, at the distance of 16 miles from the Upper Savage Islands, the Esquimaux canoes came off, according to their usual custom, to barter with the ships.[16] They were soon followed by their women as we approached the shore, in large skin boats,[17] steered by old men; and after remaining with us a few hours, they returned, appar-

14. Franklin's map shows a probable but unmapped strait, north of and parallel to the eastern half of Hudson Strait. Though Frobisher Bay had been explored by Sir Martin Frobisher in 1576 and 1577, and Davis had sailed along the east coast in 1585-87, the admiralty maps in 1823 not only failed to distinguish between Cumberland Sound and Frobisher Bay, but hinted that the latter might be another strait.

15. Saddleback Island is one of the Middle Savage Islands.

16. Just east of Big Island; offshore from the present site of Lake Harbour, Baffin Island.

17. Each of these five or six umiaks could carry 20 people in fine weather. Franklin estimated a total of 150 Eskimos and felt they must have represented a tribe of over 200 persons.

ently well satisfied with the produce of the market, which they had doubtless been long anticipating. During so short an intercourse, little knowledge was to be obtained of these people but that which fell under our immediate observation. Lieut. Chappell had a better opportunity, and has described all that we saw with such precision that I am unable to add fresh interest to a subject which is almost exhausted.[18] The Abbé Raynal's work is still interesting, but enough is now known to prove, that he is indebted to fiction for that recommendation.[19] The stature of the men does not appear to be less than five feet five inches, and some of them have agreeable countenances, notwithstanding the round fatness of their faces, and the very general disorder which disfigures their eyes.[20] The features of the women are regular, and their eyes larger than those of the men, but the extreme relaxation of their breasts renders them objects of disgust to Europeans.[21] A sailor, however, is a native of every part of the world, and some familiarities took place between them and our people, which the men seemed to regard with indifference; perhaps they countenanced this public infidelity for the sake of profit.[22] Individual property appeared to be inviolable, which is the first

18. Chappell met the Eskimos at Cape Saddleback on 31 July, 1814, and saw other Eskimos at the Upper Savage Islands on 4-6 August. [Edward Chappell, *Narrative of a Voyage to Hudson's Bay in his Majesty's Ship Rosamond* (London: J. Mawman, 1817), pp. 55-134.]

19. Abbé Guillaume Thomas François Raynal, *A Philosophical and Political History of the British Settlements and Trade in North America* (Edinburgh: C. Macfarquhar, 1776). This included second-hand, erroneous accounts of the Eskimos.

20. Probably Labrador keratopathy, a corneal scarring resulting from exposure to small ice-crystals as well as solar radiation. It occurs in older age groups. [Arnold Freedman, "Labrador Keratopathy', *Arch. Ophthalmology* 74(1965), 198-202.] Another eye disease which causes corneal scarring is Phlyctenulosis, but this usually occurs in childhood. [Clyde Farson, 'Phlyctenular Keratoconjunctivitis at Point Barrow, Alaska,'', *Am. J. Ophthalmology* 51 (1961), 585-88.]

21. All observers of the time seemed very

interested in this subject. Dr. Thomas M'Keevor, who accompanied the second group of Selkirk settlers and traded with this same group of Eskimos on 2 August 1812, observed that 'their breasts, though very long and flaccid, are by no means of sufficient length to throw over their shoulders, as some have asserted'. [Thomas M'Keevor, *A Voyage to Hudson's Bay during the Summer of 1812.* (London: Richard Phillips, 1819), p. 37.] Chappell noted that 'the pendant breasts . . . have certainly a disgusting appearance . . . one of the young girls shewed me, with conscious pride, that her breasts had not as yet been thus relaxed; intimating, that she differed from the other dusky damsels in this respect, and was therefore to be considered as an object of greater admiration.' [*Narrative,* pp. 96-97.]

22. Franklin of course does not mention such conduct; the sailors were not under his command. Chappell delicately referred to similar behaviour: 'Several of the natives brought their wives on board the ship, and, in return for a tin spoon or pot, compelled them, nothing loath, to receive our

remove from absolute barbarity. Depending chiefly on the sea for sub-sistence, they are naturally more associated than a nation of hunters, and confined by the scarcity of wood, to particular places. The country is probably the most ineligible in the world for the residence of man, yet the ingenuity of its inhabitants is equal to their wants. With no other materials than skins, whalebone, and driftwood, they have constructed machines,[23] by the aid of which they can assume the faculties of another race of creatures in their own peculiar element; can vie with them in swiftness, and trace them through all the mazes of their flight, with such admirable dexterity, that life seems to be imparted to the vehicle which obeys every impulse so readily. The world cannot pro-duce an instance of such powers invested by art in the strength of a single man.

The Hudson's Bay ships annually receive several tons of oil, and a great quantity of sea-horses' teeth,[24] for articles of very small value, during this single interview with the Esquimaux; and it is certain that a vessel annually employed to touch at every part of the coast might procure a cargo which would amply repay the cost of fitting her out, and at the same time encourage the industry, and ameliorate the condition of a race which is cut off from all other means of improvement. Some connection is, however, established with Labrador; as the Esquimaux were possessed of copper, iron, and brass, which had not been given on any former occasion by the ships. The benevolent zeal of the Moravian Missionaries has produced gratifying and wonderful changes on the east coast of Labrador, and even the northern shores of Hudson's Straits may not be considered by them, beyond the pale of their appointed work.[25] But their numbers are small, and their progress consequently slow, although they have no enemy to contend with, except ignorance.

We now began to want water, and as we had neglected to procure a supply from the ice, we stood into a large bay on the coast of Labrador, in Latitude 61°53′ N., Long. 71°40′ W. and sent a boat onshore for that

salutations. Nay, one man plainly intimated, that if I wished to hold any private conversation with his lady, he should have no objection to her visiting my cabin, provided I rewarded him with an axe.' [*Narrative*, pp. 65-66.]

23. The sealskin canoe or kayak, swift and responsive.

24. The ivory tusks, upper canine teeth of the walrus.

25. The first four Moravian brethren went ashore in Labrador in 1752 and were never heard of again. In 1771, their first permanent mission was established at Nain, followed in 1776 at Okkak and in 1782 at Hopedale. These were the three Moravian stations in operation in Labrador in 1819. [Douglas Leechman, 'Moravians to Ungava', *Beaver* 278 (Sept. 1947), 28-31.]

purpose, in which Mr. Franklin and Dr. Richardson embarked to examine the country.[26] It appeared barren and rocky at a distance but discovered some verdure in the valleys on our approach. The unfavourable aspect of the weather compelled the party to return without success, as the water flowed in small quantities from the melting snow on the hills.

On the 19th [August], Cape Diggs being in sight,[27] we parted from the *Eddystone*, her destination being Moose Factory, on the south side of the bay, which we entered on the 20th, passing between Mansfield Island and the main.[28] Here our progress was again interrupted, and we were driven by our old enemy, the northwest wind, for several days among those dangerous islands and shoals, called the Sleepers.[29] No part of the Admiralty chart is so incorrect as that in which they are laid down. The officers of the Hudson's Bay ships are well acquainted with them, and would readily communicate their information, at the desire of government. We should not have considered our difficulties serious, in any other circumstances. The leaks had lately increased unaccountably upon us, and only eight days' short allowance of water remained. But fatigue and privation were easily borne, in comparison with the apprehension that the lateness of our arrival at York Fort would confine us there till the next summer. However, on the 26th a strong gale enabled us to steer our course across the bay.

It is believed that Hudson's Bay is entirely frozen over every year. That this mass, as well as the numerous icebergs formed to the northward of Churchill, should pass to the ocean by so narrow and remote a channel as Hudson's Straits, affords curious matter for enquiry. The strong ebb tide which runs two hours longer than the flood, in the straits, cannot be wholly supplied from the bay. The flood tide, which has been observed to run with great violence between Southampton Island and Cumberland Island,[30] may be the other agent in this

26. Probably Douglas Harbour, presuming the latitude to be correct.

27. Correct spelling is Cape Digges, named after Sir Dudley Digges, 1583-1639, a shareholder in the East India Company, much interested in the Northwest Passage project.

28. Correct spelling is Mansel Island, named by Button in 1613, after Vice-Admiral Sir Robert Mansel (1573-1653).

29. The Ottawa Islands, well north of the Sleeper Islands; no wonder the charts were confusing on this point.

30. 'Cumberland Island' here refers to the southwestern extremity of Baffin Island; the channel between it and Southampton Island is Foxe Channel. The connection with arctic waters west of Baffin Island is a circuitous, ice-bound, and often narrow passage which would not explain a major water movement.

phenomenon; and if so, it certainly communicates either with Davis's Straits or Baffin's Bay. That question can only be decided by examining the tide in Cumberland Strait. But the ice from Hudson's Bay is brought into the current on the north side by the body of water flowing from many large rivers, which is too great for evaporation, especially as the bay is so long covered with ice.

The dependence of the temperature of the air upon the radiations from the earth, has long been satisfactorily ascertained. During our passage, we had an opportunity of observing the similar influence of the ocean. At our departure from the Orkneys, the thermometer was 57° in the air, at noon, and in the water 52°. Our course was nearly west, and the summer advancing; yet the temperature of the water continually decreased. We were approaching those regions where the cold northwest winds are prevalent, counteracting the heat of the sun at the surface. In the air, the thermometer sometimes rose high in the day, but fell in the night to the temperature of the water, and often much below it. On the 15th of July [August?], a heavy gale brought up the cold particles of the water, and its temperature was reduced several degrees, the thermometer in the shade immediately corresponding with it. When the gale subsided, the surface was again heated to its former temperature. Among the ice islands, and in the straits, which had just been evacuated, the water was sometimes 32°, but generally 35°. The strait, and the passage between Mansfield Island and the main, are much deeper than the bay, in which the water rose to 39°. In this last easterly gale, the water fell to 32°, and the air to 35°. On the 27th, the water still agitated, and the air at 35°, the former rose to 38°, but on sounding, we found only 45 fathoms; and this circumstance indicates the heat supplied by the bottom. On the 28th we saw Cape Tatnam, and having anchored with the ebb tide in 9 fathoms, the temperature of the water was 45°.

During the 29th we beat to windward, towards the mouth of Hayes River. The land was exceedingly low, and covered with trees. On this day, the variation of the compass was 3°49′ E. In Hudson's Straits the variation was generally 58° W., thus making a difference of 62°, in 6° of Latitude and 7° of Longitude.[31] There is one remarkable fact which

31. The map of Serson et al indicates the accuracy of Hood's readings of magnetic declination or variation. For epoch 1844, it shows readings of just under 60°W through Hudson's Straits and of just under 5°E off Cape Tatnam. ['Ground and High-Level Aeromagnetic Observations' in *Science, History and Hudson Bay*, ed. C. S. Beals and D. A. Shenstone, (Ottawa: Dept. of Energy, Mines & Resources, 1968) II, 661.]

deserves attention, but I have not anywhere seen an account of it. It is well known that the variation was observed in London in 1580, to be exactly one point of the compass easterly. At present it is more than two points westerly.[32] Since the year 1773, it has not increased more than 4°. In the year 1587, at the entrance of Cumberland Strait, Davis found the variation 30° W. In 1615 the variation according to Baffin was 24°6′ W., on the northwest side of Resolution, not more than 2° of latitude to the southward of Cumberland Strait. About a degree and a half to the southwest of this place, we found it to be 58°57′ W. Thus it appears, that in the same space of time, the magnetic poles of Resolution and of London, have moved 3 points of the compass from East to West. A close corroboration will be found in the poles of Cape Farewell and London, Pickersgill having ascertained it to be 41°31′ W., in 1776, and Lieut. Chappell in 1816, makes it 45° W. Nearly the same alteration has taken place in London. The observations of the early navigators in the East Indies, might discover the changes in the quantity or disposition of ferruginous matter, which have affected the magnetic poles of these places.

On the morning of the 30th [August], we were in sight of York roads.[33] A vessel was descried at anchor, which gave rise to a variety of speculations among us. It was generally believed that it could be no other than the Schooner employed to carry provisions and stores to Churchill. At 8 o'clock however, we had neared her so much, that we distinguished our lost consort, the *Wear*. Our satisfaction scarcely equalled our surprise at this unexpected meeting. Measures had been taken on board the *Prince of Wales* and *Eddystone* to search for her on their passage to England. Her boat came out to us, and the people were received as if they had risen from the dead. We learnt that her danger had not been much less than we supposed. She was driven upon the rocks, but saved from wreck by the interposition of a large piece of ice;

32. A compass showed 32 points, each point representing 11¼ degrees. These figures for the magnetic deviation at London of 11°E in 1580 and over 22½°W in 1820, are close to the published figures of 10 degrees E in 1580 and 24°W in 1820. [J. A. Fleming, *Terrestrial Magnetism and Electricity* (New York: McGraw Hill, 1939) p. 16.]

33. The anchorage for York Factory at 'five fathom hole'. York Factory was built in

1684 on the north shore of Hayes River and was named for the Duke of York, later King James II. It was occupied by the French in 1694-96, 1697-1713, and 1782. In 1788-93 the fort was rebuilt a mile upstream from the original site. In 1810, it became headquarters for the Northern Department of the Hudson's Bay Company, in addition to being its chief port. York Factory was closed in June, 1957, after 275 years of operation.

and though much shattered, escaped into the straits before the commencement of the westerly gale which drove us off. The rendezvous off Cape Saddleback had not been kept, because the Master of the *Wear* concluded that he was behind us. Four of his men with the carpenter were absent on board the *Eddystone*, but he arrived safely at York Fort, notwithstanding the diminution of his crew, and his total ignorance of the navigation of the Bay, being employed for the first time in the service of the company. But future events proved that this was not the most extraordinary of his adventures.

At 3 p.m., we anchored in five fathom hole, York beacon bearing SWbW, distant four miles. Shortly afterwards, the agent and general superintendent of the company's affairs came on board, and we accompanied him to the factory through a heavy storm of rain; we had sailed up Hayes River in the dark, passing rocks and shoals with a rapidity too great for observation.[34] Our voyage from Gravesend had occupied three months and seven days, which was considered a very unusual length of time.

34. Only Franklin, Richardson, and Hood accompanied Governor William Williams ashore that first night. A former ship's captain with the East India Company, Williams had been appointed in May, 1818, as a 'fighting Governor' to restore a greater share of the fur trade to the Hudson's Bay Company. When the Hudson's Bay and North West Companies amalgamated in July, 1821 (just too late to benefit the Franklin expedition), Williams became the senior of the two governors. He returned to England in 1826 and died in 1837.

2

York Factory to Cumberland House

Proceedings at York Fort.
Passage from thence to Cumberland House.

The first few days after our arrival [30 August 1819], were fully occupied by consultation with such persons at the factory as were capable of giving advice on the best route for the prosecution of our undertaking. At length, Mr. Franklin determined to proceed to Cumberland House, by the rivers affording communication; to winter at that place, and, in the spring of 1820, to commence our journey towards the Arctic Sea. Accordingly, the stores and men were landed, and lodged in the factory. Persons were employed to fit up a boat, and prepare necessaries for the journey. Our endeavours to obtain an Esquimaux interpreter were for the present ineffectual; but we were informed that a person of that nation had been employed as a servant at Churchill, and having lately taken a wife, returned to live with his countrymen. As the Esquimaux visit Churchill every year in the spring, hopes were entertained that he might be prevailed on to accompany us, and in that case, means were to be adopted for conveying him after us to Cumberland House, or the Slave Lake.

York Factory is in Latitude 57°0'0" N., and Longitude by chronometers 92°27'0" W.[1] It is situated about 200 yards from the west bank, and five miles from the mouth of Hayes River.[2] It consists of several wooden buildings inclosed by stockades or wooden spikes four or five yards in length, driven into the ground. The principal building is two stories high, with a courtyard in the interior; the upper apartments are appropriated to the officers and clerks, and the lower to their servants. The other buildings contain stores and furs prepared for embarkation. The whole has the appearance of a temporary erection by shipwrecked seamen, and the resemblance may be carried farther in the

1. Actually, 57°00' N latitude and 92°18' W longitude. The longitude is thus 9' in error, a mistake of between five and six miles at this latitude. The officers' calculations of latitude throughout this journey were very exact, determined by a sextant and artificial horizon. The longitude calculation depended on the accuracy of their pocket time pieces (chronometers), checked occasionally by the difficult and less precise observations of the moon (lunar observations).

2. Named for Sir James Hayes, a charter member and at one time the largest shareholder in the Hudson's Bay Company.

occupations and varied garbs of its inhabitants, who seemed to be clothed in what they had snatched by chance from destruction. They cultivate a small garden of greens and potatoes, but no grain. From the factory to the bank, a floor of boards is laid for the convenience of transporting goods, which are lifted from the pier by a barbarous wooden crane. Three or four small field pieces are kept here for the purpose of making signals. Such is the principal establishment of this once profitable commerce; yet the whole country does not contain another which will bear any comparison with it in size or convenience. Those who make choice of it for their residence, must shake off every lingering want which abundance has cherished, with rigid determination, and learn to think that sufficient, the deprivation of which would be fatal.

The breadth of the river opposite to the factory is a mile; full of islands and shoals. The channel, though intricate, will admit vessels of 200 tons burthen. The ships employed by the company are too large for this navigation and deliver their cargoes into smaller vessels and boats which are obliged to carry it nine miles. Stormy weather often prevents any intercourse for many days, and from this cause alone, the ships have been blocked by the ice during their passage to England. The introduction of smaller ships into the Company's service would be attended by other important advantages. They would work better in the ice and on the numerous flats near York roads; and their number would be an additional security against the accidents to which their voyage is liable.

In 1782, at the capture of York and Churchill by La Perouse,[3] the former stood on the bank, about a mile nearer the mouth of the river. But on the breaking up of the ice, it was every year in danger of being swept out to sea, and the new depot was erected in its present situation. The ground is not higher within 20 miles. When the ice gives way, some large body of it is impeded by a projecting point or shoal, and that which follows, rises upon it with irresistible force till the whole pile, with the torrent foaming in its rear, tears away the obstacle, carrying rocks, banks with trees, and sometimes men and animals out to sea. The factory is 30 feet above the ordinary level of the water, notwithstanding which, the flood frequently washes the boats from the pier against the stockades, and then instantaneously subsides.

3. Jean Francois de Galaup, Comte de la Perouse, to whom the outnumbered Samuel Hearne surrendered Churchill on 8 August 1782.

The country is flat and swampy, being towards the north, one continued marsh as far as Nelson River.[4] The soil is alluvial mud, and produces spruce, willow, currant, gooseberry and cranberry bushes. Strawberries grow spontaneously in the woods and the currants are not inferior in flavour to those of Europe. When Mr. Ellis was here,[5] and at a much later period, the trees were very large and abundant. But they have been made use of for fuel; and those who reside here during the winter find sufficient occupation in dragging five or six miles the wood necessary for their consumption. The whole coast of Hudson's Bay is the resort of various waterfowl, in the summer. It is the natural abode of grey geese [Canada Goose] and ducks, which are unwillingly driven from it by the severity of the climate. Teal, curlew, and spotted snipes [yellowlegs] feed on the banks and shores. There are few fish in the river nearer than a small creek called Pennycutaway, about 12 miles from York. The Indian hunters furnish the chief provision, which is reindeer [caribou] and geese, and they are employed here only for that purpose, as York is merely the channel through which the trade of the interior is embarked, and stores imported in return.

At this season, the masters or chiefs of the different posts inland, come down the rivers with their furs, and on the departure of the ships, return with English stores, which being a more bulky cargo than the former, they have great difficulty in conveying to so great a distance. This general rendezvous is delightful to persons who have been so long incarcerated in the snow, with no other society than their servants and the natives. They catch a glimpse of the civilized world, laugh at their own altered habits, and begin the same course again. Many of them have lived thus for 25 years, and some have visited England after amassing a competence for their support, but have returned in disgust, unable to reconcile themselves to those regulations of mankind which take from them some of the privileges of liberty, to secure the rest. So great is the love of power, and hatred of control, that having once tasted the pleasure of cutting down a tree or shooting a bird, without any license but that of their will, the charms of refinement and comfort of

4. Port Nelson, on the north shore of the peninsula and only twelve miles from York Factory, preceded York as an H. B. C. post in 1682-83. It is at the mouth of the Nelson River, discovered by Sir Thomas Button in 1612 and named after Button's sailing master, who died on the voyage.

5. Henry Ellis, who spent the winter of 1746-47 at York Factory with Moor and Smith. Their expedition was the second sent by Arthur Dobbs in search of the northwest passage. [Henry Ellis, *A Voyage to Hudson's Bay by the 'Dobbs Galley' and 'California'* (London: H. Whitridge, 1748).]

security are offered to them in vain. It is the spirit that peoples deserts, and to encourage it, is to hasten its destruction.

The disposition generated by this mode of life will not, unfortunately, admit any division of the bounty of providence with another; and the encroachments of a neighbour are regarded with a corroding jealousy, that betrays the selfishness from which the professed desire of freedom has sprung. We had here an example of this nature. One of the proprietors of the North West Company, Mr. McTavish, and several others,[6] were in confinement and preparing to embark in the ships for England, having been seized by Mr. Williams at the Grand Rapid in the River Saskashawan, for some violences alleged to have been committed by them in the interior. We introduced ourselves to these gentlemen, who gave us much valuable information. Mr. McTavish had visited the mouth of the Columbia, and the Great Bear Lake, near Mackenzie's River; and we regretted that time did not permit us to enjoy a longer communication with one who was so capable of answering our enquiries.

Before our arrival, Mr. Williams had received accounts from Canada [Montreal, Lower Canada] of our intended expedition. But being ignorant of the route which we had proposed to take, and of the number of men which we carried, he had been at a loss to know what assistance we should require. The agent of the Company at the Orkneys had misinformed us with regard to the supply of men, for we could not engage a single volunteer; and Mr. Williams was greatly disappointed in the numbers sent to him by the ships, having demanded 100, and obtained only 20. He could therefore only provide us with a steersman, in addition to our own six men.[7] The boat was not capable of carrying more than three tons, so that we were under the necessity of leaving a quantity of bacon, balls, tobacco and powder, to be carried after us at a more favourable opportunity.[8] Ammunition and tobacco, we were told,

6. John George McTavish was in charge of the North West Company post at Fort Chipewyan. The other North West Company partners still prisoner were John Donald Campbell, Angus Shaw, and Benjamin Frobisher. They had been captured at Grand Rapids on 23 June 1819 by Hudson's Bay Company Governor Williams and John Clarke with twenty armed de Meuron soldiers and ten other 'constables'.

7. An expedition of four officers and seven men in one boat. John Hepburn and Samuel Wilks, the English seamen, were aided by four Orkneymen and the steersman from York Factory. Wilks was 'unequal to the fatigue of the journey' and was discharged at Cumberland House in the spring of 1820.

8. Because of the hostility between the two fur trading companies, most of these

were abundant at Cumberland House. The Company's boats departing for the interior were compelled to leave behind many of their winter stores, from the same cause.

On the 9th of September, our boat was launched, rigged with one mast and a square sail, and stowed with the remainder of our cargo.[9] It consisted of three sextants, a transit instrument, theodolite, dipping needle, two azimuth compasses, and several artificial horizons, a sympiesometer,[10] electrometer,[11] and 12 thermometers. The other stores were ammunition, tobacco, preserved meats, portable soups, and tea. Each officer carried his pocket chronometer, compass, spy-glass and gun. At noon, we embarked and were saluted at our departure with cheers and nine guns.

The wind was favourable, and we sailed up the stream. Above York, its depth is not more than 1½ fathoms, and its breadth half a mile. But the banks and islands are covered with trees of a larger size than those on the coast. Our survey was conducted in the following manner. The bearings of every point were taken and noted, with figures to distinguish them, and the distances computed. At the same time, the outlines of the river, islands, etc., were delineated, and transferred every evening to a map of very large scale, and the whole was corrected by astronomical observations whenever they could be procured. Easy and rapid as was this method, the errors seldom exceeded two miles between the observations, and correction was sometimes found to be needless.

At sunset, we landed on a small island, pitched our tent, and made a large fire before it. Our bedding was spread upon buffalo hides and we

---

provisions, which also included some flour and rice, never did catch up with the expedition.

9. Boats, as opposed to canoes, were first used on the Hayes River in 1795. Built at York Factory, and hence named York Boats, they were pointed at both ends for easier passage over sandbars. A long mast was placed against one gunwale. The boats sketched by Hood appear little more than 20 feet in length, but larger versions were commonly 40 feet by 10 feet. With a crew of 15, they could be propelled at six knots in calm water. [Richard Glover, 'York Boats', *Beaver* 279 (March 1949), 19-23.]

10. Sympiesometer: a type of barometer for determining the air pressure, and hence altitude. The weight of the air is indicated by the compression of gas in a tube, the lower part of which is filled with an oily fluid.

11. Hood later mentioned the 'common cork-ball electrometer', used to detect the presence of an electric charge or difference of potential. This might have been a Henley or Cavallo electroscope. Although the gold leaf electrometer had been developed by Bennet in 1787, this was not the instrument they carried.

slept without molestation. At sunrise, we struck our tent and embarked.

Beyond the influence of the tide, the current is very rapid, and the boat was tracked, or dragged by the men, harnessed to a line and carrying large sticks to support themselves. This laborious manner of travelling rendered our progress slow, but there is no other method of making head against the stream. As in every other river running through an alluvial soil, that side of the bank apposed to the strength of the current is broken perpendicularly, and the earth deposited in a shelving slope on the other. The cliffs of Hayes River are 100 feet high.

On the 11th [September], the shallowness of the river greatly impeded us, and we were frequently obliged to get out of the boat, and lift it over the shoals. The weather was exceedingly fine, and the increasing beauty of the scenery was alone a source of gratification which repaid every exertion. The brilliant hues of the poplar and larch [tamarack] now relieved the dark unvarying hue of the pines,[12] and the trees opened into avenues discovering spacious lawns beyond them, with an effect which we could hardly conceive was produced by accident.

On the 12th, we entered the Steel River, which is 56 miles from York by our courses.[13] The other branch of Hayes River is called the Shamatawa.[14] Steel River is 300 yards broad, and the trees so numerous that the country beyond the banks was wholly screened from our view. On the 13th, the calmness of the weather was interrupted by squalls and rain, but it was restored on the 14th, and we entered Hill River, the Steel River dividing also at this place into two branches.[15] It is 32 miles in length. Our men continued to track, and where the river ran in rapids over the shoals, made use of poles.

Several boats belonging to the Company which left York on the 10th now came up with us, and we were informed that our boat was too heavily laden to encounter the flats of Hill River. This we quickly experienced, for it remained half the day aground in spite of the efforts of our whole party, which indeed, could not employ much strength in

12. Hood's 'pine' always refers to spruce. At that time, spruce and fir were included in the genus, *Pinus*.

13. At each fork, the party ascended the main tributary, in those days given a new name above each branching. Today the name of Hayes River is used throughout.

14. Now called God's River, but the trading post and settlement 40 miles upstream is still called Shamattawa.

15. The branch to the westward is the Fox River.

raising it, while standing in a current running seven miles an hour. These rapids are occasioned by gentle slopes of the bottom, and are broken by large stones. On the 15th and 16th, we struggled with the same difficulties, and twice, endeavouring to drag the boat over the ground, the tracking rope broke, and it was carried against stones with the whole force of the stream. The shocks were violent, but the strength of the boat resisted them. However it was obvious that a repetition of them would soon put an end to our journey, and as the Company's boats had been directed to assist us, Mr. Franklin prevailed on the persons in charge to receive a small portion of our cargo, resolving to leave more of the remainder at the Rock House which was not far distant.

Our astonishment at the delightful prospects of Hill River, was in proportion to the strength of our prejudices against the imagined barrenness and desolation of this country. It would, however, find admirers from every climate. Along the bank at the water's edge, the poplars are ranged, now in the fading yellow garb of autumn, but still tinged with bright orange at the summits. The larch is interspersed among them, in the light green hue of spring, which it preserves to the last, and behind, the tall dark wintry pine lifts its head above all, its unchanging foliage defying alike the wintry blast and the summer's heat. But the original of this picture is to be found everywhere except in those places which chance or caprice has filled with burning embers. No distant hills, or mountains wrapped in clouds, are here, to give that eternal variety of light and shade afforded by an uneven surface, and to exercise the fancy by extensive and dubious outline.

On the 17th [September], we reached the Rock Portage, a large mass of rock in the middle of the river, on each side of which is a fall of about ten feet. Here we landed and carried the cargoes across, and then the boats were dragged up, and launched into the water on the other side. This is called a portage or carrying place, and there are 16 of them in Hill River, from 20 yards to 1/4 of a mile in length. Sometimes the cargo only is carried, when the boats can pass up the rapid or fall. Every man carries a burthen of two or three pieces, which are packages weighing 90 Tlbs. each.[16]

16. 'Tlb.' is an abbreviation for 'troy pounds.' A Troy pound, now a jeweller's measure of gold and silver, contains only 12 ounces of 480 grains each. Our regular avoirdupois pound has 16 ounces of 437½ grains each. Ninety Troy pounds was equal to just over 74 avoirdupois pounds.

At noon we arrived at the Rock House.[17] This is a post of late establishment, having been erected as a depot for the canoes which come from the Athapescow.[18] Three houses form as many sides of a square, and the fourth side is open towards the water. It is situated between two small eminences; and a stream running at the foot of one of them affords abundance of trout, suckers, pike, and perch. Black bears are said to be numerous here. The place is of no importance to the Company as a trading post.

Having lodged in the store 16 packages containing sugar, biscuit, tea, rice and portable soups, we reembarked, and after this sacrifice,[19] we had the satisfaction to find that the other boats could scarcely keep up with us.

On the 18th [September], we crossed several portages and at 2 p.m. passed a hill about 600 feet high, an object so remarkable in this level country, that the river receives its name from it.[20] From this eminence, 36 lakes may be seen, intersecting the surrounding country. Its summit is bare and apparently rocky.

The breadth of Hill River cannot be determined, as its full extent is hid by islands which leave only a narrow channel on each side; sometimes the passages were so numerous and intricate that only one guide in the party would undertake to conduct us. A day was scarcely sufficient to carry us over two of the long portages, and the fatigue sustained in this constant labour disheartens those who are engaged in it for the first time. But example and habit reconcile them to a life calculated only for beasts of burthen. The people employed by the company are almost wholly from the Orkneys and Western Isles of Scotland, a choice which has been dictated by experience; for necessity has taught them frugality and education, patience.[21] Few acquainted with the profits of begging in England, would live in Hudson's Bay. Their food is a mixture of fat and meat called pemmican.[22] The meat is

17. Rock Depot, sometimes called Gordon House, was founded in 1793-94 as a terminus depot where the larger river boats often turned over their cargo to lighter canoes.

18. Athabasca, from the Cree, *Ayabaskaw* or *Arabaskaw*, meaning 'bulrushes here and there'.

19. About 1,200 pounds of food left behind; each package weighed about 75 lbs.

20. Brassey Hill, for which this part of the Hayes River was named the Hill River. The

hill is only about 800 feet above sea level and 400 feet above the river.

21. In 1799, for example, there were 416 Orkneymen among the 530 men employed by the Hudson's Bay Company in their territories. [J. Storer Clouston, 'Orkney and the Hudson's Bay Company', *Beaver* 267 (Dec. 1936), 4.]

22. Spelled *pimikkan* by Lacombe; *pimiy* meant 'grease'.

dried and pounded, and melted grease amounting to one third of the quantity is poured upon it. It is nourishing but unpalatable, and in summer, often mouldy or rancid. This article is chiefly supplied by the posts on the River Saskashawan,[23] where the herds of buffalo overspread the plains.

To the westward of the Rock Portage, the soil does not cover the primitive rocks, which form the beds of the lakes and rivers. Unable to deepen its channel, the stream flows nearly on a level with the banks, and the ledges crossing it occasion the frequent falls which obstruct the navigation. In going down the current, the boats descend some of them without danger.

The pine clung to the most naked rocks, rising loftier than ever on insulated stones destitute even of moss. At the water's edge, the willow and that beautiful shrub, the American dogwood, intermingled their bright green and red leaves with their images beneath. The moss in the woods is several feet deep, and here the cranberry flourishes in great excellence.

On the 23rd [September], we reached the head of Hill River, which, though only 60 miles in length, had cost us nine days of unintermitting exertion. We hoisted our sails and at 1 p.m., landed at the Swampey Lake House. It is a single hut, erected to contain provisions. We obtained a small supply of pemmican, and reembarked. Swampey Lake is 12 miles long and 2½ broad; it is shallow and muddy. At 6 p.m., we crossed the lower portage in Jack River [still the Hayes River], and on the 24th, the three remaining portages. During the two last days, not a cloud appeared in the sky and the temperature of the air, in the night, was far below the freezing point. Our blankets were stiffened by the congelation of our breath, but we suffered little from the cold. We had often, since we landed, seen the Aurora, but never so brilliant as on the 24th. The whole sky was streaked with parallel arches, the tracks of coruscations which took their courses indifferently from east and west towards the opposite point.

The geese, ducks, and spotted snipes are as numerous as on the coast. Loons, gulls, and cormorants frequent the lakes.

Jack River is eight miles in length, and on the 25th we entered Knee Lake. It is a large expanse of water in the shape of a knee, and full of islands of rock thinly covered with moss, but clothed with pine, aspen

23. *Kisiskatjiwan,* meaning 'rapid current' in Cree; now rendered as Saskatchewan.

and poplar. Its depth is not well known, but supposed to be very great.

On the 26th [September], we landed on an island containing magnetic ore, about 40 yards in length, and nearly circular. At the distance of 200 yards from the north end of it, when it bore nearly south, the south point of the compass began to recede towards the east, and had traversed 15 points when we reached it. On the southwest side, the dipping needle was 80° 37' 50" and on the northwest side, it was perpendicular, with the plane of the arc facing the southwest. The compass on the southwest side took its usual direction, and this circumstance, the repulsion of its south end on approaching the island and the perpendicularity of the needle on the northwest side, tend to prove that the south pole of the magnetic ore was near the surface at that side, and also, that its north pole was depressed at an angle nearly similar to the dip of the needle. This therefore is one of the many magnetic bodies, which concur in attracting the north end of the needle towards their meridians, but the influence of which, did they not counteract each other, would reverse it when it passed their parallels.[24] The Latitude of the Island was 54° 57' 0" N. and Longitude 94° 56' 30" W.

The lake was strewed with leaves, and all vegetation withered in the vigorous cold of the nights. The sandflies and mosquitoes ceased their persecutions, to languish a little longer in the heat of noon, and then resign their annual existence.

On the 27th, we arrived at the Trout Fall Portage, having sailed 46 miles in Knee Lake. At this place, the Trout [Hayes] River falls between two rocks, about 16 feet, and the portage over which the boats are dragged is very steep.[25] The river is 12 miles long and contains four portages. The difficulties of most of the portages which we have crossed might be removed by making use of trucks or carts, and taking a few stones out of the channels. Indeed, a road for horses might easily be made between Cumberland House and York Factory, with ferries established on the rivers.[26] However, one voyage is at present sufficient to transport the Company's furs, and while they continue the staple

24. Hood's observations and interpretation were correct; this was a concentration of magnetic ore forming a 'natural magnet', with its S-pole near the surface and its N-pole at lower depths. Today aircraft fly overhead carrying sensitive magnetometers to search for such magnetic anomalies.

25. See plate 19.

26. Already in 1812-15 there had been an ill-fated attempt to build a winter road from York Factory to Norway House. Colin Robertson's efforts in 1828 were to be equally unsuccessful. Such a road has yet to be built.

commodity of the country, the route will not be improved.

On the 28th [September], we arrived at Oxford House,[27] at the entrance of the Holey [Oxford] Lake. It is built like the rest, of wood, and inclosed by stockades. These lonely dwellings are more widely scattered than the cities of Siberia. There is no difference in them; they were raised for the primitive object of shelter; and variety is only to be found in decoration and arrangement, here neither attempted nor desired.

A number of Indian tents were pitched near the house, and the dreadful ravages of the hooping cough, and the measles had filled them with lamentation and despair.[28] The poor creatures felt so deeply the loss of their relations, that they forsook their hunting occupations and starvation brought them to the border of the lake, where without much trouble they obtained fish. Their tents, canoes, and dogs, constituted their whole property. The dogs were of the Esquimaux breed; large, and strongly resembling wolves.

We reembarked, at 4 p.m., with a quantity of fish. On the evening of the 29th, we passed the first portage in the River Wepanapanis [Hayes].[29] Holey Lake is 25 miles in length, and four in breadth. Its name is derived from numerous holes in the bottom, said to be unfathomable. It abounds in fish, and is remarkable for the size and excellence of its trout. The banks and islands are rocky and the trees not so luxuriant as usual.

On the 30th [September], we crossed four portages in the Wepanapanis, a little crooked rocky channel and at 1 p.m., ran through a small lake [Windy], entering the river again at its extremity. Its banks were for several miles alluvial mud, overgrown with large reeds. This portion of the river is called the Rabbit Ground, and it opens into a small lake [Opiminegoka], divided into two passages by islands in the middle. By the southern passage, it is necessary to traverse a high hill, in order to join the river again, and by the northern, two difficult portages, called the Hill Gates. We chose the northern passage, and

27. Founded by the Hudson's Bay Company in 1798.

28. Indians, lacking centuries of natural selection of those resistant to the disease, suffered a high mortality when they contracted such diseases of the white man. The repeated, spasmodic cough of whooping cough, ending with vomiting of thick, tenacious sputum, can be very debilitating. Even today, the mortality rate for whooping cough and measles remains higher among Indian than white children.

29. Spelled *Weepinapannis* by Franklin. Wipanipanis is the name of a nearby falls on modern maps.

encamped at the head of the lake.

On the 1st of October, we entered the Hill Gates, in which the river was confined to about ten yards between steep granite rocks, for a mile and a half. One mile is so straight that the whole perspective presents itself at once, the heights crowned with pine and larch, and the distant opening bounded by the sky; a magnificent defile which one would have thought too regular for nature, but too stupendous for art. In many places, the rocks appeared to have been burst by the expansive force of ice formed in the crevices. At the middle, and western extremity of the channel, the near approach of the opposite mountains redoubled the rapidity of the stream, and the cargoes of the boats were landed at these places, and carried up the face of the ascent by half worn steps; while the rest of the people tracked the boats through the current, frequently struggling for hold with extended limbs on the hard level surface, or panting at the root of a friendly tree which had stayed with outstretched arms their unwilling recoil.

At noon, we passed the Upper Hill Gate and pursued the course through a small lake [Logan], till at 7 p.m. we arrived at the White Fall Portage and encamped.

On the 2nd of October we commenced our labours at this portage, which exceeds half a mile in length; across an island, round the north side of which the river makes three falls. The north bank is a steep cliff covered with trees; along the foot of it, large masses of rock have been heaped at different periods, in such slight dependence upon each other that their huge bulk vibrates in the breeze. On the island, the descent is more gradual, and the pines, poplars, and larches rise from the brink in majestic and almost impenetrable woods, inhabited by squirrels and woodpeckers. Where they are overthrown, by lightning or by wind, the ground is spread with the ruins of several generations, and so great is the confusion of bulk and posture, that the eye could not trace the form of any single tree. On the south side, the stream is narrow and impassable.

Mr. Franklin was traversing the banks, between two of the falls, when he slipped from the edge of a rock and rolled down a declivity 15 or 20 yards into the water. The current was not rapid, but the bank for a great extent continued too steep and slippery to afford him a firm grasp, and he was tantalized by sometimes touching the bottom, while he was, in spite of all his efforts, slowly approaching a fall. At this juncture he was descried from one of the boats, which had just been carried above the fall, and some persons hastened to his relief. He had however reached a low point before their arrival, and they found him, half immersed in the water, quite exhausted by his repeated attempts to land. His recovery was rapid; and the only bad consequence of the accident was the derangement of the chronometer, which we repaired at Norway House. Since our departure from York, Mr. Franklin had been afflicted so severely with the hooping cough, that it often threatened strangulation. But his mind was too eagerly bent on the service which he had undertaken to be relaxed by the attacks of this disorder, even with the auxiliaries of cold, wet, and indifferent provisions.

The boats and cargoes were all conveyed across by the evening of the 2nd. Though the thermometer now often fell to 20° at night, the warmth of the day, and the fresh colours which still variegated the landscape, gave us reason to hope that we should reach our destination before the formation of ice in the lakes.

On the 3rd of October, we passed the Whitewater [Robinson] Lake and from thence, no current could be distinguished in the river to its source at the Painted Stone, which is a rock, about 20 yards in breadth, separating this river from the source of the Echiamamis.[30] No springs were indicated by the thermometer, nor by any motion of the water. The length of the river from Holey Lake, by our route, is 58 miles. The Painted Stone (so denominated from some rude Indian sketches on the rock), is the height of land nearest to York Factory, and one of the sources of Hayes River. It is in Lat. 54°21'50" N., and Long. 96°50'0" W. We had no means of ascertaining accurately the amount of our ascent; the sympiesometer having been deranged by the cold. The following mode of calculating it, I have carried forward throughout the country. By allowing a foot for each mile of distance from York, and 6 feet, on an average, for each fall and rapid, the former will be 324 and the latter 150, making an ascent of 474 feet.[31] This height is crossed by the Sea

30. Spelled *Echemamis* by Franklin, but *Echimamish* on modern maps. David Thompson called this 'Each away man's brook' and Malcolm McLeod in 1872 claimed that *Aitchemanus*, as he spelled it, was the indianization of 'each man his'. There were several driblets of water courses; depending on the location of the beaver dams at the time, *each man his* own way had to make. [Malcolm McLeod, ed.

Peace River. A Canoe Voyage by the late Sir George Simpson in 1828 (Ottawa: J. Durie & Son, 1872).] John Peter Turner ['The La Loche Brigade', *Beaver* 274 (Dec. 1943), 35] spelled it *Echiomameesh* and claimed it was an Indian word meaning 'water flowing both ways'.

31. The actual elevation is approximately 800 feet. Hood's rough method of calculation considerably underestimated

[Nelson] River at no great distance to the westward.[32]

As we were about to embark in the Echiamamis, two canoes came up, with Mr. Williams, on his way to Norway House. He had left York on the 23rd of September and carrying no cargo, his canoes had travelled fast. He informed us that the *Prince of Wales* had been again driven onshore by a heavy gale while endeavouring to repair the effects of her disaster at Resolution; but had at length received a tolerable repair, and sailed for England.

Mr. Williams passed on and at 7 p.m., we encamped on the banks of the Echiamamis. On the 4th, we set sail with a fair wind, but were drenched by rain the whole day. The river is about four yards wide and occasionally very winding; its current is slow and its level banks hid by willows. The stream would probably exhaust itself in summer, were it not for the labours of the beavers which inhabit it. These creatures build their dams of such strength that a body of water is generally sustained sufficiently deep to float a boat; and we even found great difficulty in forcing a passage through them. When the destroyer has passed, the poor animal issues from its concealment and closes the breaches of its work, the principal benefit from which is to be derived by its mortal enemy. The Indian hunters employed by the company have often been desired not to molest the beavers of this river, a prohibition to which however they pay no attention.

A curious optical delusion was exhibited by the mist, which I never before observed. When the river extended a few hundred yards in a straight line, the water seemed in each direction to be greatly depressed, and the boat to be sailing on the summit of a convex surface. It was perhaps occasioned by our referring the visible horizon, (which was bounded by the banks of the river, seen dimly through the fog) to a much greater than the actually existing distance. There is no such appearance in open water, because no horizon is defined.

At 4 p.m., we entered a small lake [Hairy] from which we passed by a creek into the Sea River [Nelson River, east channel], having run 24 miles through the Echiamamis.

On the 5th, a strong breeze carried us through the river and the Little Playgreen Lake. The Sea River is 200 yards wide and filled with

his ascent. The longitude on modern maps is 96°43′ W.

32. The Nelson River drains Lake Winnipeg into Hudson Bay. Major portions are not navigable, but offer sites for present and future hydro power generation.

islands which are rough naked rocks, except the fringes of moss which the pine gathers about its roots. Below the Little Playgreen Lake, we turned on the left bank, into a channel communicating with the Great Playgreen Lake, called Jack River [Gunisao], and encamped near Jack House,[33] a fishing hut belonging to Norway House.

At 5 a.m., October 6th, we embarked, and sailed through the Great Playgreen Lake. It extends towards the northwest, far out of sight, and is studded with dangerous rocks and islands teeming with waterfowl. By Sea River it discharges the waters of the Saskashawan into Nelson River.[34] At 10 a.m., we landed at Norway House.[35]

A few scattered Indian tents reeking with debauchery, announced our advance into the regions more particularly appropriated to trade. That none of these pages should have been dedicated to the natives of a country in which we had penetrated so far, will reasonably excite the surprise of those who are as ignorant of it as we were. The only features of the whole landscape which indicate the existence of man are a few abandoned and solitary huts disposed an hundred miles apart on the banks of the rivers. He whose inquiries are directed after the most rational of all objects of curiosity, the influence of situation on human nature, will pursue his researches in vain through a series of deserts which have scarce any difference but their positions on the surface of the earth.

We found here, the settlers for Lord Selkirk's colony, who had been our fellow passengers from England.[36] They were emigrants from the Hebrides, Scotland and Germany, of different ages and sexes. As it

33. This was the first site of Jack River post, built in 1796 by the Hudson's Bay Company near the North West Company post of 1795. Independent Montreal traders had been there as early as 1773. The post was abandoned in 1817, but rebuilt on a nearby island, the present site of Norway House, in 1826. This Jack River is not to be confused with another Jack River, a portion of the Hayes River east of Knee Lake.

34. The waters of the Saskatchewan are carried first to the north end of Lake Winnipeg, which in turn drains via the Nelson into Hudson Bay.

35. The post was built on Big Mossy Point in 1814-17 by the Hudson's Bay Company at what is now known as Warren Landing. It was at the site of the shanty used in October and November 1814 by a Norwegian road gang brought in to build a winter road from Lake Winnipeg to York Factory, hence the name. The correct longitude is 97°52' or some 26 miles east of Hood's calculation. The post was burned in 1824 and then rebuilt on an island 20 miles north, near the site of the earlier Jack River Post.

36. The eighteen Selkirk settlers had left York Factory one day before Franklin and Hood. Their arrival at Red River swelled the total population of the colony to 382. The colony's entire crop had been destroyed by grasshoppers that summer, at the same time that 52 horses had been brought down the Saskatchewan to the colony.

commonly happens, though with more than common cause, they lamented their precipitation, and lost all desire to proceed. On the evening of our arrival, they unwillingly embarked, and after venting their discontents by beating and ducking their conductor and medical attendant, they departed before any account of their proceedings reached the house.

The harvest at the Red River colony was destroyed by frost in 1817, by locusts in 1818, and again in 1819, while the inhabitants were swept away by the measles and hooping cough. Famine, disease and rapine have joined their forces to crush this first agricultural attempt in its birth, although yet too weak to resist its natural enemy, the rigour of the climate. It is a rock upon which the noblest enterprise has split, and providence seems to have marked it out as a boundary beyond which even speculation shall not wander. But the extermination of a colony is no ordinary offence against mankind. To blast in the germ, the provision of future multitudes, to deprive poverty of an asylum from guilt, and industry of its last retreat, is a complication of crimes in those people who have effected it, in which the murderer's share is the least atrocious.[37]

Norway House is in Latitude 53°41'38" N., Longitude 98°31'8" W., and distant from the mouth of the Echiamamis 62¼ miles. Its central position, being at the junction of the routes from the Athapescow country and Canada, towards York Factory, is advantageous for a depot. The Playgreen Lake is stocked with fine fish, particularly sturgeon, which are not found in the rivers to the eastward of the Painted Stone, nor in those to the northward of the Frog Portage. The Indians trading at this house, as at all those between it and Hudson's Bay, are Crees; a chain of establishments which are now nominally trading posts, whatever profit the company might once have derived from them. The change has been produced by the diminution of natives and almost total annihilation of beavers.[38]

On the 7th [October], at 1 p.m., we embarked, in company with

37. Hood alludes to the Seven Oaks Massacre on June 19, 1817, when the Métis under North West Company clerk Cuthbert Grant shot and killed Governor Semple, five officers, and fourteen men of the Red River colony.

38. As early as 1795, the numbers of beaver had begun to decline, coincident with the introduction of steel traps and the use of castoreum as bait. Only three years later, in 1822, the amalgamated Company first advocated conservation measures and tried to discourage Indians from hunting out of season and from killing cub beavers, a delicacy to them, for food.

two boats, carrying Mr. Williams and the winter stores for Cumberland House. At 2 p.m., we entered Lake Winnipeg.[39] The passage between the lakes is narrow, and the current strong, being the only known outlet of many great rivers from the westward and southward. We coasted along the north border of this great body of water, in which not a single island was visible. It extends 250 miles to the southward and a moderate gale raises the waves so high, that boats seldom venture from the shore, and are sometimes detained many days, with a small stock of provisions. Having a fair breeze, this consideration induced us to run all night. The air was clear but intensely cold, and the Aurora stole silently across the northern sky, fluttering in half-formed circles, and glowing with brilliant colours.

On the 8th, the wind became contrary, and increased so much that we were forced to land on a small island at the northwest extremity of the lake. It was connected by a bank with a point [Limestone Point] which extended 10 or 12 miles from the main, inclosing a portion of water called Limestone Bay. Here the primitive formation ceases, and the country to the westward as far as Cumberland House is lime and clay stone rocks, with alluvial soil. The long promontory was sandy, with pebbles of quartz and granite; the only trees were pines, stunted by exposure to the wind.

The gale brought round us cormorants, gulls, loons, spotted snipes, and golden plovers. The two latter afforded us much sport and some excellent meals. On the 9th, a favourable wind tempted us, though late in the evening, to embark. Our course was along the west side of the lake; and before darkness enveloped us, we distinguished that we were passing between a chain of islands and the main. We were driven by heavy squalls accompanied by hail at the rate of seven or eight miles an hour. Once we endeavoured to land, but the surf rendered it impracticable. The gale blew directly towards the mouth of the Saskashawan, and indeed, the waves left no other course in our choice; a circumstance which prevented us from losing our way. At midnight, the yard [arm] was broken by a squall, and our companions immediately disappeared. We contrived to fish the yard with poles, keeping the boat before the waves with a few oars, and found ourselves in another hour at the mouth of the Saskashawan, where we rejoined Mr. Williams and encamped.

39. Lacombe gives the derivation of the name Winnipeg as from the Cree root *win* 'dirty' or 'stinking' and *pek* 'an expanse of water'.

The distance run in Lake Winnipeg was 88 miles, including the north and part of the west sides.

On the 9th [10 October], we proceeded three miles up the current to the Grand Rapid.[40] The Saskashawan is here ¼ of a mile wide, and runs with extraordinary noise and fury for three miles, round a long peninsula, fretted into a sheet of foam by the rocks which interrupt it. In winter its surface is a snowy plain, undistinguishable from any other part. The portage is a mile in length, across the peninsula, with a high bank at each extremity, and a ravine in the middle, across which a wooden bridge has been built by the Hudson's Bay people. The place is not provided with any other facility for transportation, although the whole trade of the interior is detained two days by that operation as it is at present conducted. The cause of it, according to both the trading companies, is the same, each party alleging that carts or trucks were once made use of and, being left at the portage, destroyed by the other; which, if true, changes the subject of censure from folly to crime.

It was here that Mr. Williams had seized Mr. McTavish's party which we saw at York Factory. In this country, justice cannot act without force; but the latter is by no means dependent on the former, which, having sometimes employed its aid, is now compelled to serve any end which it proposes. The Hudson's Bay people suspected that their opponents had secured justice on their side, and thus prepared for retaliation, were concealed in the neighbourhood. However, they did not make their appearance, and we were spared the humiliating spectacle of the expected contention.[41]

The woods on the banks are thick, and well stocked with partridges and rabbits. Pelicans and fishing eagles frequent the rapid. One of the latter birds was killed with a ball, after having sustained several discharges of small shot, many of which did not pierce the scales of its talons. It plumage was brown, with a mixture of grey and a white belly, and its wings extended eight feet.[42]

40. At Grand Rapids, the Saskatchewan River dropped 75 feet in three miles. Since 1965, a Manitoba Hydro dam at this site has raised the level of Cedar Lake a further 12 feet, flooding the lower river area and forming a reservoir covering 1,350 square miles. It generates 472 megawatts, presently about one quarter of Manitoba's electric power.

41. In retaliation for the seizure of their partners in June, 1819, the North West Company men were indeed lying in wait here the next summer (1820). Colin Robertson was captured, but Governor Williams wisely took the rarely used Minago route and avoided capture.

42. Hood has greatly exaggerated the wing span of this osprey, at most six feet.

On the 12th [October], we left the portage, and the 13th passed Cross Lake and a portage on its west side, at the opening of the river.[43] The lake is four miles in breadth, and the river between it and Cedar Lake is very rapid, wheeling in a thousand intermingling eddies among the islands which concealed the banks. Some of these wood-crowned clusters displayed the remains of beauty which in its prime was superior to that of the prospects in Hill River. So quickly is the face of nature altered by the decay of summer, that it may be viewed each day with new interest. But this was the last scene. The yellow leaf hung quivering, though the wind was still, and the next storm left the forest bare.

We had made some progress in Cedar Lake on the 14th when we were driven by bad weather on a small island, which, producing nothing but stones, we could not even pitch a tent. The shore which we had left was not more than three miles distant; but, as we dreaded no inconvenience so much as delay, we kept our ground, and were relieved the next morning by a fair wind, which brought us at 4 p.m. into Muddy Lake.[44] Cedar Lake is so called from a species of white cedar found on its bank;[45] its length is 16 miles, and its extent to the northward, where it receives another branch of the Saskashawan [Summerberry River], has not been explored. At the borders of Muddy Lake, we found some tents of Indians, who were occupied in shooting geese, of which we obtained a plentiful supply for a small quantity of rum. On the 16th, we entered one of the principal branches of the Saskashawan, which discharges itself into the lake by several channels formed of muddy banks, which the river has brought down. The most tedious and uninteresting part of our journey now commenced. The rapidity of the current prevented us from making more than one mile in an hour, and the shore was one continued quagmire. The river is generally 1/4 of a mile wide, and divided into many branches by large islands. The soil is alluvial mud, with limestone rocks. On both sides, the banks declined towards the stream in long shelves, indented at different heights by the water, and fenced above by impervious thickets of willows, regular as a clipped

43. Demi-charge Rapid, so named because boats could make their way up the rapid only if half the cargo was unloaded. Now submerged beneath the dam reservoir.

44. The name given to an expansion then present in the Saskatchewan River delta at

the west side of Cedar Lake.

45. This isolated occurrence, 230 miles to the northwest of the continuous range of the cedar, was fortuitously situated for the repair of fur trade canoes.

hedge; so that our view was for six days confined to the unvarying space within their boundaries.

On the 19th [October], we landed on the north bank at the borders of a small lake,[46] where we found a large encampment of Indians belonging to Cumberland House. They all recognized Mr. Williams, whom they saluted by the appellation of father, desiring drams of spirits as an acknowledgement of their relationship. The Cree Indians were never informed of the object of our mission, and they confounded us with the traders, till long after our arrival at Cumberland House; a mistake of no importance to us in this part of the country.

We were enabled to proceed much faster than before by tracking the boats, as the mud was frozen. Many trees of the largest dimensions which had been brought down by the ice in the spring, were scattered over the banks, and furnished us with fuel, of which we should otherwise have been almost destitute. Some showers of snow seemed to be the signal of departure to the geese and ducks. This river is the last of their summer haunts, and they linger till the ice threatens to cut off their subsistence. They now put themselves in motion with so much expedition, that after the 22nd no more were visible.

On the 21st [October], we encamped at the entrance of a little river [Tearing River] connecting the Saskashawan with Pine Island [Cumberland] Lake, and on the 22nd endeavoured to force our way through it, against a current and a wind so strong, that nothing but the certainty of being, in another day, blocked by the ice, could have induced us to persevere. We were a little sheltered by the river, but at the entrance of a small lake,[47] the wind kept us stationary for an hour and a half. The spray froze in falling, and encrusted the boat, the rowers and the oars, in ice. Violent exertion was the only resource against the cold, and our difficulties thus operating to destroy each other, we at length crossed the lake, but were compelled by darkness to encamp within four miles of Cumberland House.

On the 23rd [October], the temperature of the air was 20°, and of the water 33°. The river was choked by driving ice and we tracked to the entrance of Pine Island Lake, from which we distinguished our intended winter abode at the distance of three miles on the south side. A very short delay would have subjected us to serious embarrassment, for

46. Adjacent to Reader Lake, a few miles west of The Pas.

47. Merely a dilatation of the Tearing River. October 23 was an unusually early date for ice.

the margin of the lake was already frozen two hundred yards from the beach. At 10 a.m., we landed, and were lodged in the Hudson's Bay Company's house.

Here our journey terminated for the year 1819—having travelled 685½ miles into the interior, from York Factory.

3

Cumberland House and Pasquia Hills

*Proceedings at Cumberland House
during the winter.*

*Departure of Messrs. Franklin and Back on
the snow to Lake Athapescow.*

*Final departure of the remaining part of
the expedition in canoes.*

The arrival of the Expedition having been wholly unexpected at Cumberland House, we were not accommodated without difficulty, but our men were immediately employed to prepare a house for our reception, within the stockades, which had been partly erected in the summer. It was built of wood, the interstices being choked up with mud, and the roof boarded. The chimneys were made of stones, and the windows of moose skin parchment. Our tardy people were a month in completing it, and it proved rather too airy for this climate. We kept the chimneys in a constant blaze, notwithstanding which our pens and brushes were frozen to the paper, and we felt at the same time the extremes of cold and heat at each side of our persons. We retained two of our men as servants, and permitted the rest to serve with the people belonging to the post, on condition that they should not interfere in the business of trade.

Our next care was to introduce ourselves to the gentlemen in charge of the North West Company's house, Mr. Conolly.[1] He promised all the assistance in his power to our future plans, and his conduct gave us ample reason to be satisfied of his sincerity.

The North West house is of recent erection, but the Hudson's Bay Company house was built and named Cumberland House about 40 years ago, by Mr. Hearne.[2] Its Latitude is 53°56′40″N., and Longitude by

1. William Connolly. One of the North West Company traders seized at Grand Rapids on 18 June that year, he evidently had been released. Born near Lachine about 1787, he had joined the N. W. Co. as a clerk in 1801. After amalgamation, he was Chief Factor of the New Caledonia district on the west side of the Rocky Mountains in 1828. In 1831 he retired to St. Eustache in Lower Canada.

2. Actually, 45 years before. Hearne in 1774, two years after returning from his overland trek to the mouth of the Coppermine, founded Cumberland House,

chronometers 102°16′40″ W. It is on the north side of Pine Island, which is 15 miles in length, and bounded on the north by the lake, on the south by the Saskashawan, and on the east and west by little rivers running into the Saskashawan.[3] The soil is calcareous and not very deep, the limestone rocks appearing in many places above the surface. The trees, though much exhausted, are still numerous at some distance from the houses. They are said to harbour mosquitoes in summer, and the people are obliged in consequence to deprive themselves of the relief afforded by their shade. It is a remarkable and unaccountable circumstance, that wherever the pine tree is cut down, the poplar springs up in its stead, and this island, originally a forest of pines, is now covered with groves of the balsam poplar.[4]

The animals frequenting the country are moose deer, and a few reindeer [caribou], black and brown bears, grey, black and yellow wolves, red, cross and silver foxes, wolverenes, martens, cats or lynxes, fishers, otters, skunks, minks, muskrats, porcupines, beavers, ermines, and mice. The birds remaining at our arrival, were ptarmigans, partridges, ravens, owls, woodpeckers, grosbeaks, crossbills, magpies, whiskey jacks,[5] blackbirds, and snowbirds [snow buntings]. All these

---

the first inland post of the Hudson's Bay Company and now the oldest settlement in the present province of Saskatchewan. It was built first in the bay two miles west of the Tearing River, as shown on Peter Fidler's map of 1792. [J. B. Tyrrell, ed., *Journals of Samuel Hearne and Philip Turnor between the years 1774 and 1792* (Toronto: Champlain Society, 1934).] Soon thereafter it was moved west to the North West Company post at the present townsite, about one mile further west on the south shore of the lake. The longitude given by Hood is exactly correct.

3. The west channel was the Bigstone River. In 1819 Cumberland Lake was a deep, clear lake, with the Bigstone and Tearing Rivers as its outlets to the Saskatchewan. About 1875, spring ice jams blocked the old passage of the Saskatchewan, which flooded and then flowed northward, cutting a channel through to the lower Torch River and thence by a maze of channels into Cumberland Lake. Since that time, most of the waters of the Saskatchewan have

flowed down the new channel into the west end of Cumberland Lake, forming a delta of mud flats at its entrance, and generally silting and muddying the lake. The name of Pine Island is no longer used for the island at Cumberland House, but inexplicably has been assigned on modern topographic maps to a large uninhabited island at the northwest side of Cumberland Lake.

4. This is a perceptive account of the usual succession. After a coniferous stand is destroyed by fire or logging, the tree that thrives in the open sunlight is the aspen poplar. After the poplars grow up and provide sufficient shade, seedling spruce once more appear; their dense stands in time choke out the decaying poplars. Thus the spruce [Hood's 'pine'] is the climax or end-stage species.

5. The gray jay. 'Whiskey jack' is a corruption of its Cree name, variously rendered as *wiskatjan* by Lacombe, *whiskae-shawneesh* by Richardson, *uskashoan* by Drummond, and *whiskey-jonish* by Sabine. It is a year-round resident in northern woods.

were seen at intervals till the month of January, after which they buried themselves, except the raven, in the inmost recesses of the woods. The lake contains sturgeon, pike, trout, perch, suckers and tittameg or whitefish; but their numbers are not great.

Both the Hudson's Bay and North West Company's houses are surrounded by stockades and flanked with wooden bastions. They have grounds inclosed which supply them with potatoes, barley, and Indian corn. It is gratifying to contemplate the successful efforts of cultivation on this hitherto neglected land. Mr. Williams has done much, the possibility of which was disputed by two parties that only agreed, in not making the attempt.[6] He has conquered incredulity; but it is merely the outwork of indolence, a fortress impregnable by nature.

Horses are sent from the plains near Carlton House and from Edmonton to all the neighbouring posts, where they are eminently useful in dragging fuel for the houses. These animals are found in a wild state on the Columbia, beyond the Rocky Mountains, where, in some places, neither natives nor Europeans have any other food. Their flesh, however, is said to be very good. From the Lesser Slave Lake and Peace River they have been taken to Fort Chepewyan, and a few of them are there domesticated. So extensively have they propagated themselves since their first introduction by Hernando Cortez into Mexico.[7] They must have become known to many nations of the new world, ages before any other inhabitant of the old. Some of them are equal in size and beauty to any of the European breed. When their labour is not required, they are sent into the woods to subsist, and sometimes are not seen for a month in the severest part of winter. They scrape through two or three feet of snow to reach their food, and sleep in swamps among the long reeds. This treatment renders them lean and wild, and they contract many vicious habits, dashing their riders against trees, and rolling

6. The new governor, with official headquarters at York Factory, had spent his first winter at Cumberland House from October 1818 at least through February 1819. By 1833, 'the implements of tillage and the capacious barns were silent monuments of waste; the horses were becoming wild...and a solitary hog stood every chance of dying without issue.' [Richard King, *Narrative of a Journey to the Shores of the Arctic Ocean in 1833, 1834, and 1835* (London: Richard Bentley, 1836), p. 54.]

7. Cortez brought horses to Mexico in 1519. By September 1754, the Indians southwest of present Battleford were already using horses when visited by Anthony Henday, the first Englishman and probably the first white man to watch a buffalo hunt. Henday bought a horse to carry his provisions and saw several wild horses.

themselves in the snow. Some of them will chase the dogs from their meals, and devour the frozen fish themselves. Those which have been accustomed to hunt the buffalo, incline themselves when galloping on one side; a practice taught them by the Stone Indians,[8] which enables them to turn quickly, and to avoid the badger holes on the plains. If the wolves fall upon a single horse, it is devoured by them, but not till it has made a desperate defence.

Cattle and pigs have been brought to Cumberland House by Mr. Williams, and are rapidly thriving. There is some excellent pasture for sheep, but it requires an extensive and lofty inclosure to protect them from the wolves. The cold has the effect of increasing the length and quantity of hair on the skins of all animals, whether native or transported hither from warmer climates.

The dog is the most useful, though troublesome, animal in the country. Horses can travel with burthens only on a beaten path; but three dogs will drag a sledge load of 200 Tlb., in snow through which no man can make any progress without snow shoes. They resemble wolves, both in appearance and disposition. Domestication does not improve their manners and no kindness attaches them. They are cowardly, stupid and ravenous. At the houses, nothing is secure from them; they eat their way through the parchment windows and devour every animal substance without distinction. In the night they bury themselves in the snow, from which they rise at certain periods and exercise themselves in a long, melancholy, and unnatural howl, all joining in the same key, and ceasing almost at the same instant. No rest can be procured by those unaccustomed to this dismal serenade. But their hardships are without comparison among the creatures allotted to the use of man. Often they carry for many days a heavy load of provisions, of which they have no share, and are at last destined by necessity to supply its place.[9]

The inhabitants of Cumberland House subsist on salted geese, fish, moose and buffalo meat. The fish is brought on sledges from Beaver

8. Assiniboine or Stony Sioux tribe. 'One who cooks by the use of stones' in Ojibwa. *Assini* means 'stone' in Cree. The tribe had originated near Lake of the Woods and spread westward to share the prairies with the Plains Cree.

9. The best account of the Cree Indian dog, or *attim,* is by Dr. Richardson, who considered it the domesticated cross between the prairie wolf, or coyote, and the timber wolf. It was smaller than the Eskimo dog, with a total length of about four feet. Its flesh was eaten by the Crees and highly esteemed by the voyageurs. [John Richardson, *Fauna Boreali-Americana* (London: John Murray, 1829), I, 80-82.]

Lake,[10] which is stocked much better than Pine Island Lake, and Indian hunters furnish the moose meat from the Basquiau Hill [Pasquia Hills], about 40 miles to the southward. A person resides there in a leather tent, to traffic with them for provisions and furs. The buffalo meat is smoke-dried at Carlton House. We have no reason to complain of our fare. The fish of North America, especially the tittameg and sturgeon are, perhaps, the best in the world. The Indians do not use salt, and the Europeans indulge a little indolence at the expence of living without it; for though it is found in many parts of the country, in springs and on the earth, they eat fish the whole year unprovided with it, with bread, or with vegetables, except at Cumberland House; a proof that industry is not to be excited for the mere gratification of the palate.

A short time after our arrival, the thermometer rose above the freezing point, and the ice disappeared from the Saskashawan and the middle of the lake. By the latter end of November, it formed permanently, and the snow began to collect. The partridges [willow ptarmigan] and rabbits became white, and traps were set to catch martens, foxes and wolverenes. All the productions of the earth were buried till the spring. No sound disturbed the silence of the woods, but the frequent strokes of the axe. It is during this long interval of rest that the traders contract those habits of supineness which are always found in the extremities of climate. Few of them have books, and the incidents of their lives do not furnish much subject for thought, nor could any source supply a consumption so perpetual. In such a state one might be disposed to envy the half year's slumber of the bears.

It was easy by exercise to keep the body warm in the open air. No additional clothing is required except flannels, and the feet are wrapped in several folds of duffil. The shoes [moccasins] worn both by natives and Europeans are made of moose skin, and tied with thongs above the ankles. Mittens are suspended by a cord round the neck, for the hands. Many expedients have been tried to protect the face, of which a mask is the best. The breath freezes and forms a coat of ice on the inside, to which every respiration adds a fresh surface, but it is a defence against the wind.

It is a curious fact, that the sudden abstraction of heat from the human body produces the same feeling as if it was burnt, and the

10. Amisk Lake. *Amisk* is the Cree word for beaver.

place assumes the same appearance. It is scarcely to be credited that natural cold is ever so great as to cause sensations instantaneous and violent. No good conductor of heat can be touched without severe pain. A piece of metal put into the mouth inadvertently immediately freezes all the moisture about it, and the part in contact loses its skin. Large pike and trout, which when taken struggle with great strength, are thrown on the ice and become motionless in a minute, and before they are carried to the house might be pounded to powder. It is necessary to thaw every kind of meat before it can be cut with a knife.

It was impossible to use astronomical instruments without freezing the hands. Our observations, especially lunars, were rendered erroneous by the disproportionate contraction of the arcs of the sextants.

In the beginning of December, Mr. Franklin came to the resolution of going forward, accompanied by Mr. Back, to Lake Athapescow; thinking that his presence there would be more effectual, in providing hunters and guides, than the letters which had been sent before him. On the removal of the ice, the rest of the expedition was to follow in canoes. The chief motive of our stay here was the hope of procuring the Esquimaux interpreter in the ensuing spring; otherwise we should have endeavoured to get our stores forward on sledges during the winter. Mr. Franklin determined to commence his journey in the middle of January.

The Indians seldom visit the trading posts in winter. In spring and autumn they receive credit, in a certain quantity of cloth, ammunition and tobacco, and this credit is renewed every year, though they continue debtors their whole lives. Some of them accurately remember their debts and exert themselves to discharge them, but others are seduced by the traders of the opposing company, to whom they carry their furs, considering all their former obligations cancelled. To avoid this persons are sent out with them to take charge of every fur when it is obtained, who accompany them through the winter, and share their want and their filth. The Indians provide them with food, but expect them to cut wood and perform several other offices in the tents. They soon learn to speak the language of the natives, and to adopt the same improvident habits. It often happens that a party of their opponents claims a right to their furs, on the plea that the Indians have disposed of property which was already due, and the dispute ends in plunder, or murder. Such examples have fortunately lost their pernicious effects, from a people whom the Indians now heartily despise. But the perversion of their minds by the use of spirits will soon complete the triumph of European vices.

The multiplied distresses of the Cree Indians this year, occasioned a univeral stagnation of trade. Every family had to deplore the loss of several of its members by the hooping cough or measles. In vain they were urged to hunt; their sole occupation was the performance of religious ceremonies, to arrest the progress of the disease, till want compelled them to seek the trading posts. There they cast themselves on the earth, and nothing but spirits could rouse them from the torpor of their grief.

On the 16th of January, a packet was dispatched to the Red River,[11] and we availed ourselves of the opportunity to send letters by Canada to England. On the morning of the 18th, Messrs. Franklin and Back set out on the Saskashawan, with four sledges and five men, belonging to both the houses, except John Hepburn, who had joined the expedition in London. Their intended route was by Carlton House and Isle-à-la-Crosse, in order to relieve the dogs and men at those posts. Mr. Franklin left two chronometers for the continuation of the survey by water.

The numerous connections between the traders and the Indian women have given birth to a race called Metiss or Bois Brulee's [sic] by the Canadians, and half bred by the Europeans. The former are uneducated, volatile and vicious, like the Canadians; but the latter add the qualifications of an Indian hunter, to the sedateness and industry of Europeans.[12] They gladly learn to read and write, are proud of the advantages which they derive from their birth, and will not be persuaded to adopt the wandering and uncertain manner of life recommended to them by their Indian relations.

They have dark hair and eyes, regular features, and intelligent countenances. Many of the women are fair and exceedingly handsome. Both Canadian and English Metiss are the most useful persons in the service of the fur traders, by whom they are regularly engaged as guides and interpreters.

Mr. Williams has made an excellent regulation, obliging those who take Indian women, to contribute annually a small sum which is set

11. A 400-mile trip by snowshoes or dogteam.

12. The English and Scotch were 'Europeans' whereas this term was not applied to the French, who were perhaps justifiably considered 'Canadians' after nearly 200 years residence along the St. Lawrence. The 10,000 original colonists in Lower Canada had by this time increased to about 200,000.

apart for their future support. They were before frequently deserted with their children, from motives of convenience or caprice, and either became a heavy burthen to the trading posts, or returned to the Indians, totally disqualified for the performance of those laborious duties which are exacted from the women by their own countrymen. Mr. Williams is also endeavouring to establish schools, and should his project succeed, he will confer on these people the only real benefit which they have received in their long intercourse with a civilized nation.

On the 2nd of February, a packet arrived from York Fort. The brig *Wear*, which had been sent to Moose Factory with three of the prisoners taken at the Grand Rapid, was stopped by the ice at the entrance of Hudson's Straits, and had returned to York. The bearers of the packet were the master of the *Wear*, and a single Indian. They had been thirty-six days on their journey.[13]

On the 10th of February, the wolves attacked and carried off the fish sledges on their way from Beaver Lake. About Cumberland House, they became numerous and ferocious. One of them devoured a dog at the gates of the North West house, although his leg had previously been broken by a ball. They generally fly from man; but on the 18th, a wolf attacked two men armed with hatchets at Moose Lake and wounded them both. On the 20th [of February] the Canadians who went with our party, returned from Carlton House, bringing letters from Mr. Franklin. Their journey had occupied 14 days, the track being exceedingly bad from a heavy fall of snow. Mr. Franklin had frozen his arms [fingers][14] in attempting to observe for the latitude, but proposed to leave Carlton on the 10th.

In March, the snow on the lakes was more than three feet deep, and drifted in some places so as to render them impassable. It began however to thaw in the sun's rays, and the thermometer sometimes rose above the freezing point in the shade. On the 19th, the Saskashawan opened in several places which were alternately frozen and thawed till the 5th of April, when a channel formed itself in the middle which closed no more.

Being desirous of obtaining a drawing of a moose deer, and also to

13. A commendable mail service, considering the time of year and the distances involved. The *Wear* had sailed from York Factory 7 September and disembarked J. D. Campbell and four lesser prisoners at Moose Factory 26 September.

14. 'Fingers' has been substituted in pencil, possibly by Franklin himself.

make some observations on the height of the Aurora, I set out on the 23rd [in March] to pass a few days at the Basquiau Hill. Two men accompanied me, with dogs and sledges, who were going to the hill for meat.

The snowshoes and sledges of this country have been accurately described by Mr. Hearne; but I shall endeavour to spare the reader the trouble of referring to his work. A snowshoe is made of two light bars of wood, fastened together at their extremities and projected into curves by transverse bars. The side bars have been so shaped by a frame, and dried before a fire, that the front part of the shoe turns up like the prow of a boat, and the part behind terminates in an acute angle. The spaces between the bars are filled up with a fine netting of leather thongs, except that part behind the main bar which is occupied by the foot. The netting is there coarse and strong, and the foot is attached to the main bar by straps passing round the heel, but only fixing the toes, so that the heel rises after each step, and the tail of the shoe is dragged on the snow. Between the main bar, and another in front of it, a small space is left, permitting the toes to descend a little, which prevents their extremities from chafing [in the act of raising the heel to make the step forward].[15] The length of a snowshoe is from four to six feet, and the breadth, $1\frac{1}{2}$ to $1\frac{3}{4}$ feet, being adapted to the size of the wearer. The weight [of] a man, embracing so large a surface, does not sink more than a foot in the softest snow. The motion of walking in them is perfectly natural; for one shoe is level with the snow, when the edge of the other is passing over it. It is not easy to use them among bushes, without frequent overthrows, nor to rise afterwards without help. Each shoe weighs about two Tlb., unclogged with snow; but in a long journey the feet, though well covered with socks, are much galled by the bars and straps.

The northern [Chipewyan] Indian snowshoes differ a little from those of the southern [Cree] Indians, having a greater curvature on the outside than on the inside of each shoe; one advantage of which is, that when the foot rises, the overbalanced side descends, and throws off the snow. All the superiority of European art has been unable to improve the native contrivance of this useful machine.

Sledges are made of two or three flat boards, curving upwards in front and fastened together by transverse pieces of wood above. They

15. Another addition in pencil in the same handwriting, not Hood's.

are so thin, that if heavily laden, they bend with the inequalities of the surface. The ordinary dog sledges are eight or ten feet long and very narrow, but the lading is secured to a lacing round the edges. The sledges or carioles used by the traders are turned up at both ends, and have sides of painted leather or wood, and a covering for the legs.

Besides snowshoes, each individual carries his blanket, hatchet, steel, flint and tinder. Firearms are also indispensable; not that there is much reason to dread the attacks of any carnivorous animal, or that the natives of this country have ever shown any hostile disposition towards the traders; but to repel the assaults of their own fellow subjects, or to commit outrages which admit of no defence, but from such weapons.

We found the Saskashawan open and were obliged to follow it several miles to the eastward. We did not then cross it without wading in water which had overflowed the ice, and our snowshoes were encumbered with a heavy weight for the remainder of the day. On the south bank of the Saskashawan were some poplars 10 or 12 feet in circumference at the root.[16] Beyond the river, we traversed an extensive swamp, bounded by woods. In the evening we crossed the Swan Lake, about six miles in breadth and eight in length.[17] On its south side we halted, 24 miles SSW of Cumberland House.

Nothing in this climate will afford more matter of astonishment than the manner of sustaining life while traversing snowy wildernesses, destitute of lodging, in a degree of cold once considered impossible:—and when proved to be possible, deemed insupportable. A single description of the method practiced both by Europeans and natives, of sheltering themselves during the night, will convey a general idea of it under all circumstances. A place is selected, if it can be found, inclosed by trees. Some of the party cut wood and the rest scrape with their snow shoes, a large hole in the snow, which is piled up as a barricade against the wind. At one end of the hole, a fire is kindled; a very tedious operation when the wood is green or the fingers benumbed. The remaining space is spread with small pine branches, and the travellers unload their sledges, placing their provision before the fire to thaw, and drying their snowshoes and socks.

16. A balsam poplar of this diameter is hardly credible, but is confirmed by the following: 'In the river valleys north of the prairies it has been known to reach a height of 100 feet and diameters of more than four feet.' [Native Trees of Canada, Forestry Branch Bulletin No. 61 (Ottawa, 1956), p. 94.]

17. Now known as Wapisew Lake; wapisew is Cree for 'swan'. It is only 16 air miles south-south-west of Cumberland House.

The chief article of food is pemmican, which does not require cooking.[18] Fish are thawed and given to the dogs. Snow water has some disagreeable qualities which may be destroyed by boiling it. When the meal is finished, a stock of fuel is collected and the fire renewed. Everything upon which the teeth of the dogs can make any impression must be placed in trees out of their reach. The party then roll themselves in their blankets with their feet next to the fire, and the dogs lie among them without distinction, all repugnance to filth giving way to the desire of warmth. Fatigue produces so sound a rest that no disturbance is suffered, unless the flame seizes a blanket, or an exposed part is frozen.

At 4 in the morning, March 24th, we continued the journey. We crossed some creeks in the woods and another large swamp. These swamps are covered with water in summer, to the depth of several feet, which is the melted snow from the higher grounds. The tracks of foxes, wolves, wolverenes and martens, were very numerous. The people employed in carrying meat set traps on their way out and take possession of their captures at their return, for which they receive a sum from the Company, proportioned to the value of the fur.

In the evening, we crossed the Goose Lake, which is a little larger than Swan Lake, and afterwards the River Sepanack,[19] a branch of the Saskashawan forming an island extending 30 miles above and 40 below Cumberland house. We turned to the westward on the Root [Carrot] River which enters the Sepanack, and halted on its banks, having made a SWbS course and direct distance not more than 20 miles since the 23rd.

From the Root River we passed to the Shoal Lake on the 25th and then marched 12 miles through woods and swamps to the hunting tent mentioned at the beginning of this chapter.[20] It was in a grove of large poplars, and would have been no unpleasant residence if we could have avoided the smoke. Three large stages supported by trees were covered with moose meat purchased from the Indians.

18. Plains forts, such as Carlton, supplied the forest forts, such as Cumberland, with pemmican. Dry, pounded buffalo meat with fat tallow added was a concentrated food; a day's ration for a voyageur was 1½ pounds, considered equivalent to eight pounds of fresh meat.

19. The Sipanok Channel, which carries the overflow from the Saskatchewan River into the Carrot River system, and vice versa. *Sepanuk* in Cree meant 'a branch of river, running around an island'.

20. Probably near the present junction of Highway 163 and its branch road into the Red Earth Indian Reserve.

A heavy gale from the westward, with snow, confined us for several days to the tent. On the 30th, two Indians arrived, one of whom, named the Warrior, was well known at the house. We endeavoured to prevail upon them to set out in quest of moose, which they agreed to do, on receiving some rum. Promises were of no avail; the smallest present gratification is preferred to the certainty of ample reward at another period; an unfailing indication of strong animal passions and a weak understanding.[21] On complying with their demand they departed.

The next day [31 March], I went to the Warrior's tent at the distance of 11 miles SWbS.[22] The country was materially changed. The pine disappeared, and gentle slopes with clumps of large poplars formed some pleasing groups from the open heaths which afforded a view of them. Willows were scattered over the swamps. When I entered the tent, the Indians spread a buffalo robe before the fire, and desired me to sit down. They were eating and sleeping, many of them without any covering except the breech cloth and a blanket over the shoulders: a state in which they love to indulge themselves, till hunger drives them forth to the chase. Besides the Warrior's family was that of another hunter named Long Legs, whose bad success in hunting had reduced him to the necessity of feeding on moose leather for three weeks, when he was compassionately relieved by the Warrior. I was an unwilling witness of the preparation of my dinner by the Indian women. They cut into pieces a portion of fat meat, using for that purpose a knife and their teeth. It was boiled in a kettle and served in a platter made of birch bark, which, being dirty, they had peeled off the surface. However, the flavour of good moose meat will survive any process that it undergoes in their hands, except smoking.

Having provided myself with some drawing materials, I amused the Indians with a sketch of the interior of the tent and its inhabitants. An old woman who was relating with great volubility an account of some quarrel with the traders at Cumberland House, broke off from her narration when she perceived my design; perhaps supposing that I was employing some charm against her; for the Indians have been taught a

21. Hood is rather unfair here; nomadic tribes cannot carry many possessions or lay things in store for the future. It is simply an adaption to their nomadic existence that they must feast and share whenever they make a kill.

22. Somewhere along the northwestern edge of the Pasquia Hills.

supernatural dread of particular pictures. One of the young men drew with a piece of charcoal, a figure resembling a frog, on the side of the tent, and by significantly pointing at me, excited peals of merriment from his companions. The caricature was involuntary; and I soon fixed their attention by producing my pocket compass and affecting it with a knife. They have great curiosity, which might easily be directed to the attainment of useful knowledge.

As the dirt accumulated about these people was visibly of a communicative nature,[23] I removed at night into the open air, where the thermometer fell to 15° below zero, although it was the next day 60° above it.

In the morning [1 April], the Warrior and his companion arrived. I found that instead of hunting, they had passed the whole time in a drunken fit, at a short distance from the tent. In reply to our angry questions, the Warrior held out an empty vessel, as if to demand the payment of a debt, before he entered into any new negotiation. Not being inclined to starve his family, we set out for another Indian tent, ten miles to the southward but we found the frame only, or tent poles standing when we reached the spot. The men, by digging where the fireplace had been, ascertained that the Indians had quitted it the day before, and as their marches are short, when encumbered with the women and baggage, we sought out their track and followed it. At an abrupt angle of it, which was obscured by trees, the men suddenly disappeared, and hastening forward to discover the cause, I perceived them both still rolling at the foot of a steep cliff, over which they had been dragged while endeavouring to stop the descent of the sledges. The dogs were gazing silently with the wreck of their harness about them, and the sledges deeply buried in the snow. The effects of this accident did not detain us long, and we proceeded afterwards with greater caution.

The country was similar to that which we passed on the 30th. The air was warm at noon, and the solitary but sweet notes of the [gray] jay, the earliest spring bird, were in every wood. Late in the evening we

---

23. Probably body lice, *Pediculus humanis corporis*, or head lice, *P. capitis*. Samuel Hearne related that the Chipewyans did not consider it a disgrace to have lousy clothing, since they would 'amuse themselves with catching and eating these vermin; of which they are so fond, that the produce of a lousy head or garment affords them not only pleasing amusement, but a delicious repast.' [Samuel Hearne, *Journey 1769-1772* (London: Strahan & Cadell, 1795), p. 325.]

descried the ravens wheeling in circles round a small grove of poplars, and according to our expectations found the Indians encamped there. The men were absent hunting and returned unsuccessful. They had been several days without provisions, and thinking that I could depend upon the continuance of their exertions, I gave them a little rum. The next day they set out with their dogs.

The tents commonly used by the Indians are constructed by forming a cone of poles 14 or 15 feet long, one of which is forked to receive the rest; round the poles is rolled parchment or dressed skins, leaving an aperture above which gives light, and vents the smoke. The Cree Indians of the plains on the Saskashawan, paint figures on the outside of the skin with earths of various colours. The fire is in the middle and there is not room elsewhere for a person to stand upright. Pine branches are strewed on the ground, and every Indian possesses, besides his blanket, a buffalo hide dressed with the hair upon it, which is impenetrable by the cold. A pole is elevated above the fire, across the tent, to which their cooking utensils are suspended and it serves also to dry meat in the smoke.

Our hunters did not return, but they swept past us at midnight, in close pursuit, with their dogs. In the morning we found that a moose had eaten the bark of a tree near our fire. The hunters, however, again failed and they attributed the extreme difficulty of approaching the chase, to the calmness of the weather, which enabled it to hear them at a great distance. They concluded, as usual when labouring under any affliction, that they were tormented by an evil spirit, and assembled to beat a large tambourine and sing an address to the Manito or deity, praying for relief, according to the explanation which I received, but it consisted of only three words constantly repeated. One of the hunters yet remained abroad, and as the wind rose at noon, we had hopes that he was successful. In the evening he made his appearance and announcing that he had killed a large moose, immediately secured the reward which had been promised. The tidings were received with apparent indifference by people whose lives are alternate changes from the extremity of want, to abundance. But as their countenances seldom betray their emotions, it cannot be determined whether their apathy is real or affected. However, the women prepared their sledges and dogs with the design of dismembering and bringing home the carcass; a proceeding to which, in their necessitous condition, I could have had neither reasonable nor available objections, without giving them a substitute. By much solicitation, I obtained an audience, and offered them our own provisions, to suspend the work of destruction till the next day.

They agreed to the proposition and we set out with some Indians for the place where the animal was lying. The night advancing, we were separated by a snow storm, and not being skillful enough to follow tracks which were so speedily filled up, I was bewildered for several hours in the woods, when I met with an Indian, who led me back at such a pace, that I was always in the rear, to his infinite diversion. The Indians are vain of their local knowledge, which is certainly very wonderful. Our companions had taken out the entrails and young of the moose, which they buried in the snow. The Indians then returned to the tents and one of my men accompanied them. He was the person charged with the management of the trade at the hunting tent, and he observed that the opportunity of making a bargain with the Indians, while they were drinking, was too advantageous to be lost. It remained for us to prevent the wolves from mangling the moose, for which purpose, we wrapped ourselves in blankets between its feet and placed the hatchets within our reach. The night was stormy, and apprehension kept me long awake. But finding my companion in so deep a sleep that nothing could have roused him except the actual gripe of a wolf, I thought it advisable to imitate his example as much as was in my power, rather than bear the burthen of anxiety alone. At daylight, we shook off the snow which was heaped upon us and endeavoured to kindle a fire; but the violence of the storm defeated all our attempts. At length, two Indians arrived, with whose assistance we succeeded, and they took possession of it to show their sense of our obligations to them. We were ashamed of the scene before us: the entrails of the moose and its young, which had been buried at our feet, bore testimony to the nocturnal revel of the wolves, during the time we had slept. This was a fresh subject of derision for the Indians, whose appetites, however, would not suffer them to waste long upon us, a time so precious. They soon finished what the wolves had begun, and with as little aid from the art of cookery, eating both the young moose, and contents of the paunch, raw.[24]

24. Since the rutting season is late September and early October and the calving season is late May, the moose was perhaps six months pregnant in an eight months gestation. The unborn calf, possibly half its expected birth weight of 30 pounds, was considered a delicacy.

I had scarcely secured myself by a lodge of branches from the snow, and placed the moose in a position for my sketch,[25] when we were stormed by a troop of women and children, with their sledges and dogs. We obtained another short respite from the Indians, but our blows could not drive, nor their caresses entice, the hungry dogs from the tempting feast before them.

As the American moose deer is an animal of which I have not seen any perfect account, I shall add to what is already known, the information procured on this occasion.

This animal measured from the breast to the rump, 5 feet 1 inch. The height of the hump from the ground was 6 feet 3 inches. The length of the head was 2 feet 2 inches, and of the ears, 1 foot 1 inch. Its eyes were not larger than those of an ox, and situated 5 inches from the ears. The profile of the head is nearly a straight line, rising a little at each extremity, and gradually curving so as to form a very large nose. The hump is an elevation of four inches from the back, immediately over the fore shoulder, and the neck is short and very broad. The legs are well proportioned and delicate in appearance; but though not fleshy, they are sinewy and the bones large. The hoofs are disproportionately small, and do not open much when the foot is on the snow, in which it sinks almost to the ground. It must be observed that all these dimensions are larger in the male species. The females have no horns.

The throat, as far as the underlip, is furnished with hair two or three inches long; and the male is said to have a beard of 5 inches. The neck is covered with shaggy hair, which is shorter on the rest of the body, and erect on the back; the tail is a small tuft of hair and the legs are as smooth as those of a horse. The general colour of the hide is dark brown, with a tinge of red in summer, and of grey in winter. The thighs, belly, and throat are very dark, and the legs, light brown. The iris of the eye is burnt umber, and the pupil black.

The moose is not remarkable for quickness of sight, but its nose is sensible, and its large ears exceedingly acute. The female brings forth one or two young in May, and the horns of the male begin to shoot rather earlier. The young moose which I saw was completely formed. In August the horns of the male have attained their full growth, and he is then heard in the woods, bellowing and rubbing the skin off them against the trees. The hunters easily decoy him within their reach, by

25. For the result, see Hood's drawing [plate 9].

imitating the noise which he makes with them. The rutting season commences in September and the horns are cast in December; so that I had not an opportunity of seeing them.

This animal observes a singular regularity in its habits, lying down, and feeding at particular hours in the day. The shortness of its neck prevents it from reaching the ground without inconvenience, which the nature of its food does not require. It lives upon the tops of willows and the bark of young trees, and consequently cannot subsist in a barren country. It is much annoyed in summer by the mosquitoes, and the whole year, by a large and disgusting insect which breeds in its head.[26]

The weight of a male including the horns, exceeds 800 Tlb. The flesh is coarser than other venison, but juicy and well flavoured. The liver is sometimes entirely composed of fat. The nose is justly esteemed a great delicacy. The general mode of hunting the moose, practised by the Crees, is on foot, with the gun; which, from the hardship and difficulty attending it, few Europeans will attempt. When there is snow on the ground, its track is easily followed, but in summer, the eye only of an Indian can trace its footsteps on the bare rock and through the watery swamp. A single unwary step upon a decayed branch is sufficient to betray him, and it stretches at once across the country, generally against the wind with extended nostrils, to avoid a sudden advance upon new danger. Its quickest pace is a kind of trot, lifting its legs high, from the habit of walking in deep snow and fallen wood. The hunter does not attempt to keep it in sight, but pursues the track with unremitting perseverance, scarcely taking either food or rest, and thus the chase has been known to continue three or four days. The moose is said to make use of a manoeuvre when fatigued, which indicates a high degree of sagacity. It doubles on its track, and returning some miles, lies down to rest its limbs till the hunter passing at a distance gives it timely notice for flight. But the faculties of the human mind concentrated, and continually exercised in one employment, are too powerful for the instinct and superior organs of sense bestowed on the animal creation. An experienced hunter will, by frequent examinations of the impressions, determine nearly the time at which they were made, especially when snow or rain is falling. He leaves the track, if it is fresh, and makes a circuit till he has crossed it returning in a parallel line. After thus

26. Probably maggots of *Cephenemyia,* which occur in the nasopharyngeal cavities of the moose.

circumscribing the place which contains the object of his pursuit, he casts aside every incumbrance and creeps forward towards the centre: having reached, unobserved, a suitable distance, he supports his gun on a stone or tree and, breaking a small branch, his victim starts, rises, and stretches itself, and then receives the fatal blow. While life remains, it strikes violently with its fore feet and sometimes amply revenges itself on an enemy too eager to take possession of the spoils.

In spring, when the snow is deep and its surface frozen, the moose is the prey of boys or women, and carnivorous animals. The hunters scarcely sink in their snowshoes, while the moose plunges to the belly at every step, wounding its legs against the hard edges of the snow. Dogs are brought to the chase, which confound and impede it by their noise, for they are not courageous enough to seize it. In stormy weather, the uproar of the wind in the forest renders the quickness of its ears useless, but it usually seeks the plains to escape the falling trees.

I had not finished my sketch before the impatient crowd tore the moose to pieces and loaded their sledges with meat. On our way to the tents, a black wolf rushed out upon an Indian who happened to pass near its den. It was shot, and the Indians carried away 3 black whelps, to improve the breed of their dogs. I purchased one of them intending to send it to England; but it perished for want of proper nourishment.

The Latitude of these tents, was 53°12′46″ N. and Longitude [by] chronometers, 103°13′10″ W. On the 5th of April, we set out for the hunting tent by our former track and arrived there in the evening. As the increasing warmth of the weather had threatened to interrupt communication by removing the ice, orders had been sent from Cumberland House to the people at the tent to quit it without delay, which we did on the 7th. The Latitude was ascertained to be 53°22′48″ and Longitude 103°7′17″ W. Some altitudes of the Aurora were obtained, the results of which shall be noticed elsewhere.

We had a fine view at sunrise, of the Basquiau hill, skirting half the horizon with its white sides chequered by forests of pine. It is seen from Pine Island Lake, at the distance of 50 miles, and cannot therefore be less than ¾ of a mile in perpendicular height, probably the greatest elevation between the Atlantic Ocean and the Rocky Mountains. But it is the most remarkable mountain in the world for extent, being about 200 miles in circumference.[27] The direction of its length is NEbE and

27. The actual height of land is 2,680 feet above sea level. [The Cypress Hills in

SWbW. The ascent is gradual, except at the eastern extremity, and so beset by fallen wood as to be almost inaccessible. It is probably formed of limestone like the surrounding country.[28]

A small stream runs near the hunting tent, strongly impregnated with salt. There are several salt springs about it, which are not frozen during the winter.[29]

The surface of the snow, thawing in the sun, and freezing at night, had become a strong crust which sometimes gave way in a circle round our feet, immerging us in the soft snow beneath. The people were afflicted with snow blindness, a kind of ophthalmia occasioned by the reflection of the sun's rays in the spring. It is a tormenting disorder, but not attended by lasting bad consequences.[30]

At the borders of the Swan Lake we halted, having marched 48 statute miles.

The miseries endured during the first journey of this nature are so great, that nothing could induce the sufferer to undertake a second, while under the influence of present pain. He feels his frame crushed by unaccountable pressure, he drags a galling and stubborn weight at his feet, and his track is marked with blood. The dazzling scene around him affords no rest to his eye, no object to divert his attention from his own agonizing sensations. When he rises from sleep, half his body seems dead, till quickened into feeling by the irritation of his sores. But fortunately for him, no evil makes an impression so evanescent as pain. It cannot be wholly banished, nor recalled with the force of reality, by any act of the mind, either to affect our determinations, or to sympathize with another. The traveller soon forgets his sufferings, and at every future journey, they recur with diminished acuteness.

A hard frost enabled us to reach the Saskashawan early the next day, which we crossed in a boat, and arrived at Cumberland House.

---

southwestern Saskatchewan reach 4,567 feet.] Measured at 1,800 feet elevation, the Pasquia Hills are just under 130 miles in circumference.

28. An incorrect assumption; it is mostly Cretaceous shale. The Palaeozoic limestone begins just north of Cumberland Lake.

29. When I flew over on 20 March 1971, I failed to locate open water in this immediate area. Twenty miles to the south, near the probable site of Hood's moose painting, Larry Stevenson reports two

springs on the Papikwan River that remain open all winter.

30. Snow-blindness is commonest in the bright sunshine of spring, when the unmelted snow reflects the dazzling rays. Swelling of the eyelids and conjunctiva may prevent opening of the eyes in the acute stage, but this subsides without residual damage. Dr. Richardson reported relief in 20 to 30 hours, after direct instillation of a drop of laudanum [opium tincture] twice daily.

Letters had been received from Messrs. Franklin and Back, dated at Isle-à-la-Crosse February 27. Their march to that place was performed without any of their former misfortunes, and they were preparing to proceed to Lake Athapescow.

Between the 10th and 12th [April], the return of the swans, geese, and ducks, gave certain intelligence of the advance of spring. The juice of the [Manitoba] maple tree began to flow, and the women repaired to the woods for the purpose of collecting it. This tree, which abounds to the southward is not, I believe, found to the northward of the Saskashawan. The Indians obtain the sap by making incisions into the tree. They boil it down and evaporate the water, skimming off the impurities. They are so fond of sweets, that after this simple process they set an extravagant price upon it.

On the 15th fell the first shower of rain we had seen for six months, and on the 17th the thermometer rose to 77° in the shade. The whole face of the country was deluged by the melted snow. All the nameless heaps of dirt, accumulated in the winter, now floated over the very thresholds, and the long imprisoned scents dilated into vapours so penetrating, that no retreat was any security from them. The flood descended into the cellar below our house, and destroyed a quantity of powder and tea, a loss irreparable in our situation.

The noise made by the frogs, which this inundation produced, is almost incredible. There is strong reason to believe that they outlive the severity of winter.[31] They have often been found frozen and revived by warmth; nor is it possible that the multitude which incessantly filled our ears with its discordant notes, could have been matured in two or three days.

The fishermen at Beaver Lake, and the other detached parties, were ordered to return to the post. The expedients to which the poor people were reduced, to cross a country so beset with water, presented many uncouth spectacles. The inexperienced were glad to compromise with the loss of property, for the safety of their persons, and astride upon ill-balanced rafts with which they struggled to be uppermost, exhibited a ludicrous picture of distress. Happy were those who could patch up an old canoe, though obliged to bear it half the way on their shoulders, through miry bogs and interwoven willows. But the veteran trader, wedged in a box of skin with his wife, children, dogs and furs, wheeled

31. By hibernation.

62

triumphantly through the current, and deposited his heterogeneous cargo safely on the shore.

The woods re-echoed with the return of their exiled tenants. An hundred tribes as gaily dressed as any burnished native of the south, greeted our eyes in our accustomed walks, and their voices, though unmusical, were the sweetest that ever saluted our ears.[32]

From the 19th to the 26th [April], the snow once more blighted the resuscitating verdure, but a single day was sufficient to remove it. On the 28th, the Saskashawan swept away the ice which had adhered to its banks, and the next day a boat came down from Carlton House with provisions. We received such accounts of the state of vegetation at that place, that Dr. Richardson determined to visit it, in order to collect botanical specimens, as the period at which the ice was expected to admit of the continuation of our journey, was still distant. Accordingly he embarked on the 1st of May.

The Indians, as usual, crowded into the [H. B. Co. and N. W. Co.] houses with their families, and various merchandise to pay their debts, or rather, to procure credit for the ensuing year. No bargain was concluded without the necessary libations of liquor, and they danced, sang and wept, declaring that such happiness was alone worthy of their toil.[33] The night was no hindrance to their enjoyment, which however, proved very much so to our repose: for when at last refused admittance, they thundered at the parchment windows, and pleased with this acquisition of noise, their hands continued mechanically to produce it, after the power of utterance had failed. When sober, they were harmless and tranquil, stalking silently through our rooms, and viewing with admiration the instruments and drawings spread on the tables. They

32. 'An hundred tribes': This suggests an Indian population of about 100 men trading at Cumberland House. Richardson that year estimated 120 hunters or a total population of 500 men, women and children in the large trading area. Back in 1779, Philip Turnor had said that 'no Indians reside nigh unto' Cumberland House. [Tyrrell, ed. *Journals 1774-1792*, p. 254.] The modern population is roughly 1000 in the settlement alone.

33. Mandelbaum has claimed that an anthropologist can predict the attitudes of a people to liquor by studying the value system of that culture. The Indian of greatest value to his community was the one who was somewhat reckless in the hunt or in stealing horses from another tribe; liquor only accentuated these desirable characteristics, so no stigma was attached to the drunken state. [David G. Mandelbaum, *Anthropology and People: the World of the Plains Cree*, University Lectures, No. 12 (Saskatoon: University of Saskatchewan, 1967), p. 13.]

nevertheless remarked that we were wretched chiefs, because we had no rum.

In the course of the month, the ice gradually wore away from the south side of the lake, but the great mass of it still hung to the north side with some snow visible on its surface. By the 21st [May], the elevated grounds were perfectly dry, and teeming with the fragrant offspring of the season.[34] When the snow melted, the earth was covered with the fallen leaves of the last year, and already it was green with the strawberry plant, and the bursting buds of the gooseberry, raspberry and rose bushes, soon variegated by the rose and blossoms of the chokecherry. The gifts of nature are disregarded and undervalued till they are withdrawn, and in the hideous regions of the Arctic zone, she would make a convert of him for whom the gardens of Europe had no charms or the mild beauties of a southern clime had bloomed in vain.

Mr. Williams found a delightful occupation in his agricultural pursuits. The horses were brought to the plow, and fields of wheat, barley, and Indian corn promised to reward his labours. His dairy furnished us with all the luxuries of an English farm.

Preparations were busily made for the embarkation of the furs which had been collected, by pressing them into packs of 90 Tlb. each, averaging in value 100£.[35] People were employed to build canoes, and as these are the only vessels now used to the northward of Cumberland House, they deserve particular description. They are constructed of birch bark, which is stripped from the tree in April, by making a fire round it, or by cutting it down, and hewing it into logs of the length required for the bark. A canoe house is erected, open at the sides, and floored, or crossed by several timbers.[36] Pieces of bark are sewed together with the root of the pine,[37] of a sufficient length to form the bottom, and upon it is laid a frame, pointed at each extremity, and

34. In part, the pungent fragrance of the 'Balm of Gilead' or balsam poplar.

35. Harold A. Innis [*The Fur Trade in Canada* (Toronto: University of Toronto Press, rev. ed. 1956), pp. 240-41 and 265-67] gives some values for 90-pound packs without specifying whether Troy or avoirdupois pounds. Such a pack would contain about 67 beaver skins, which weighted 1⅓ pounds each, with a fluctuating value of from 8½ to 15½ shillings per beaver skin. It seems that few packs would realize £100 when sold in London; average packs of mixed fur more commonly were worth £20 and £30.

36. Robert Longmoor, in 1776-77 at Cumberland House, was the first white man to master the art of making a birchbark canoe, *Waskwey-osi* in Cree. One wonders whether it was his innovation to do so within a special canoe house.

37. Again, 'pine' means spruce; these small roots are *watapiy* in Cree.

pressed down by posts introduced between it and the beams of the house. Other pieces are attached on each side to the first; and the sides being kept together by stakes, the canoe is cut out while thus doubled, so that they are exactly similar. The ends are curves including about two thirds of a circle, and the middle rises in proportion to the breadth intended for the canoe. The sides are then separated and wooden gunwales, 1¹/₂ inches square, pierced to receive the timbers, are strongly sewed to them.

Frames of thin laths confined to a curve by a piece of wood joining the extremities, are fitted to the stem and stern, and the edges of the bark sewed round them. The inside is rubbed over with a mixture of pitch and grease, and covered with thin splints placed along the bottom and sides, the frame having been taken out. The timbers, of which there are 60 or 70, made of cedar, are bent by the hand, and the ends inserted into the gunwales; after which they are driven gradually by a mallet into a vertical position. The bark is wetted with hot water, and the canoe occasionally lifted by slings from the beams to force out the inequalities of the surface. Nine small bars are fixed to the gunwales, across the canoe, and the seats for the paddlers are suspended at each end. The last office is to cover all the seams on the outside with a mixture of pitch and grease boiled together. The shape of the canoe is now a round bottom, sharp extremities, gunwales in a plane parallel to the horizon, and circular prows and sterns, elevated one foot above them, the former of which is larger than the latter. The paddles are four feet long, with narrow blades, and a small square sail completes the equipment; but a canoe, having no keel, can only cross the direction of the wind at a very oblique angle. The largest canoes are 32 feet in length, 5¹/₂ in breadth and 2¹/₂ in depth. They are borne across the longest portages by two men, the foreman and steersman; and though their materials are so slight, they will carry 3200 Tlb. each, besides the crew.[38] A loaded canoe has six paddlers, two of whom sit upon each bench, the foreman being single and the steersman standing in the stern with a long paddle. A lightly loaded canoe can stow conveniently ten paddlers and is capable of going seven miles an hour for a

38. Larger than the usual north canoe or *canot du nord,* said by Turnor to be 24 to 27 feet in length. A Montreal canoe or *canot du maître* was 36 feet long and could carry 65 packs of 90 pounds each, more than double the load of the north canoe. [Tyrrell, ed., *Journals 1774-1792,* p. 222; Eric Morse, *Fur Trade Canoe Routes of Canada Then and Now* (Ottawa: Queen's Printer, 1969), p. 20.]

whole day. The large flat heads and sterns greatly impede their speed when not paddling directly against the wind. This injudicious model has been adopted by the Canadians, who imagine that it is an additional beauty.

The canoes of the Southern Indians are built in the same manner, but without a house, and they are small enough to be managed if necessary by one man, who sits in the bottom and uses a single paddle.[39]

On the 25th [May], the ice vacated Pine Island Lake. We were, however, informed that Beaver Lake, which was likewise in our route, would not afford a passage before the 4th of June. According to directions left by Mr. Franklin, applications were made to the chiefs of the Hudson's Bay and North West Companies' posts, for two canoes, with their crews and a supply of stores, for the use of the expedition. They were not in a condition to comply with this request, till the arrival of their respective returns from Isle-à-la-Crosse and the Saskashawan departments. Of the six men whom we brought from England, the most serviceable, John Hepburn, had accompanied Mr. Franklin, and only one other desired to prosecute the journey with us. Mr. Franklin had made arrangements with Mr. Williams for the employment of the remaining five men, in bringing to Cumberland House, the ammunition, tobacco, etc., left at York Fort, which stores were, if possible, to be sent after us in the summer.

On the 30th, Dr. Richardson returned from Carlton House and on the 31st, the boats arrived belonging to the Hudson's Bay Company Saskashawan department. We obtained a canoe and two more volunteers.

On the 1st of June, the Saskashawan, swelled by the melting of the snow near the Rocky Mountains, rose 12 feet and the current of the little rivers, bounding Pine Island ran back into the lake, which it filled with mud. On the 5th, the North West Company's people arrived, and Mr. Conolly furnished us with a canoe and five Canadians. They were engaged to attend us till Mr. Franklin should think fit to discharge them, and bound under the usual penalties in case of disobedience or other improper conduct. These poor people entertained such dread of a ship of war, that they stipulated not to be embarked in Lieut. Parry's vessels, if we should find them on the coast; a condition with which

39. Surely Hood has made a slip of the pen here and refers to the Northern or Chipewyan, rather than the Southern Indians. The canoes of the Chipewyans tended to be smaller than those of the Cree Indians which he has just described.

they would gladly have dispensed, had that desirable event taken place.

As we required a Canadian foreman and steersman for the other canoe, we were compelled to wait for the appearance of the Isle-à-la-Crosse canoes under Mr. Clarke. On the 8th, Mr. Williams embarked for York Fort. He gave us a circular letter, addressed to the chiefs of the Hudson's Bay Company posts, directing them to afford us all possible assistance on our route, and he promised to exert every endeavour to forward the Esquimaux interpreter, upon whom the success of our journey so much depended. He was accompanied by eight boats, well armed, expecting a retaliation for the affair at the Grand Rapid. With him we sent our collections of plants, minerals, charts, and drawings, to be transmitted to England by the Hudson's Bay ships. [40]

After this period, our detention, though short, cost us more vexation than the whole time we had passed at Cumberland House, because every hour of the short summer was invaluable to us. On the 11th, Mr. Clarke arrived, and completed our crews.[41] He brought letters from Mr. Franklin, dated March 28th at Fort Chepewyan, where he was engaged in procuring hunters and interpreters. A heavy storm of wind and rain from the northeast, again delayed us till the morning of the 13th. The account we had received at York Factory, of the numerous stores at Cumberland House, proved to be very erroneous. The most material stores we received, did not amount in addition to our own, to more than two barrels of powder, a keg of spirits, and two pieces of tobacco, with pemmican for 16 days. The crew of Dr. Richardson's canoe consisted of three Englishmen[42] and three Canadians, and the other carried five Canadians. Both were deeply laden, and the waves ran high in the lake. No person in our party being well acquainted with the rivers to the northward, Mr. Conolly gave us a pilot, on condition that we should

40. Williams would have been captured at Grand Rapids, as Colin Robertson was a little later that summer, in retaliation for the capture of the North West Company men in 1819, had he not taken the difficult Minago route used much earlier by Kelsey, Henday, and others. This followed the Summerberry River to Moose Lake, thence over a portage, down the Minago River to Cross Lake and after another portage, down the Bigstone and Fox Rivers to the Hayes. In spite of the difficult and little-used portages, the collections of natural history reached England safely.

41. John Clarke, who had been involved in the disastrous Peace River expedition of 1815-16, was in charge of the Hudson's Bay Company post at Ile-à-la-Crosse in 1819-20.

42. Three Hudson's Bay Company employees, probably Orkneymen. Hood spoke of Scots as 'Englishmen', an appellation they would scarcely have appreciated.

exchange him, when we met with the Athapescow brigade of canoes. At 4 a.m. we embarked.

Bounding once more on the disenthralled and yielding element, we felt a long opposing barrier removed; yet the spot was associated with pleasing recollections, in which our irksome confinement had been often cheered by hospitality; a virtue that empowers man to overthrow every distinction set by nature between the climates of the earth.

4

Account of
the Cree Indians

Some account of the Cree and
other Indians

The North American Indians, called indifferently Knistineaux, Crees, and Southern Indians,[1] inhabit the country from Churchill and York Factory to the head of the Saskashawan, being there bounded by several of the Rocky Mountain tribes, and towards the southeast their language is spoken almost to the boundaries of Canada.[2] They do not reside in the country to the northward of the Athapescow Lake, where they are intermixed with the Chepewyans. The numbers occupying this prodigious space are exceedingly small.[3] In describing them, however, a general view is given of the manners and pursuits of all the neighbouring tribes. The same rigorous climate and the same means of support, modify the whole.

The Southern Indians are equal in stature to the natives of Europe. Their eyes are small and dark and their black hair hangs in coarse tresses over the shoulders. The forehead is low, the cheek bones high, and the cavity of the eye, deep. The nose is sometimes aquiline and often broad and flat; but I have seen no countenance approaching the Grecian among them. The mouth is wide, with thick lips, and a short chin. They pluck out their beards, which are only seen on individuals of an advanced age.[4] It is perhaps possible for these features to be so placed as to form an agreeable countenance; but nature has not tried the experiment, or the gift has been bestowed where it was impossible to preserve it. None of the women are exempt from toil and hunger; and against the ravages of such enemies, beauty cannot long contend for her dominions. Their complexion, which is naturally a dark copper colour,

1. Since the earliest days of trading at York Factory and Churchill, 'Southern Indians' had been a synonym for the Crees and 'Northern Indians' a synonym for the Chipewyans.

2. The boundaries of Upper Canada, established in 1791, extended north-east of Lake Superior to the height of land, to meet the Hudson's Bay Company territories draining into Hudson Bay.

3. The pre-European Cree population was estimated at 15,000 and the Chipewyan population as 3,750, including the 'Caribou-eaters', [James Mooney, 'The Aboriginal Population of America North of Mexico', *Smithsonian Misc. Coll.* 80 (1928), 26.]

4. It is characteristic of Indian men to have little facial hair; plucking would at most accentuate this natural tendency.

is only to be discovered when accident has removed the dirt, that from their childhood is unmolested by design. Their breasts undergo a distention, from their early marriage, and other causes, the sight of which is irreconcilably repugnant to a stranger; and the deformity is increased by the effect of a disorder that sometimes destroys one of them.[5]

The shoulders of the men are broad and their arms muscular; but their legs are thin and ill-shaped. The practices of sitting with them doubled under the haunches, and of walking in snowshoes, have assisted to render them crooked. Their gait is a long awkward stride, and they do not possess the bodily strength of Europeans, but are capable of sustaining hunger much longer. Few of them are corpulent except when young. Their personal ornaments are silver and brass trinkets suspended from the nose and ears. The men tie the hair about the crown into a small bunch, and the women are tattooed from the corners of the mouth to the chin. Both sexes paint on particular occasions, making blotches of vermilion on the cheeks, and black circles round the eyes.

Their clothing is made of leather and cloth, the latter being preferred. The dress of the men is composed of the following articles. A cloth, or bandage, is passed between the legs and fastened to the waist at each extremity. The leggins extend to the hips and are also attached to the waist. They are called Indian stockings and if made of cloth are bound with various colours on the outside seam and bottom, but if of leather, the seams are fringed by cutting the border into strips. The muskasins [moccasins] or leather shoes have been before noticed. A long waistcoat is worn tied or buttoned in front, and over it a frock which covers the thighs, furnished with a hood above, and tied round the waist with a belt. The cap is an otter or marten skin, decked with the feathers of an eagle's tail, which the Indians hold in great estimation. In winter, they carry a blanket over the shoulders which is their only bedding when hunting. Though all that is here enumerated is necessary to constitute a complete dress, an Indian must be the most fortunate or the most prudent man of his nation, who possesses them at the same time.

The stockings of the women are gartered at the knees, and ornamented at the ankles with rows of beads. An undergarment covers the body from the neck to the feet, the sleeves not being sewed to it, but attached to one another by a strip of cloth across the back. Their hoods

5. One suspects that Hood saw one or two Indian women with carcinoma of the breast and generalized from this small sample. Breast cancer is not more common among Indian women than among white women.

are fastened at the neck, forming a tippet on the shoulders, which, as well as the breast of the undergarment, is adorned by stained porcupine's quills, beads, and tassels of leather or worsted. A blanket is constantly worn about the neck and a belt round the waist.

The women do not suffer much in childbirth, performing their ordinary duties immediately afterwards.[6] The contrary has, however, been observed of those who are resident at the trading posts. They are married at the age of 13 or 14 years, and sometimes produce numerous families, but more than half their children are destroyed by hardship at an early age.[7] On the birth of a child, it is encased in a leathern bag of moss, its arms are placed at its sides, and its head only left at liberty. The bag is laced to a board fringed with rows of beads.[8] In this state of durance, it is pinioned for more than a year, being occasionally released to change the moss. When the mother travels, the board is carried at her back by a strap round the head or shoulders, and in a tent, the poor little mummy is suspended to the cross beam, while the inhabitants are abroad. Whether its cries proceed from pain, from fear, or from caprice, they have one universal mode of pacifying it; which is to cram it with food, and the complaint ceasing, they consider the evil to be removed. One consequence of the constant application of this remedy, is an unwieldy protuberance of stomach, and another, excessive and debasing gluttony. The first disappears with the privations incident to an Indian mode of life; but the second entails a want which industry could not supply, and which indolence renders a source of misery.[9]

6. Cree women tend to have above average dimensions of their bony pelvis. Morton S. Adams and Jerry D. Niswander [*Human Biology* 40 (1968), 226-34] found that Cree babies have an above average birth weight. Difficult labours due to a small bony pelvis, and breech presentations are remarkably uncommon among Cree women to this day. In a nomadic society in an extreme climate, natural selection may have eliminated those incapable of delivering large infants without difficulty.

7. Even today, there are high neonatal and infant mortality rates among Indian children, due to socio-economic and cultural factors and remoteness from medical facilities.

8. The cradleboard (*tikonagan, tikinakun,* or *takkunigan* in Cree) facilitates transport and care of infants in a nomadic society. The mossbag without a backboard is called in Cree, *waspisun,* from the verb *waspisuw* 'he is laced up'. These infants are very close to their mothers at all times, receive instant attention to their needs, are pacified, cry less, and sleep more. However, swaddling predisposes to dislocation of the hip in infants with a family history of the condition, or with joint laxity. When moss is used, diaper rash is unknown.

9. Again, an unsympathetic appraisal of the 'feast and famine' adaptation to the life of a nomadic hunter. A kill meant that everyone within reach ate to satiety—an efficient way to carry meat was in one's stomach.

The first efforts of the infant's strength are applied to procure freedom; and, though it sometimes succeeds in moving its limbs, it cannot restore them to their original straight posture, which they never afterwards recover.[10]

The women employ herbs to procure abortions,[11] out of hatred to their husbands; and it has been said that they destroy their female children. No instance, however, of that crime came under my observation.

The child is emancipated from its trammels in the beginning of the summer, that it may learn to walk, and the next winter it totters on snowshoes after its mother. The days of boyhood are passed in the exercise of the bow and arrow, and in acquiring the management of a canoe. He quickly becomes dextrous enough with the former to strike the smallest bird from its perch. When his strength enables him to carry a gun, he casts away his bow and his independence at once. He is the particular care of his father, who brings him to the chase, and points out to him the leaves turned up, or the moss brushed away by the foot of an animal, till his perception by degrees has attained the perfection so surprising to Europeans.

The girls are taught the duties of their sex, which, in all savage countries, are the most laborious. They dress skins and make clothing, cut firewood, and when travelling, drag the sledges. They net the snowshoes, pitch the tents, and sew and gum canoes; in their leisure hours, they split sinews, and embroider gunpowder and tobacco pouches. The art exhibited in some of these offices is not unworthy of notice. The most valuable skin which the country produces, for clothing, is that of the moose deer. It is stretched on four sticks, and one side being elevated, several women mount upon it, with sharp instruments of iron or bone, scraping off in their descent the hair and adhering flesh. With the hair, they unfortunately rub away the most tenacious

10. This is a surprising statement. The infant, bound always in a fully extended position in the *tikonagan,* should have straight legs when released; even today if a Cree child is bowlegged or knock-kneed, its mother is criticized for not binding its legs tightly enough in infancy.

11. Abortifacients: Usually irritant volatile oils were taken orally. In the northeastern United States, this oil was obtained from the tops of *Juniperus alba.* It caused irritability of the bowel, and secondarily increased the irritability of the uterus, comparable to the use of castor oil for the same purpose. The 'treatment' was often ineffective and since the dose was difficult to regulate, some of the recipients died. The Indians of Montana used sweet flag or calamus, *Acorus calamus,* for this purpose. [Alex Johnston, 'The Old Indian's Medicine,' *Sask. Archaeology Newletter* 26 (1969), 12.]

and impermeable part of the skin. They next dry and then rub it, with a mixture of the brains and other parts of animals, after which it is soaked in warm water and scraped, alternately, and smoked over a fire of decayed wood, which prevents it from becoming hard when it has been wet; for it absorbs water immediately. No skin is more durable or agreeable to the touch, and a knowledge of the means of tanning it would be inestimable to the Indians.

Their nets are manufactured of the skin of the reindeer or of the red deer [elk], cut into strips, and they have borrowed the mode of making them from the Orkney fishermen employed by the Hudson's Bay Company. The operation is so tedious, that they generally endeavour to purchase them.

They embellish their muskasins with representations of birds, animals, and flowers, worked with porcupine's quills. The quills are split, and coloured with dyes extracted from cloth. The process of embroidering ammunition pouches displays much ingenuity. They make a kind of tambour frame, with sinews stretched in parallel lines by a bow. Across these they interweave beads and quills into gay and sometimes elegant patterns.

To hold their meat and water, they have utensils of birch bark, and if unprovided with an iron kettle, they can boil water in them, by immersing heated stones.

The men provide food for their families by hunting and fishing. They cut and shape timbers for canoes, make paddles, sledges, and the frames of snowshoes. The birch tree supplies them with wood for all these purposes. Their only tools are the hatchet and crooked knife, an instrument shaped like a piece of iron hoop, sharp at one edge. They use it very expertly, drawing it towards them in cutting, with the palm of the hand upwards.

The Crees do not fish unless unsuccessful in hunting. To set a net in winter, they make a certain number of holes in the ice, and by means of a long stick, they lead a cord under water from hole to hole, bringing the end up at a sufficient distance from the first. The head of the net is attached along the line with floats, and weights are suspended at the foot. It is then dragged through the hole into the water and the extremities of the line tied to large sticks on the ice. The nets are oblong, 20 or 30 fathoms long, and three feet deep, with meshes of five or six inches. Another mode is to attract fish to a hole at night with a piece of blazing pitch pine, and spear them when they rise.

If pressed by hunger, they fish in streams with an eagle's claw, which they prefer to a hook. They often catch trout and pike with a stick, to which the line is fastened in the middle, and also slightly at one end. The bait covers the stick, and the fish gorging it, the upper end is detached by a jerk of the line, and falling across within his jaws, he is easily taken.

The Indian traps are made of wood, and will answer for any kind of carnivorous animal. A space is inclosed with stakes, against the root of a tree, leaving several openings. On the ground, through the center, is laid the trunk of a poplar, and a stick cleft at one end is placed with the other resting upon it. At that end, also, of the cleft stick, stands another stick perpendicularly, supporting a heavy beam or trunk of a tree. Other trunks are laid upon it, like the rafters of a house, so that they may all descend through the openings in the inclosure and fill up the whole space. The bait is held by the cleft stick, and the animal pulling it away, the perpendicular stick slips from the other end, and the beam falls, with its superincumbent burthen. Some Indians use a forked stick to support the beam, and in that case it is cut into two parts, fitted to rest upon each other. Stakes are driven on both sides of the beam, that the wolverenes may not tear the trap to pieces, which notwithstanding they often do.[12]

The women make snares for rabbits and partridges with running nooses of sinew, attached to long sticks called tossing poles. The tossing pole is unequally balanced upon a mound of stones, or wood, and the most weighty end upheld by a stick, the snare being at the other. The rabbit in struggling, displaces the stick and is lifted into the air, so that it cannot use its teeth or feet to effect its escape.

To take the beaver, several Indians furnish themselves with trenches, or flat pieces of iron, sharp at the ends, and hooks, both [of] which are fixed upon poles. The beaver houses, or lodges, are built with a descent towards the water, and the only holes or openings are below its surface and underneath the ice. The walls are three or four feet thick, except on the side exposed to the sun, where the beavers sleep. There, the Indians are directed by experience to make their attack. The beavers, alarmed by the noise, escape into the water and take refuge in holes, which they dig at the sides of the banks in summer. The water does not rise to the upper extremity of these holes, but leaves small spaces, like

12. See Hood's painting of the deadfall trap (plate 5)

their lodges above it. Some of the Indians break the ice near the banks, and carefully examine the surface of the water, which, when a beaver is within his hole, is gently agitated by his breath. They then plant stakes before the entrance, and trench into the bank, till they can draw him out with their hooks. In the meantime, one Indian gets into the breach which has been made in the lodge, and lying motionless, with his hook and gun prepared, the beavers which again venture to their violated dwelling betray themselves into his hands. When the stream or channel in which the lodge is built is narrow, a net made of strong leather thongs is stretched across it under the ice, and the beavers entangle themselves in swimming away. If the net is not quickly drawn up, they will regain their liberty with their sharp teeth.

In summer, the beavers desert their lodges, and the Indians watch their favourite haunts with guns. They build in August, and may be traced by their labours at that period.

The Crees hunt all the larger animals with the gun, and only snare them when wholly unprovided with ammunition. The manner of hunting the moose and buffalo is related in the description of those animals. The guns trafficked with the Indians by the Companies, are of a very bad quality, and occasion accidents every year. A poor man whose hand had been dreadfully shattered by the bursting of his gun, the year before our arrival, was brought down from Carlton House to Dr. Richardson, who amputated it above the wrist and restored the use of his arm. He bore the operation with an unchanging countenance, and afterwards manifested much gratitude.

Some of these misfortunes are doubtless to be attributed to the Indians themselves who, sometimes in haste, discharge their guns without wadding, and the balls have rolled half way through the barrels, before the powder explodes. They straighten crooked barrels with great precision by their hands and knees.

They practice various devices to entrap the waterfowl. Mimic geese are constructed in various postures, and the hunters, concealed in long reeds, imitate the cries of those birds, and decoy within reach of their guns a passing flock. The geese readily answer this cry in spring and autumn. To snare ducks they plant stakes across a little bay, projecting above the water, and scatter branches about them, so as to make them appear like a natural accumulation of driftwood. Several openings are left in which running nooses are stretched. The ducks, swimming through the openings without suspicion, are caught round the body by the nooses. A fence of the same kind on a bank frequented by geese is equally successful.

The Crees are not good marksmen with the gun—their whole art consisting in making an approach, unperceived by the animal which they pursue. They impel their prostrate bodies through the leafy labryinth, with slow but indefatigable progress, solicitously intent upon each motion of their limbs, or glide by silent and invisible effort over the smooth current, till their aim is more certain than the utmost dexterity could render it, at a greater distance. In this their skill is unrivalled.

Their snowshoes, sledges, canoes, and tents have already been described. In summer, several families sometimes live together in large oblong tents, which have ridge poles, supported by posts at each end.

The Cree religion is a tissue of absurdities, interwoven with some articles of the Christian faith, imbibed during their long intercourse with Europeans. That they believed themselves to be created by, and subservient to, a superior being is the most important fact we have ascertained; because, unless derived from tradition, it is a distinguished proof of the reasoning faculty extended to all mankind. The morality of a heathen people exhibits their disposition, and their arts display their genius; but the mode in which they worship their idols, the follies and inconsistencies which enter into their ceremonies, are common to all who labour under the same ignorance, and are only worthy of relation as they affect the moral conduct, or cast lights on the origin of a nation. It is natural for the human mind to identify existence and material substance; and if men be disposed to superstition, there is no reason with the exception of the heavenly bodies, why divinity should be attributed to any one visible object more than to another. The desire of pre-eminence induces some individual to make his choice, and his descendants confirm it, because it was the religion of their forefathers. They improve in arts, make discoveries in science, and become formidable in arms; their religion alone remains unchanged. And this does not demonstrate their inferiority as a people, but the necessity of revealed religion.[13]

The supreme being is adored by the Crees, under the title of the Manito, or great spirit.[14] They consider him as their creator, and the

13. Hood, like most Christians of his day, took a patronizing attitude towards other 'more primitive' religions.

14. *Kijemanito* or *Kitchemanito*, from *kitchi* 'great' and *manito* 'spirit'.

avenger of those crimes by which mankind sustain injury from one another. They believe also in the existence of several evil spirits, to which the Manito has given the power of assuming the forms of animals, to punish offences and to exercise their malice. Their idea of a future state is, that both men and animals are transported to a delightful region, where there is neither want nor misery. But they think that all are admitted into this paradise without distinction, as the wicked are corrected by their sufferings on earth. Long life without misfortunes is therefore deemed a peculiar proof of divine favour.

The Crees on the Athapescow river have small wooden idols, carved like human heads. They sacrifice dogs to them by hanging them on trees. Their temples are rude huts, made of branches. Another religious ceremony is to inclose themselves in a tent, well secured from the air, and pour water upon hot stones, which occasions the most profuse perspiration. They sit in a circle without covering except the breech cloth, and smoke their pipes. During their confinement, they address a prayer to the Great Spirit, recommending themselves to his care, and at the same time detailing their good actions. No women are suffered to be present. Sir Alexander Mackenzie[15] has described the ceremony of opening the medicine bag and smoking the medicine pipe: a kind of sacrament binding the Indians to the performance of promises, and forgiveness of injuries which none dared to violate. But this laudable rite is now much neglected. The depravation of their characters by the corruption introduced in the course of the late contentions, has abolished an engagement which would have secured their morality. The feasts also, have generally fallen into desuetude.

Their priests are conjurors, who obtain credit in the usual manner, by prophetic interpretations of dreams, or by acts in which preternatural agency is supposed to be required. They pretend that they can only communicate their mysteries to children and they select one accordingly, to be initiated at an early age. They permit themselves to be bound hand and foot, and placed in a small hut of wood and leather; their friends surround it and sing in chorus, beating a piece of parchment stretched on a large hoop, with a flat instrument upon which are

15. Sir Alexander Mackenzie, a Scots highlander, who began employment in the fur trade at Montreal in 1779 and explored to the mouth of the river which bears his name in 1789. He returned to Scotland to learn the accurate use of surveyor's instruments and in 1793 was the first white man to reach the Pacific by an overland route north of Mexico. He died in Scotland in 1820.

carved the figures of birds, quadrupeds and fish. This tambourine is an attendant on all religious ceremonies; in times of sickness or famine, its doleful sounds are heard on every side, continued through day and night. When the conjuror has liberated his limbs, he announces that the Great Spirit has released him; and his dexterity imposes, not only on the Indians, but has made converts of Europeans.

The conjurors are consulted on the means of recovering articles which are lost, and they also act in the capacity of physicians. They sometimes employ their arts to obtain the property of their country-men, or to revenge an affront. An Indian labouring under the law of a conjuror, imagines if he misses his aim at an animal, that an evil spirit has assumed that shape to torment him; and he pines or starves to death unless accident throws provision in his way. Such was the case of the Indian who lived on moose skins at the Basquiau Hill, mentioned in the former part of this narrative.

The conjuror himself is not the last to be persuaded that the Great Spirit actually interferes in his behalf. With the view of exposing these follies to derision, Mr. Williams bound two conjurors, on different occasions at Cumberland House, when many Indians were present. The enthusiasts smiled with contempt on their bonds, but their efforts to free themselves were unsuccessful, and so was the attempt to unde-ceive the Indians.

They discover several notions of the Deity, similar to those of the ancient heathens. If they are threatened by any great calamity, they throw into a river the most valuable of their possessions, in the hope of averting the wrath of the Great Spirit by self-privation. They never taste spirits without previously pouring a small quantity on the earth as an offering to propitiate the Manito. Suicide has been prompted by grief for the loss of a relation; and is sometimes committed by old people, who, summoning their children, declare that they have long been unable to support themselves, and that they will not live upon the earth to be a burthen to their relations. It is the duty of the children not to oppose this resolution, and the magnanimous victim expires with the fortitude of a Roman sage, but uninfluenced like him by promise of reward, unsupported by the admiration of a multitude, and hopeless of fame. This self devotion evinces less love of life, or stronger belief of futurity, than is to be found in the civilized world.[16]

16. An infirm person is an infinitely greater burden upon a nomadic society.

On the death of a relation, the Indians assemble and make a feast. The body is doubled, with the knees against the breast and the feet under the hams, and a blanket fastened round it.[17] The depth of the grave is four or five feet. By the side of the deceased is laid his property, and the body is covered with small logs, laid at right angles to each other. They seldom put earth into the grave, but arch it over with branches and place mounds of earth or stones at the extremities. If the deceased is a chief, his flag (which is given by the Europeans) is left flying near the grave, and an oration is made in celebration of his virtues. The bodies of the dead are, in some places inhabited by Crees, elevated on high stages, and the funeral ceremonies also vary. The practice of making what is called a sacrifice, mentioned by Sir Alexander Mackenzie, is general. A number of articles are suspended to a tree, which any distressed person may appropriate, provided that he leaves a trifling substitute.

The Indian men deem it effeminate to weep except when they are drunk and they procure liquor for this occasion, if possible. But their mourning is sincere and affecting. For many weeks afterwards, they burst forth into a melancholy cry, at the rising and setting of the sun. Their grief is of that amiable character which excites compassion, though attended by the most extravagant absurdities. They grovel in the dust, piercing their limbs with knives, and introducing feathers to prevent the wounds from closing. Their families are compelled to subsist on the bounty of their friends.

A nation of hunters scattered through so wide a region, neither needs nor desires the control of laws. The dread of retaliation prevents personal injury, and they have no wealth to protect. Every wood furnishes materials for their abode, and the creation is their common store. They have some chiefs, whose influence over them has been obtained by eloquence, or superior skill in hunting. To those of the latter description they are attached by necessity and the orators preserve authority over them while they can engage their inclinations. The band of a chief is composed principally of his relations; but each individual is governed by his will, in making his choice. An Indian is often selected by the traders and treated with particular attention, to confer distinction on him and secure his services; but such chiefs are

17. Many peoples, including those of the ancient cultures of South and Central America, buried their dead in the fetal position – the position before birth and after death being the same.

generally ridiculed by their countrymen.

The Cree Indians had long traded with Europeans, when the fur trade was carried into the interior, and were habituated to the use of the gun, before the surrounding nations, except the Chepewyans, were acquainted with the nature of that weapon. The first use which they made of the advantage, proves that ambition and rapacity are the crimes of barbarous as well as of civilized nations, though not equally their disgrace. The Crees made irruptions in every quarter, destroying the unarmed natives and carrying off their women. They even penetrated to Mackenzie's River and across the Rocky Mountains near the Saskashawan, and to commemorate their transitory power, bestowed the contemptuous appelation of slaves upon the Dogrib Indians, the Thickwood Indians,[18] and those of the Rocky Mountains in Mackenzie's River, and at the source of the Saskashawan. The Chepewyans, or Northern Indians, were numerous enough to resist them, and they could make no impression on the Stone Indians. But they drove back the Beaver Indians from the river which bears their name to the main branch of the Slave River, and that brave tribe defended their retreat so obstinately, that a peace was concluded about 35 years ago, from which circumstance the river received the name of the Unjigah or Peace River. Their progress received a final check, and their last incursion to Mackenzie's River took place in the year 1796. The gun is now almost universally substituted for the bow, and the superiority of the Crees is at an end; but the scornful epithet of slaves, and the resentment of the people to whom it was applied, has survived. Since that period, the whole country has been depopulated by the smallpox and other disorders, and this cause added to the extension of European commerce, has produced one solitary good effect; that of rendering wars less frequent, and more partial.

The natives of North America are extremely jealous of their reputation for courage. When two Indians of the same tribe have cast the imputation of cowardice upon each other, they choose to wipe off the

18. Thickwood Indians is a most confusing term. There are Thick Woods northwest of Carlton near the present village of Mullingar, and another Thick Woods west of Fort McMurray, Alberta. La Verendrye mentioned Thick Woods on the east side of Lake Winnipeg. Richardson spoke of Thick Wood Crees and Beaver Hill Crees, while Franklin used the term as a synonym for the Beaver or Strongbow Indians. The ambiguity of the term as used by both the Hind and Palliser expeditions has been discussed by Frank Gilbert Roe. [*The North American Buffalo*, (Toronto: University of Toronto Press, 1951), p. 763.]

stain either by making war on their neighbours, by attacking a grizzled bear, or by stabbing themselves in the fleshy parts of the body. If war is resolved upon, the chief sends a pipe of tobacco to the young men; those who smoke, assent to the proposal, and the rest are branded with the denomination of old women. Another motive for war is to obtain women; or to revenge a similar depredation of their enemies. The warriors disfigure their countenances with charcoal and earths of various colours. They provide themselves with shields, made of doubled buffalo hide, dried so hard that it will repel arrows. Their weapons are the gun, a spear made of the blade of a dagger fixed on a shaft four or five feet in length, and a kind of club, called a Paccamawgon.[19] It is a crooked piece of wood furnished with a heavy ball of bone, at one extremity. The ball is sometimes wood, and a spike of bone projects from it. This instrument is curiously and ingeniously carved. Thus prepared, they commence their excursion, and the war is conducted, like their hunting, by stratagem. They never meet their enemy openly in the field, but practice the most subtle artifices to surprise him; and such is the universal character of Indian warfare. When they have succeeded in this, they dispatch the sleeping foe with the spear and paccamawgon, using the gun against those who fly. If they are not exasperated by injuries, they spare those who throw themselves between their legs, which is the mode of claiming protection among all known tribes of North American Indians; and the suppliant, by this acknowledgement of his enemy's superiority, converts him into a zealous defender. The prisoners are led home in triumph but treated with kindness. The Crees scalp the dead, taking the whole skin of the skull, and the ears. They stretch and dry it, painting the ears red, and plaiting the hair with beads and buttons. In the war dance, they wear the scalps on their heads, and compel the prisoners to do it also. The women become the wives of their captors,[20] and the men, though called slaves,

19. This bone-ended club, spelled *pakamagan* by Lacombe, is not to be confused with the stone hammer. The tomahawk, of the Hurons and Iroquois, which appeared after contact with the white man, had either a stone or bone end. *Otamahuk* in Cree means 'stun it' or 'knock it out'. [Diamond Jenness, *Indians of Canada*, Nat. Mus. of Canada, Bull 65 (1934), 289, 298.]

20. Had it not been for such events, inbreeding might have become a serious problem among dispersed tribes. Later there was considerable admixture of genes, particularly from the French and Scots traders. Now that the Indians have taken up permanent residence in communities, in part to allow for schooling of their children, their socio-economic isolation from white people is paradoxically more complete, and inbreeding is becoming a serious genetic and medical problem in some areas.

are permitted to hunt, and their condition of life is in no respect altered by their captivity. Their tribe considers them alienated, and will not again receive them.

It is said that the Crees drink the blood of their adversaries, on the field. War is now so uncommon, that I could obtain no account of the ceremonies practised in making peace, nor of the war dance.

The Crees have no marriage ceremony. When an Indian wishes to marry, he is at liberty to take any woman not already engaged; otherwise, the father has a right to prevent him. Those who connect themselves with their aunts, nieces, or women who have been their stepdaughters are held in abhorrence. The men do not marry the daughters of their uncles, but are not prohibited from taking the daughters of their aunts. Polygamy is admitted by them; the necessity however of supporting their wives limits the number to two or three. The first wife maintains a degree of authority over the rest, which is countenanced by the husband. The Indians are not indifferent to what we consider a pleasing exterior; but they prefer those qualifications in a woman which render her useful to them; the usual choice of every labouring class among mankind.

During the continuance of a certain periodical disorder, the women dwell apart, and their presence is not suffered, when setting or drawing nets, nor at any other familiar occupation. This general superstition is amply described by Hearne.[21]

The Cree are sometimes guilty of barbarous cruelty to their wives, which is occasioned by jealousy; but the instances are rare. They desert them on suspicions of this kind, and the women are then taken by other persons who adopt their children. The quarrels that arise from so fertile a source are productive of fatal consequences, if the parties are inebriated, for they are decided with the knife or the gun. Such is the strife to which they condemn themselves, in making a property of creatures which have the right, and the inclination, to dispose of themselves; and we cannot expect to find constancy among the virtues of those, the object of whose duties is so often changed.

The moral character of the Crees, with all these blemishes, is honourable to human nature. The afflictions of an individual are com-

21. It was the custom for a young girl on returning from her first absence due to menstruation to 'wear a kind of veil or curtain of beads, for some time after, as a mark of modesty, as they are then considered marriageable'. [Samuel Hearne, *Journey 1769-1772*, p. 314.]

mon to his whole tribe and distress gives him a claim to relief, which in this country has never been questioned. Economy, providence, and all the long list of worldly virtues, are swallowed up by universal benevolence: for the sole lesson which calamity has taught them, is the benefit of mutual dependence. They preserve food only for their children, who often enjoy abundance, when hunger is gnawing the bosoms of their parents; and filial kindness repays the debt to the aged and infirm. No sooner is an Indian equipped at a trading post than he is uneasy till he can share it with his companions, and returns with the crowd, ragged and destitute as the rest, and unconscious of the surprise which he raises in the traders.[22]

Though much of their misery results from lavish generosity, yet the habits of their youth, which have so ill formed them for self denial, must be allowed to contribute the chief proportion. But this cause at the same time enhances the merit of their privations in favour of their offspring.

No offence can provoke an Indian to strike his child. Correction is the province of the women; and those of the Cree nation are said to inflict it with greater severity than any others. In general, however, it is so mildly exercised that the children have no dread of it, and no temptation to practice falsehood. From hence perhaps, sprung the sincerity which was once the boast of North American savages. A contempt for dishonesty is still carefully inculcated. When we read the history of what they were, and contemplate what they are, the conviction that they have deplorably degenerated is fixed on a solid basis, raised by innumerable facts; a monument of ignominy to civilization. Their minds have suffered more by European principles, than their health by European diseases. The deleterious effects of spirituous liquors have transformed the inoffensive and independent Indian into the slave of debilitating vice; his care is transferred from his family to the means of gratifying an inordinate appetite, and his maddened arm is raised to commit crimes at which he would before have shuddered.

The most prominent feature in the Indian character is, at present, indolence. The desire of spirituous liquors alone contends with it. They consider it the very essence of liberty, and will rather submit to extreme want, than acknowledge the dominion of their own necessities. An Indian seldom brings his furs to a trading post but desires the Master or

22. To this day a problem for the Indian who works hard and earns considerable money; as many as forty relatives may wish to share it with him.

Chief of it, to dispatch his slaves for them. Tobacco is presented to him, and he will answer no questions till he has seated himself on the floor and adjusted his pipe. He sits in sullen taciturnity with a countenance which physiognomy would scrutinize in vain, for there is little connection between his mind and his features; he listens with suspicion to the mention of his name, and takes umbrage at laughter, if he attributes the cause to himself. He addresses the chief by the title of father, and his speech is a composition of native eloquence, and of that art, without which commerce would be only an exchange, equally beneficial to both parties. Mixed spirits are then given to him, and after the first draught of the seducing poison, his reserve vanishes, and he becomes an abject suppliant, or an outrageous maniac.

The traders have urged in their defense, that spirits are not trafficked, but given as presents. However, they are not accused of defrauding the Indians of their property; but of their health and their mental faculties. The present servants and proprietors of the companies, I fully acquit of having caused these evils. On the contrary, they lament them in common with other Christians, and have forbidden the introduction of spirits among the newly discovered nations on Mackenzie's River. But the Crees, from long habit, are now so attached to the destructive beverage, that the fur trade would be ruined, or would undergo a suspension equivalent to it, if spirits were withheld. That consequence will be derived at no distant period, from other causes; the violent contentions of two parties, animated against each other by a series of injuries which will never be forgiven; and the diminution of Indians and animals throughout the country. The original adventurers were not bound to improve the natives: it formed no part of their charter, and by what other code could they have been expected to govern their conduct? Even if they had established themselves for that purpose only, the French traders from Canada would have counteracted their labours. The Americans have set the first example of prohibiting the use of spirits by their fur traders. It is too late for the application of a similar remedy in the British Indian territory.[23] With the increase of the Metiss, or half breed race, the country will revive. The aborigines, like all others will be forgotten, and the hand of culture will draw, from a

23. In 1820-21, the fur trade distributed 50,000 gallons of spirits, in or for trade. In 1821-22, the first year of amalgamation, this decreased to 10,000 gallons and by 1825 it was 'discountenanced'. [Malcolm McLeod, ed., *Peace River. A Canoe Voyage by the late Sir George Simpson in 1828*, p. 62.]

new source, an imperishable tribute.

The Crees eat the flesh of the lynx, the wolverene, and the dog. They prefer their meat cooked; but seldom boil it. They detest cannibals, though the unhappy persons have been rendered so by extreme necessity.[24] At Cumberland House, they were curious to see the cattle, and turned with loathing from milk and butter.[25] Of vegetables they are very fond, but when asked why they do not cultivate the earth to procure them, they answer disdainfully that they are not slaves. Both Europeans and Indians smoke tobacco with a mix of the dried leaves of a small shrub called Jackashapucca, which softens and improves the flavour of the former.[26]

The Crees have several games of hazard, at which they stake their whole property. They have learned the use of cards from the traders, and also the game of drafts, at which many of them evince considerable ability.

Of their diseases and remedies, I am not qualified to give an account. They are subject to an epidemical disorder which carries off men and animals. Water is poured upon hot stones in a close tent, to recover the sick, and the healthy also often use this perspiratory bath which is deemed very salubrious. One good effect of it, is the removal of some filth from the pores of the skin, though in an uncleanly manner. They certainly bathe in summer, otherwise their dirt would become an intolerable burthen.

Their language is a corruption of the Sautaux, from which nation they are descended.[27] It is tolerably copious, but extremely easy and harmonious. They have peculiar names for each month of the year, which, with other specimens of the language have been published by Sir Alexander Mackenzie.[28] Their songs are monotonous and unpleas-

24. F. G. Roe listed the 'three recorded instances of Northern cannibalism', including the case of Michel, and noted that all were by Iroquois. [*The North American Buffalo*, p. 891.]

25. Most non-Europeans, including people from India and China, have a deficiency of the enzyme lactase in their intestines; consequently milk or milk sugar gives them diarrhea. Milk intolerance is still common among Cree children, but in some cases seems due to milk allergy.

26. The bearberry. The leaves were dried

at the fire, pounded, and mixed with tobacco to render it more mild. The Cree name of *kinnikinnick* was given to these leaves alone, to the mixture with tobacco, and later to the inner bark of the red Osier Dogwood, also used as a smoking mixture.

27. Saulteaux Indians, so named from their meeting place at the falls or rapids (*sault*) of Sault Ste. Marie. They were a tribe of the Ojibwa or Chippewa, 'people whose moccasins have puckered seams'. Cree and Saulteaux are both Algonkian dialects.

28. They had thirteen moons of

ing, but they observe an exact measure in them.

The Northern Indians or Chepewyans are probably not inferior in number to the Crees. Nearly at the same time as that nation, they adopted the gun, and quitting the barren country about Deer [Reindeer] Lake, and the borders of the Missinnippi, they established themselves on the fertile banks of the Athapescow and Slave Rivers, which they now inhabit; but many tribes of them continue to visit Churchill, and some remain on their native hills, where they are supplied with European goods at very advanced prices by their countrymen. They are as much corrupted by spirituous liquors as the Crees. Mr. Hearne has given a correct description of their character. As hunters and warriors they are greatly inferior to the Crees. They do not scalp their enemies, but merely rub their own teeth and lips with blood. Their denial of support to the old and helpless, and unfeeling ridicule of misery, is perhaps a little exaggerated by Mr. Hearne, or their dispositions have in some measure altered since that time; but their practice of fighting to obtain the women, renders the condition of the female sex the most degraded among barbarians.

The Stone Indians occupy the South border of the Saskashawan, including the space between that river and the Assineboine. They are the most powerful and independent nation that trades with Europeans. They have not yet been tainted by spirits, and their material wants are easily supplied from the abundance of the plains. They chase the buffalo on horseback, with no other weapon than the bow and arrow. Some of the arrows are pointed with triangular pieces of iron; but they have others which are blunt and hardened at the extremity by fire; and these will penetrate through a buffalo. They clothe themselves in skins, which they whiten with clay, and decorate with paint and beads. The only article which they will carry to the forts, is provisions. They often threaten to destroy the traders and have cut off several persons singly. They are very treacherous and dishonest, but there is something bold and enterprising in their thefts. They steal horses very adroitly in the presence of the owners, and follow persons sowing potatoes, which they dig up and carry off, in the face of superior numbers. The traders travelling on the plains are compelled to practice various manoeuvres

----

twenty-eight or, more accurately, twenty-seven and a third days. Alexander Mackenzie [*Voyages 1789-93*, p. cv] listed two moons for November to convert the thirteen moons to twelve months.

to preserve themselves and their horses. At sunset, they light their fire and cook their food. As the flame is seen to a great distance, the straggling Indians are attracted towards it, designing to steal the horses while the traders sleep. But the traders, when their provisions are cooked, remount their horses, and continue their journey for eight or ten miles, and then dismounting, rest with some security.

The dread inspired by the Stone Indians is so great that at Edmonton, or Fort George, the rival companies compromise their animosities, and inclose both forts in the same stockade, which is boarded to repel arrows, and pierced with loop holes for muskets.[29]

The Stone Indians are addicted to odious and abominable vices, arising from extreme depravation of the passions, and, if their prowess has given them a superiority over the Crees, their dispositions have placed them lower in the scale of humanity.

Their language is harsh and dissonant, bearing no resemblance to that of any other northern tribe.[30]

The Beaver Indians inhabit the Peace River, and though their tribe is now diminished to 70 men and boys they deserve some notice for the stand which they made against the Crees.[31] Their language is a dialect of the Chepewyan; but their general character resembles that of the Crees. Like them they scalp the dead and naturalize their prisoners. Their weapons are very various, consisting of the gun, bow and arrow, paccamawgon, shield, and a dart, which is headed like the Cree spear, in the use of which they are extremely skilful. The feathers of the shaft are suspended by a string to its extremity.

A tribe of these Indians is settled on Mackenzie's River.

29. The Fort George of Duncan McGillivray (North West Company), on the north bank of the North Saskatchewan, seven miles southeast of the present village of Elk Point, was the precursor of Fort Edmonton, the name of a Hudson's Bay Company post which occupied three widely separated sites on the North Saskatchewan during four successive periods. During the first period, from 1795-96 until 1802, it was two miles downstream from the present site of Fort Saskatchewan; during the second, from 1802 until 1810, and the fourth, from 1813 until today, at the present site of Edmonton; during the third, from 1810 to 1812, eighty miles downstream at the mouth of the White Earth River, ten miles southeast of present Smoky Lake.

30. Assiniboine is a Siouan dialect.

31. Mooney estimated the Beaver Indians' pre-European population at about 1,250. The Beavers and Slaves had both been displaced to the northwest by the Crees. ['The Aboriginal Population', p. 26.]

5
The Buffalo,
Climate,
Aurora Borealis,
Magnetic Phenomena

Animals; Climate; Aurora Borealis; Magnetical Phenomena

A. THE BUFFALO

The dimensions of a large male buffalo were as follows. The height of the hump, or boss from the ground, 5 feet 11 inches, and the length from the horns to the insertion of the tail, 9 feet. The length of the fore leg was 2 feet 3 inches and of the hind leg, 2 feet 5 inches. The head was 1 foot 2 inches in length, and 1 foot 8 inches in breadth, between the roots of the horns, which are not more than 1 foot 2 inches in length, and form about 60° of a circle. The neck declines so much, that the ordinary posture of the head is 1 foot nearer the ground than the hump, and the flesh of the throat hangs between the fore feet below the knee. The colour of the hide varies from dark brown, to red brown, and the hair is long. The neck and head are clothed with a shaggy black mane, which conceals the small fiery eyes and the ears, discovering the points of the horns. The beard, and the hair on the throat, almost sweep the ground; that on the head is coarse wool. The tail is 9 or 10 inches in length, and twisted like that of a hog, when the buffalo is running. The disproportion between the length of the body and of the legs, the enormous size of the fore quarters and profusion of mane, conspire to render the buffalo of North America, or the Bison, the most hideous and terrible looking animal that nature has produced.[1]

It appears that there are two species of buffaloes, those of the woods, and of the plains. The only difference is, that the former is more solitary and larger than the latter, which is gregarious. Its food is grass and hay, for which it scrapes through the snow in winter. The rutting season is in August, and the cow brings forth one or two calves in April. Its postures and pace are similar to those of tame cattle, and its voice is a short, deep grunt.

It is hunted at all seasons on horseback. The hunter singles an individual from the herd, and pursues it till he has approached sufficiently near to depend on his weapon. The buffalo flounders

1. See plate 8.

through the snow, leaving a track by which a heavy piece of artillery might follow it, and its amazing strength enables it for a short time to outstrip the horse. If it is not killed by the first fire, it turns furiously on the hunter, and its onset is frequently fatal to the horse; the rider may possibly conceal himself in the snow, and at a convenient opportunity, repeat the blow, or effect his escape. On foot the method of hunting is more tedious. It is necessary to make a large circuit in order to advance against the wind, for the nostrils of the buffalo are very acute. The hunter propels himself flat on the snow, but lies without motion when the animals lift their heads from their pasture, which they do at intervals to assure themselves of security. The Chepewyans creep under the snow, which is softer below than at the surface, making holes above, occasionally, to ascertain their position. Against this insidious enemy, the vigilance of the buffalo does not avail it. Though mortally wounded, it tosses the snow in the air, and seeks its foe in vain: sometimes it runs bellowing from the herd, brushing down small trees in its course; but its career is soon finished by the wolves, which hover in its rear, watching the decay of its strength.

When a large band of Indians is collected, the buffaloes are taken in a kind of pound, which is a circular space, inclosed by stakes, having a narrow entrance at the edge of a declivity above the level of the pound. From the entrance, two hedges of stakes gradually diverge to such a distance that the mouth of the road opens two or three miles. Some hunters on horseback drive a herd towards the opening and others conceal themselves behind the hedges. When the buffaloes begin to perceive the hedges on each side, the hunters stationed there rise and terrify them by shouts, so that they rush forward and precipitate each other down the declivity into the pound, where they are dispatched at leisure with spears or arrows. In the barren parts of the plains, the buffaloes are so numerous that their bones are used to make the pounds, and their dung serves for fuel.

The weight of a buffalo is between 1,400 and 1,500 pounds. The meat is coarser than beef, but very fat; the tongue, whether dried or salted, is preferable to that of an ox, and the boss is the best food in this country. The hides, dressed with the hair, are the bedding of the Indians, and of the horns, which are capable of receiving a high polish, they make powder flasks. Some of the hair has been manufactured into strong, warm cloth in England; and if the water carriage between Lake Winnipeg and Hudson's Bay was rendered less difficult, it might prove a

more lasting source of emolument to the Hudson's Bay Company than
the fur trade.*

*I had intended to add accounts of many animals and of birds. But other occupations
have frustrated that design at present. [Robert Hood.]

B. OBSERVATIONS ON THE CLIMATE

On this interesting subject, our observations have been necessarily
limited by the few instruments which the nature of our expedition
would admit of carrying. Without a barometer, little can be expected
from meteorological observations, worthy of scientific notice.

The following table contains the mean temperatures for each
month, deduced from two daily observations taken nearly at the extremes of temperature, that is, at sunrise, and at 2 p.m. The temperatures were also observed at 8 p.m., and by including them, the
mean temperatures would be diminished half a degree, for the winter
months, and increased a degree, in September, April and May.

1819	MEAN TEMP	GREATEST HEAT	WIND, ETC.	LEAST HEAT	WIND, ETC.
September	+46.33	+60	SSW (light & clear)	+30	Calm & clear
October	+36.77	+57	Ed mod.; rain	+19	N light; clear
November	+16.23	+45	SW strong; cloudy	−20	WSW mod.; clear
December	+2.67	+40	SW strong; snow	−31	WNW, mod.; clear
1820					
January	−13.87	+10	W strong; snow	−44	EbN, light; clear
February	−1.25	+20	NW light; variable	−34	W, mod.; clear
March	+12.98	+54	W strong; cloudy	−22	WNW, mod.; clear
April	+34.68	+77	S strong; clear	−13	WNW, mod.; clear
May	+50.49	+84	NW light; variable	+20	WNW, strong; snow

In the other columns are noted the greatest and the least degrees of heat observed in each month, and the state of the weather and direction of the wind at those times.[2]

The greatest cold was always felt during clear and calm weather, or light breezes. Clouds, though unaccompanied by wind, raised the thermometer, and a strong wind, in clear weather and from the coldest quarter, produced the same effect. My meteorological information is so slight that I am not acquainted with any theory accounting for this familiar phenomenon; which I conceive to be caused by the rapid motion of the air, carrying the radiations of the earth along its surface, which on the contrary, rise perpendicularly in calm weather.[3] A continued gale gradually exhausts the earth and lowers the thermometer, and if followed by a calm, the temperature of the air sinks many degrees. We have often had an opportunity of remarking these particulars during the NW gales.

Although the thermometer is never very low, in high winds, yet the sensation of cold produced by the quick succession of frigid particles, is never so painful as at those periods.[4]

The coldest wind is from NNW, which passes over a high ridge of the Rocky Mountains. The warm vapours of the Pacific Ocean are intercepted and condensed, while the cold current passes to the eastward, and the difference of climate, on the east and west sides of the mountains amounts, I have been informed, to that which takes place in 10° of the meridian of Cumberland House. The easterly, westerly, and southerly winds were almost invariably accompanied by clouds and snow; especially the two former, which are the most prevalent.[5] To the

2. As implied by Hood, the average of the lowest and highest temperatures closely approximates the average temperature for that day. Since in January at very low temperatures the mercury sank into the bulb and froze, the temperature may have fallen below Hood's lowest recording of 44° below zero. The mean monthly temperatures deduced by Hood are remarkably close to present corresponding normal temperatures at The Pas, Manitoba, the nearest weather station. [Balfour W. Currie]

3. Hood's explanation of the rise in temperature during windy periods in winter is only partially correct. During the long

winter nights the earth's surface is cooled by radiation. If there is little wind, a temperature inversion occurs, the air near the surface becoming much colder than the air above. A wind mixes the colder surface air with the warmer air aloft. [B.W.C.]

4. Here Hood anticipates the modern concept of wind-chill.

5. Hood is correct; most precipitation in this area occurs with southerly and easterly winds, the low pressure centre bringing anti-clockwise winds with cloud and precipitation. Late in the 19th century when the telegraph allowed study of synchronous observations, the succession

continuance of easterly winds, the unusual accumulation of snow in the winter of 1819 was attributed. It is the evaporation of the Atlantic Ocean which is thus carried across the great portion of continent to the eastward of Hudson's Bay; or it may be deemed a proof that the bay is not frozen in the center, where the depth is greatest.[6]

Thunder is never heard in this climate, between the months of November and April, nor is any electricity to be distinguished in the air. The intensity of the cold renders many bodies electric which are conductors at a higher temperature, but confines the electricity by destroying the ordinary conducting powers.[7] The evaporation going forward with so little heat, must necessarily be very slight. Indeed, the winds from the north and west so seldom brought clouds that we may conclude none are formed in that quarter; but that they are driven into the track by other winds.

The daily temperature is liable to the most extraordinary changes, produced by clouds, after clear weather, amounting sometimes to 40°. The difference of thermometrical extremes in April is 90°.

The temperature of the water was observed on our route between York Fort and Cumberland House; but I have not inserted them because the communication was in so many places interrupted by lakes and portages. The lakes presenting an undisturbed surface to the sun, were always the warmest, and for the same reason the soonest frozen. The whole body of the rivers is cooled in its descent through shallow rapids before the surface is frozen, and they recruit their warmth at the bottoms of the lakes. The thickest ice observed in this latitude was at God's Lake where it was six feet in depth. From the best information I could obtain, the ground is not perpetually frozen at any depth, but, not

---

of centres of low and high pressure travelling from west to east was first recognized. With the approach of the following high, the wind changes to northerly and westerly, the skies clear and the temperature drops. In winter, these temperature drops are most noticeable as the winds bring in cold air from higher latitudes. [B. W. C.]

6. Until 1948, many people inferred from the fog over open water about six miles offshore, that the central deeper waters of Hudson Bay did not freeze. Only with

R.C.A.F. reconnaissance flights over the bay in March, 1948, was it proved that the bay freezes centrally and that the open water is only a narrow strip at the junction of the central ice with the landfast ice. [Margaret Montgomery, 'Does the Bay Freeze?' *Beaver* 282 (June 1951), 12-15.]

7. Probably Hood noticed this phenomenon only indoors. In low humidity, which results when cold winter air is warmed indoors, static electricity is more evident.

far to the northward, the frost is found to retain its hold, at the distance of four feet from the surface, in the last month of summer.[8]

In January, our mercury thermometers were all frozen, and rendered totally useless. The great diminution of the mercury, when congealed, seemed to expel some air from it, which had resisted the effect of boiling; for we could not perceive the smallest flaw in the bulbs, examined with a microscope.

The extreme rigour of the North American climate, so much greater than that of any other country situated between the same parallels, had been long an inexplicable enigma to philosophy, which could not obtain sufficient knowledge of the country to furnish materials for theory; when, from that circumstance, it became the province of invention. It was alleged that the land extended to the pole, and that it was covered with high and frozen mountains. The first of these allegations is destroyed by the strong probability now existing of a sea verging the parallel of 70°, and with regard to the second, there is surely no space of the same extent in the world, except perhaps the deserts of Africa, less diversified by irregularities of surface.

The Rocky Mountains on the west coast are insignificant in comparison with those on the west and south sides of Russian Tartary.[9] The winds that pass over the Rocky Mountains are certainly the coldest; but they have little influence on the summer, which is oppressively hot.[10] This mystery appears to me to be solved by a geographical fact, which I am enabled to state from the experience of the inhabitants added to our own; that half the country is covered by water, throughout the year. Such is the case, whether the rivers of America are more numerous than those of Asia, or the quantity of rain and snow greater,

8. In the western half of Canada, continuous permafrost is present north of a line from near Churchill to the northeastern extremity of Great Bear Lake. South of this line, discontinuous permafrost is encountered from the northern extremity of Lake Winnipeg to north of Lac La Ronge in Saskatchewan, McMurray in Alberta, and the southwestern tip of the Yukon. [R. J. E. Brown, 'Permafrost in Canada', *Geol. Survey Canada Map* 1246A, N. R. C. Publ. 9769 (1967).]

9. Tartary: that part of Russia between the Pacific Ocean and the Dnieper River.

Hood is correct when he intimates that the Himalayas are higher than the Rocky Mountains. However, the Ural's highest peak of 6,184 feet is well below the peaks of the Canadian Rocky Mountains.

10. Hood is misleading here. Air coming over the Rocky Mountains has a warming effect. It is warm as it leaves the Pacific Ocean, cools because of expansion as it rises over the mountains, then gains heat from the water vapour that condenses and falls as rain or snow, and finally is heated by compression as it flows downward over the plains. The warmest of these winds are called Chinooks. [B. W. C.]

though the latter might be presumed as America is the narrowest of the two continents. The snow in melting, and the rivers in their course, overspread the low country, and form lakes, pools, and swamps, which the summer is too short to evaporate. When the surface of this great body is frozen, the atmosphere can receive no more heat, except from the motionless particles immediately in contact with it, which give out their heat also, and the mass congealed may be estimated at five feet in depth, or 4¹/₂ feet of water.

The whole heat, therefore, obtained by the atmosphere is that which is radiated by the reduction of the 4¹/₂ feet of water, to the lowest temperature of winter. Whereas the earth, having a much greater capacity for heat, gives out much more in reducing its temperature to the same degree, and, though constantly supplied by radiations from its inner surfaces, is frozen three or four feet every year. To this must be added the emanations from all the objects upon it, which receive the sun's rays directly, including the animal and vegetable creations and the irregularities of the surface, which increase the superficies by one fourth.[11] Upon these considerations, I have ventured to found the opinion that the excess of cold in North America, above that of Siberia, is caused by the greater proportion that the water bears to the land, in the former, than in the latter.[12]

The fact which supports this hypothesis is at least important, and other conclusions may hereafter be drawn from it, more in consonance with philosophical principles.

C. AURORA BOREALIS

The most material information we had obtained at this period, regarded the height of the Aurora from the earth. The following is the result of the observations that were made at the Basquiau Hill and at the same

11. The physics of heat energy and heat transfers was not established until later in the 19th century. The heat transferred to the atmosphere as the numerous lakes and rivers cool to the freezing point, and as the land radiates heat outwards, delays the drop in temperature as winter approaches. Ice and snow are good insulators and poor conductors of heat, so only a small amount of heat is supplied to the atmosphere from the earth during the winter. The sun in winter provides little heat owing to the inclination of its rays and the short days at these latitudes. [B. W. C.]

12. Actually, the coldest temperature in the Northern Hemisphere was recorded at Oymyakon, Siberia, where it reached minus 96° F. in 1964. At Snag, Yukon, it was minus 81° F. in February 1947.

time by Dr. Richardson at Cumberland House. The instruments used for the purpose were two small wooden quadrants, revolving on pivots and furnished with plummets. Our chronometers were previously regulated; though great accuracy was not necessary in this particular, as the arches of the Aurora are sometimes stationary for many minutes. On the 2nd of April, the altitude of a brilliant beam was 10°0'0"at 10:01 p.m., at Cumberland House. Fifty-five miles south-southwest, it was not visible. As the trees rose about 5° above the horizon, it may be estimated that the beam was not more than seven miles from the earth, and 27 from Cumberland House. On the sixth of April, the Aurora was some hours in the zenith at that place, a confused mass of flashes and beams, and in Lat. 53°22'48" N., Long. 103°7'17" W. [at the 'hunting tent'], it appeared in the form of an arch stationary about 9° high, and bearing NbE. It was therefore seven miles from the earth. On the 7th of April, the Aurora was again in the zenith before 10 p.m. at Cumberland House, and in Lat. 53°36'40" N. and Long. 102°31'41" W. [Goose Lake], the altitude of the highest of two concentric arches at 9:00 p.m., was 9°. At 9:30 p.m., it was 11°30' and at 10:00 p.m., 15°0'0", its center always bearing NbE. During this time it was between six and seven miles from the earth. After 10 p.m., it covered the sky at Cumberland House, and passed the zenith at the other place.

This is true, these observations are opposed to a host of theories entertained by the first meteorologists, but not to a single fact. We have sometimes seen an attenuated aurora flashing across 100° of the sky, in a single second; a quickness of motion inconsistent with the height of 60 or 70 miles, which has been ascribed to it.[13] This kind of Aurora is not brighter than the Milky Way and resembles sheet lightning in its motions.

For the sake of perspicuity, and having no authority at hand, I shall describe the several parts of the Aurora, which I have termed flashes, beams, and arches. The beams are little conical pencils of light, ranged in parallel lines, with their pointed extremities towards the earth, generally in the direction of the dipping needle.[14] The flashes seem to

13. Hood is very much in error. The visual aurora reaches from about 40 miles to 1000 miles above the earth. For accurate measurements, two observers at separate stations must be certain they are looking at the same feature and must record its altitude and azimuth values at exactly the same time, since forms can move many miles in a few minutes. Further, because of perspective, 'auroral draperies' may appear as a bright beam seen from point A, but 55 miles away they may be viewed almost at right angles and appear as a kink in the drapery. [John Black]

be scattered beams approaching nearer to the earth, because they are similarly shaped, and infinitely larger. I have called them flashes, because their appearance is sudden and seldom continues long. When the Aurora first becomes visible, it is formed like a rainbow, the light of which is faint, and the motion of the beams indistinguishable. It is then in the horizon. As it approaches the zenith, it resolves itself at intervals into beams, which by a quick, undulating motion project themselves into wreaths, afterwards fading away, and again brightening, without any visible expansion or concentration of matter. Numerous flashes attend in different parts of the sky. That this mass, from its short distance above the earth, would appear like an arch, to a person posted at the horizon, may be demonstrated by the rules of perspective, supposing its parts to be nearly equidistant from the earth. An undeniable proof of it, however, is afforded by the observations of the 6th and 7th of April, when the Aurora which filled the sky at Cumberland House, from the northern horizon to the zenith, with wreaths and flashes, assumed the shape of arches at some distance to the southward.

But the Aurora does not always make its first appearance as an arch. It sometimes rises from a confused mass of light in the east or west, and crosses the sky towards the opposite point, exhibiting wreaths of beams or coronae boreales in its way. An arch also, which is pale and uniform at the horizon, passes the zenith without displaying any irregularity or additional brilliancy; and we have seen three arches together, very near the northern horizon, one of which discovered the beams and even colours, but the other two were faint and uniform.

On the 7th of April, an arch was visible to the southward, exactly similar to that in the north, and it disappeared in 15 minutes. It had probably passed the zenith before sunset. The motion of the whole body of Aurora is from the northward to the southward, at angles not more than 20° from the magnetic meridian.[15] The centers of the arches were as often in the magnetic as in the true meridian.

The colours do not seem to depend on the presence of any luminary, but to be generated by the motion of the beams; and then only when that motion is rapid and the light brilliant. The lower extremities

14. Hood correctly noted that the beams or rays are nearly parallel to the direction of the dipping needle. [B. W. C.]

15. Hood again is correct in noting the general motion of auroral display from northward to southward, at angles up to 20° from the magnetic meridian. This angle was almost certainly eastward from the meridian, since displacement to the west at Cumberland House is rare. [B. W. C.]

quiver with a fiery red colour, and the upper, with orange. We once saw violet in the former.

The number of Aurorae visible in September was two, in October three, in November three, in December five, in January five, in February seven, in March sixteen, in April fifteen, and in May eleven.[16] Calm and clear weather was the most favourable for observation; but it is discernible in cloudy weather and through mists. We could not perceive that it affected the weather.

The magnetic needle in the open air was disturbed by the Aurora, whenever it approached the zenith.[17] Its motion was not vibratory, as observed by Mr. Dalton,[18] and this was perhaps owing to the weight of the card attached to it. It moved slowly, to the east and west of the magnetic meridian, and seldom recovered its original direction in less than eight or nine hours. The greatest extent of its aberration was 45'.

A delicate electrometer, suspended at the height of 50 feet from the ground, was never perceptibly affected by the Aurora, nor could we distinguish its rustling noise, of which, however, such strong testimony has been given to us, that no doubt remains of the fact.[19]

The conclusions to be drawn from the above, will be found in the observations for the winter of 1820.

D. MAGNETICAL PHENOMENA

The variation of the compass at York Factory was 6° easterly, and during our passage to Cumberland House, its increase was gradual, though not regular. When the course tended to the westward, it was

16. The 67 reported auroras (presumably nights with aurora) at Cumberland House from September to May inclusive is somewhat higher than one would expect for 1819-20, which was close to minimum for the sunspot cycle. During sunspot minima, auroras are less frequent to the south of their zone of maximum occurrence than at other times. The large number observed during March, April, and May agrees with the well-known maximum occurrence during the spring months. [B. W. C.]

17. The motion of the magnetic needle during an auroral display is one aspect of what is now referred to as a geomagnetic storm.

18. John Dalton, famous English chemist and physicist, 1766-1844, who kept a meteorological diary including 200,000 observations in a period of 57 years. He was the author of the atomic theory and of Dalton's law of partial pressures.

19. The problem of a noise associated with the aurora on occasion has not been settled to this day. Some reliable observers claim to have heard it but there has been no combined audio-phonographic recording system to prove it. Sixty miles above the earth's surface, the air is very thin and any sound would be attenuated. [John Black]

most rapid, but when to the southward, approaching the magnetic meridian of York, it sometimes decreased. At Cumberland House, it was 17°17′30″ E. By such former observations as one could procure an account of, the easterly variation has increased throughout, and this motion of its magnetic poles is directly contrary to that of the poles of England and Hudson's Straits.

It was the opinion of Mr. Cavallo,[20] founded on all the known principles of magnetism, that the magnetic poles of the earth were the centers of attraction of all the ferruginous bodies contained in it. In these centers, therefore, the attraction is strongest, and the poles of particular bodies there situated will have one common direction. But, in every other place, the direction of the needle must differ, and consequently the position of no body can be altered, without likewise altering its pole—although a large ferruginous mass, surrounded by many smaller masses, may attract the poles of several places very near its own center. I have made this statement in the hope of obtaining an elucidation on a subject involved in much obscurity, by writers who descant on their approach to a magnetic pole, as if that pole was fixed in a place where the dipping needle happens to be perpendicular. To use a familiar example, the common center of gravity between a comet and the earth, might be brought so near the latter, as to effect their conjunction; but the earth is not therefore one of the foci of the comet, when it is beyond the orbit of the Georgium sidus.[21]

On these principles, there are various modes of accounting for the opposite changes of variation in Hudson's Straits, and on the continent of America. First: It may be supposed that a ferruginous mass, below the parallel of 70° N., has moved from west to east, drawing the poles of Hudson's Straits to the westward and those of the continent to the eastward. Secondly: The movement of a mass from north to south, on the meridian of 90° W. which would also account for the increase of westerly variation in England. Thirdly: A body of iron has been rendered magnetic by electricity, or by communication with other mag-

20. Tiberius Cavallo, 1749-1809, who published eight books on electricity and magnetism between 1775 and 1798. The son of a Naples physician, his adult life was spent in England.

21. Sidus is Latin for star, and Sir William Herschel in 1781, when he discovered the seventh major planet, named it for his royal patron, King George III. Although it was known as 'The Georgian' for many years, other countries disliked calling a planet after an English monarch, and it then became known as Uranus.

nets in the vicinity of the pole of Hudson's Straits. But, whatever has occasioned it, the poles of the continent, of Hudson's Straits and of the Bay and Welcome, have approached each other, so that the intersections of the planes of their meridians are almost in the same diameter; and it is most probable that the poles themselves are situated in that diameter, at such distances from the earth's surface, as are indicated by the depression of the dipping needle. Admitting this hypothesis, the above mentioned diameter terminates about 150 miles northwest of Repulse Bay, [22] and the pole of York Fort is half the earth's radius immediately below that place. The only argument afforded by the data is, that if it was nearer to York, the variations on the continent would be more easterly, and if farther from York, its influence would render them more westerly than they really are.[23]

At York Factory, the dip of the magnetic needle was 79°29'17", and at Norway House, it was 83°40'0", the variation being 14°25' E. At Cumberland House, the dip on November 24th was 83°9'45". Both these places, notwithstanding the increase of the dip, are more than 3° of latitude to the southward of York. As their variation increases in proportion to their distance from the meridian of the latter place, I should infer, that if not influenced by some local attraction, their poles are still farther from Earth's surface.

The needle at Cumberland House performed a mean vibration in 3"-90. It was 6 inches in length, and the result is obtained by taking the mean of its vibrations with the face of the arch east and west: the interval of time commencing when its position was horizontal. At the Orkneys, we found that a mean vibration occupied 2"-58: and in London a needle of 12 inches, according to Mr. Whiston, vibrates in 6". The pole therefore, of Cumberland House, must be more deeply situated in the earth, or much weaker than that of the Orkneys, or of London, as the dip is greater.

22. James Clark Ross placed the magnetic dip pole at 70°5'17" N and 96°46'45" W, when he was the first to reach it in southwest Boothia peninsula on 1 June 1831. It was then only 350 miles northwest of Repulse Bay, so Hood's calculations were a good approximation, considering that local influences in the earth's crust may prevent a compass from pointing directly towards the magnetic pole. Hood seems to have understood that the magnetic poles would move gradually.

23. Here Hood seems to grasp the theory that the earth is a spherical magnet with one pole in the north and the other in the south. Some confusion occurs, however, when he speaks of various localities having their own 'poles' at varying distances beneath the earth's surface.

The following table contains the mean diurnal variations of the compass for four months at Cumberland House.[24] Many unavoidable interruptions prevented the number of days in each month from being complete, and some irregularities have been caused by the motion of the compass box. Those days are not included, on which the needle was affected by the Aurora.[25]

1820	8 a.m.	9 a.m.	1 p.m.	4 p.m.	8 p.m.	12 p.m.
February		17°16′E.	17°-11′2″	17°-9′-9″	17°-12′-4″	17°-13′
March		17°14′9″	17°-9′-5″	17°-9′-7″	17°-12′-1″	17°-13′-4″
April	17°15′7″ E.		17°-8′-8″	17°-9′-6″	17°-12′-3″	17°-13′-9″
May	17°-16′-9″		17°-7′-8″	17°-8′-3″		17°-14′-7″

As in other places, the diurnal variation increases with the advance of summer, and the needle reaches the extremes of variation at nearly the same hours. But the maximum is at the coldest period, and the minimum at the warmest; which is the reverse, I believe, of the observations which have been made in Europe and in the East Indies.

I have not inserted the diurnal variations of the dipping needle, because they differed very unaccountably, and as that instrument admitted the air, I cannot determine whether the Aurora affected it.[26] The amount varied from 10′ to 25′; and the general uniformity of its motions with those of the horizontal needle indicates that the same cause operated upon both.

The dip was observed on June 11, 1820, at Cumberland House, and, to our surprise, it was found to have increased 1°25′44″ since November 24th, being 46′45″ less than before, with the face east, and 3°48′12″ greater with the face west.

24. In 1947, the magnetic deviation or declination at Cumberland House was just under 16° E; i.e. the compass pointed 16° east of true north. This has changed very little since 1820, in spite of the movement of the north magnetic pole, which in 1970 was located on Bathurst Island at 76.2° N and 101° W and was moving north and west at the rate of six miles per year.

25. The connection between magnetic disturbances and the aurora had been known for 60 years.

26. The magnetic inclination, or dip, is measured at right angles to the magnetic deviation or declination with a special instrument, the dipping needle. It is as though a compass were held on edge. It measures the other dimension of terrestrial magnetism. At a magnetic pole, the needle is vertical.

6
Cumberland House to Fort Chipewyan

Journey from Cumberland House to
Fort Chepewyan.

We soon found that canoes were not calculated to brave rough weather on a large lake [Cumberland], for we were compelled to land on the opposite border, to free them from the water which had already saturated their cargoes. The wind became more moderate, and we were enabled, after traversing a chain of smaller lakes [Cross and Namew], to enter the mouth of the Sturgeon River, at sunset, where we encamped.[1] The lading of the canoes is always, if possible, carried on shore at night, and the canoes taken out of the water.

At 3 a.m., June 13th [14th], we embarked and at 4, passed a portage at the confluence of the Rat River,[2] which takes its rise at a height of land about 20 miles northeast and beyond it a river rises which communicates with Nelson River, and with several establishments of the Hudson's Bay Company. At 5 p.m., we reached Beaver [Amisk] Lake and landed to repair some damage sustained by the canoes. A round stone will displace the lading of a canoe, without doing any injury, but a slight blow against a sharp corner penetrates the bark. For the purpose of repairing it, a small quantity of gum or pitch, bark, and pine [spruce] roots is embarked, and the business is so expeditiously performed, that the speed of the canoe amply compensates for every delay.

The Sturgeon River is justly called by the Canadians, La Riviere Maligne, from its numerous and dangerous rapids.[3] Against the strength of a rapid, it is impossible to effect any progress by paddling; and the canoes are tracked or if the bank will not admit of it, propelled with poles, in the management of which the Canadians show great dexterity. Their simultaneous motions were strongly contrasted with

1. At the present Indian-Métis settlement of Sturgeon Landing.

2. Now known as Goose River. One can ascend it to Athapapuskow Lake, cross 210 yards of flat limestone to the Cranberry Lakes, follow the Grass River to Reed Lake, portage to File Lake, and descend the File River to the Burntwood and thence to the Nelson River. This was not a practical route for the fur trade.

3. 'The wicked river'; this section of the Sturgeon-Weir River drops 91 feet in 23 miles with almost continuous rapids.

the awkward confusion of the inexperienced Englishmen, deafened by the torrent; who sustained the blame of every accident which occurred.

At sunset, we encamped on an island in Beaver Lake, and at 4 a.m. the next morning, passed the first portage in the River La Pente.[4] Beaver Lake is 12 miles in length and six in breadth. The flat limestone country rises into bold rocks on its banks, and at the mouth of the Pente, the limestone discontinues. The lake is deep, and has already been noticed for the number and excellence of its fish.

The River Pente is rapid and shallow. We had emerged from the muddy channels through an alluvial soil and the primitive rocks interrupted our way with frequent portages through the whole route to Ile-à-la-Crosse Lake. At 2 p.m., we passed the mouth of the River d'Avoine,[5] running from the westward and the Pente above its confluence takes the name of the Grande Rivière,[6] which rises at the height of land called the Frog Portage.

The thermometer was this day 100° in the sun, and the heat was extremely oppressive from our constant exposure to it. We crossed three portages in the Grand Rivière, and encamped at the last.[7] Here we met the director of the North West Company affairs in the north, Mr. Stuart,[8] on his way to Fort William in a light canoe. He had left the Athapescow Lake only 13 days, and brought letters from Mr. Franklin, who desired that we would endeavour to collect stores of every kind at Ile-à-la-Crosse, and added a favourable account of the country to the northward of the Slave Lake.

On the 16th [June] at 3 a.m., we continued our course, the river increasing to the breadth of half a mile, with many rapids between the rocky islands. The banks were luxuriantly clothed with pines, poplars,

4. *La Pente* means 'the slope' or 'the ascent', emphasizing the steep gradient. Here again we meet the practice of giving new names to each section of a river, now named the Sturgeon-Weir throughout its length. Franklin called this section the Ridge River.

5. *D'Avoine* 'of oats', the Hanson River. Franklin called it the Hay River. It comes from Hanson Lake.

6. Still the Sturgeon-Weir. The present name is derived from the practice of using a weir to trap sturgeon in the fast shallow waters.

7. The Scoop Rapids, where fish were scooped in the eddies below; the Leaf Rapids, now crossed by a bridge on Highway 106; and Birch Rapids.

8. John Stuart, who had accompanied Simon Fraser in 1805-6 and for whom Stuart Lake in British Columbia was named by Fraser. In the winter of 1819-20, John Stuart was in charge of the North West post at Pierre au Calumet on the Athabasca. He brought Franklin's 'favourable account' of a country that Franklin had not yet seen.

and birch trees of the largest size; but the different shades of green were undistinguishable at a distance, and the glow of autumnal colours was wanting to render the variety beautiful. Having crossed two portages at the different extremities of the Island [Corneille] Lake,[9] we ran through the extensive sheets of water under sail, called the Heron [Mirond] and Pelican Lakes; the former of which, is 15 miles in length and the latter five; but its extent to the southward has not been explored. An intricate channel, with four small portages, conducted us to the Woody Lake [Wood]. Its borders were indeed, walls of pines hiding the face of steep and high rocks, and we wandered in search of a landing place till 10 p.m., when we were forced to take shelter from an impeding storm on a small island, where we wedged ourselves between the trees. But, though we secured the canoes, we incurred a personal evil of much greater magnitude in the torments inflicted by the mosquitoes; a plague which had grown upon us since our departure from Cumberland House, and which infested us during the whole summer.[10] We found no relief from their attacks, by exposing ourselves to the utmost violence of the wind and rain. Our last resource was to plunge ourselves in the water, and from this uncomfortable situation we gladly escaped at daylight, and hoisted our sails.

The Woody Lake is 13 miles in length, and a small grassy channel at its northwestern extremity,[11] leads to the Frog Portage, the source of the waters descending by Beaver Lake to the Saskashawan. The distance to the Missinnippi or Churchill River[12] is only 380 yards, and as its course crosses the height nearly at right angles to the direction of the Grande Riviere, it would be superfluous to compute the elevation at this place. The portage is in Latitude 55°26′0″ N. and Longitude 103°34′50″ W. Its name, according to Sir Alexander Mackenzie, is

9. *Corneille* was the French-Canadian word for raven, though in Europe *corneille* means rook.

10. The mosquitoes caused a sleepless night of torment after 19 hours of strenuous travel. These explorers risked their lives as part of their routine, but it was the mosquitoes that really drove them to distraction. Perspiration attracts mosquitoes, so these hard-working men would be prime targets. The bites often cause larger welts in Englishmen than in native-born Canadians, who develop a certain tolerance.

11. Via Lindstrom Lake, a stagnant lagoon.

12. The big water, from the Cree, *misi*, meaning 'much' or 'very big' and *nipiy*, 'water'. The Churchill River was named after John Churchill, first Duke of Marlborough (1650–1722), the third Governor of the Hudson's Bay Company.

derived from the Crees having left suspended, a stretched frog's skin, in derision of the Northern Indian mode of dressing the beaver.[13]

The part of the Missinnippi in which we embarked we should have mistaken for a lake, had it not been for the rapidity of the current against which we made our way.[14] At 4 p.m., we passed a long portage,[15] occasioned by a ledge of rocks 300 yards in length, over which the river falls seven or eight feet. After crossing another portage,[16] we encamped.

On the 18th we had rain, wind and thunder, the whole day, but this weather was much preferable to the heat we had borne hitherto. We passed three portages,[17] and at 6 p.m., encamped on the north bank. Below the third portage is the mouth of the Rapid River,[18] flowing from a large lake to the southward, in which a post was formerly maintained by the North West Company.[19]

At 3 a.m., June 19th we embarked, and found ourselves involved in a confused mass of islands, through the openings of which we could not discern the shore.[20] The guide's knowledge of the river did not extend beyond the last portage, and our perplexity continued till we observed some foam floating on the water, and took the direction from which it came. The noise of a heavy fall at the Mountain Portage reached our ears at the distance of four miles, and we arrived there at 8 a.m. The portage was a difficult ascent over a rocky island [a narrow peninsula],

13. It was also called Portage du Traite or Trade Portage, since the Frobisher brothers traded there in 1774. The latitude is 55°24′ N and longitude is 103°31′ W. A large concrete control structure would be necessary here, if a proposed hydro dam is built below the confluence of the Reindeer and Churchill Rivers.

14. This widening of the Churchill River is now called Trade Lake. Through much of its length the Churchill is more a series of lakes joined by rapids than it is a river.

15. The Grand Rapid or Great Rapid, a soggy 675 yard portage.

16. The Barrel Portage around Keg Falls, above which they entered a widening of the river called Keg Lake.

17. Island Portage between Keg and Drinking Lakes, then another to ascend the falls between Drinking Lake and Nistowiak Lake, and then the Stanley Rapids above the mouth of the Montreal River. A Hudson's

Bay Company post, Stanley House, had been established in the area in 1798, with intermittent occupancy. The Church of England's Stanley Mission was later founded above the rapids in 1853-60 by Rev. Robert Hunt with Saskatchewan's first church completed in 1856.

18. The Rapid River, draining Lac la Ronge via Iskwatikan Lake, plunges over the beautiful Nistowiak Falls into the Churchill.

19. Lac la Ronge. Jean Etienne Waden established there in 1779 and died in 1782, allegedly killed in a quarrel with Peter Pond. Simon Fraser occupied a fort on the east shore in the winter of 1795-96, and when David Thompson explored the lake in 1798 Joseph Versailles had a post at the present townsite of La Ronge.

20. In the northwesterly extension of Mountain Lake.

between which and the main shore were two cataracts and a third in sight above them, making another portage. We surprised a large brown bear, which immediately retreated into the woods. To the northward of the second portage, we again found the channels intricate, but the shores being sometimes visible we ventured to proceed.

The character of the country was new and more interesting than before. The mountainous and stony elevations receded from the banks, and the woods crept through their breaches to the valleys behind; the adventurous pine alone ascending their bases, and braving storms unfelt below.

At noon, we landed at the Otter Portage, where the river ran with great velocity for half a mile, among large stones. Having carried across the principal part of the cargo, the people attempted to track the canoes along the edge of the rapid. With the first they succeeded, but the other, in which were the foreman and steersman, was overset, and swept away by the current. An account of this misfortune was speedily conveyed to the upper end of the portage, and the men launched the remaining canoe into the rapid, though wholly unacquainted with the dangers of it.[21] The descent was quickly accomplished, and they perceived the bottom of the lost canoe above water in a little bay, whither it had been whirled by the eddy. One man had reached the bank, but no traces could be found of the foreman, Louis Saint Jean. We saved the canoe, out of which two guns and a case of preserved meats had been thrown into the rapid. So early a disaster deeply affected the spirits of the Canadians, and their natural vivacity gave way to melancholy forebodings, while they erected a wooden cross on the rocks near the spot where their companion perished.

The loss of this man's services and the necessity of procuring a guide, determined us to wait for the arrival of the North West Company people from Fort Chepewyan and we encamped accordingly. The canoe was much shattered, but as the gunwales were not broken, we easily

21. Franklin, [*Journey 1819-22*, p. 182] gives a footnote from Dr. Richardson's journal: 'Mr. Hood himself was the first to leap into the canoe and incite the men to follow him, and shoot the rapid to save the lives of their companions.' Saint Jean, the Canadian foreman, may not have been able to swim, or he may have been stunned when his canoe broke loose and was carried backwards or broadside in the thundering waters. In August 1972 my two younger sons and other members of their boy scout troop 'shot' these rapids a number of times, but when I tried it we overturned. My first three attempts to get air coincided with four-foot waves; without a lifejacket I would probably have drowned.

repaired it. In the evening a North West canoe arrived, with two of the partners. They gave us an account of Mr. Franklin's proceedings, and referred us to the brigade following them for a guide.

During the 20th [June] it rained heavily, and we passed the day in anxious suspense confined to our tents. A black bear came to the bank on the opposite side of the river, and on seeing us, glided behind the trees.

Late on the 21st Mr. Robertson,[22] of the Hudson's Bay Company arrived, and furnished us with a guide, but desired that he might be exchanged when we met the northern canoes. We took advantage of the remainder of the day, to cross the next portage [Great Devil], which was ³/₄ of a mile in length. On the 22nd, we crossed three small portages and encamped at the fourth. At one of them we passed some of the Hudson's Bay Company canoes, and our applications to them were unsuccessful. We began to suspect that Ile-à-la-Crosse was the nearest place at which we might hope for assistance. However, on the morning of the 23rd, as we were about to embark, we encountered the last brigades of canoes belonging to both the companies, and obtained a guide and foreman from them. Thus completely equipped, we entered the Black Bear Island Lake, the navigation of which requires a very experienced pilot. Its length is 22 miles, and its breadth varies from three to five, yet it is so choked with islands, that no channel is to be found through it, exceeding a mile in breadth. At sunset, we landed and encamped on an island, and at 6 a.m. on the 24th left the lake and crossed three portages into another, which has probably several communications with the last, as that by which we passed is too narrow to convey the whole body of the Missinnippi. At one of these portages, called the Pin [Needle] Portage, is a rapid about 10 yards in length, with a descent of 10 or 12 feet, and beset with rocks. Light canoes sometimes venture down this fatal gulph, to avoid the portage, unappalled by the warning crosses which overhang the brink, the mournful records of former failures.[23]

22. Colin Robertson of the Hudson's Bay Company. When he reached Grand Rapids he was captured by the North West men and taken to Montreal. The previous summer, Robertson had helped Governor Williams escort the captured North West men to York Factory—after Robertson had first been prisoner of the North West Company from 11 October 1818 at Lake Athabasca until mid-June 1819, when he escaped at Cumberland House.

23. The previous summer, Colin Robertson shot these rapids by canoe while travelling as a prisoner of the North West Company, all but two of whose men portaged. Some have alleged this was an attempt to drown Robertson, but he shot the rapids skilfully and did not add another white cross to those already placed over the brink.

The Hudson's Bay Company people whom we passed on the 23rd, going to the Rock House with their furs, were badly provided with food, of which we saw distressing proofs at every portage behind them. They had stripped the birch trees of their rind to procure the soft, pulpy vessels in contact with the wood, which are sweet, but very insufficient to satisfy a craving appetite.

The lake to the westward of the Pin Portage is called Lac Souris [Sandfly]; it is seven miles long and a wide channel connects it with the Serpent Lake [Pinehouse, formerly Snake], the extent of which to the southward we could not discern. There is nothing remarkable in this chain of lakes, except their shapes being rocky basins filled by the waters of the Missinnippi, insulating the mossy eminences, and meandering with almost imperceptible current between them. From the Serpent to the Sandy Lake, it is again confined in a narrow space by the approach of its winding banks, and on the 25th we were some hours employed in traversing a series of shallow rapids, where it was necessary to lighten the canoes. As we could find no path in the woods, we walked two miles in the water upon sharp stones, from which some person was incessantly slipping into deep holes, and floundering in vain for footing at the bottom; a scene highly diverting, notwithstanding our fatigue. We were detained in Sandy Lake till 1 p.m. by a strong gale, when the wind becoming moderate we crossed five miles to the mouth of the river, and at 4 p.m. left the main branch of it and entered a little rivulet called the Grassy River, running through an extensive reedy swamp.[24] It is the nest of innumerable ducks, which rear their young among the long rushes, in security from beasts of prey. At sunset we encamped on the banks of the main branch.

At 3 a.m., June 26th, we embarked in a thick fog occasioned by a fall of the temperature of the air 10° below that of the water. Having crossed Knee Lake, which is nine miles in length, and a portage at its western extremity, we entered Primos Lake,[25] with a strong and favourable wind, by the aid of which we ran 19 miles through it, and encamped at the river's mouth. It is shaped like the barb of an arrow, with the point towards the north, and its greatest breadth is about four miles.

24. An unusually narrow, slow-moving portion of the Churchill River called the marshes of Haultain.

25. Spelled Primeau by Franklin and by modern maps; named for Louis Primeau, a Canadian who was hired by the Hudson's Bay Company in 1765 and ascended the Churchill in 1766. The western portion is

During the night, a torrent of rain washed us from our beds, accompanied by the loudest thunder I ever heard. This weather continued during the 27th,[26] and often compelled us to land, and turn the canoes up, to prevent them from filling. We passed one portage, and the confluence of a river said to afford, by other rivers beyond a height of land, a shorter but more difficult route to the Athapescow Lake than that which is generally pursued.[27]

On the 28th, we crossed the last portage,[28] and at 10 a.m. entered the Ile-à-la-Crosse Lake. Its long succession of woody points, both banks stretching towards the south till their forms were lost in the haze of the horizon, was a grateful prospect to us, after our bewildered and interrupted voyage in the Missinnippi. The gale wafted us with unusual speed, and as the lake increased in breadth, the waves swelled to a dangerous height. A canoe running before the wind is very liable to burst asunder, when on the top of a wave, so that part of the bottom is out of the water; for there is nothing to support the weight of its heavy cargo but the bark, and the slight gunwales attached to it.

At 6 p.m., our view to the southward was closed by islands, and turning to the westward at sunset we landed at the forts. Dr. Richardson's canoe was forced by the wind into a deep bay on the west side, and he did not arrive till the next day.

On making known our exigencies to the gentlemen in charge of the Hudson's Bay and North West Companies' forts, they made an assortment of stores, amounting to five bales; for four of which we were indebted to Mr. McLeod of the North West Company who shared with us the ammunition absolutely required for the support of his post;[29] receiving in exchange, an order for the same quantity upon the cargo which we expected to follow us from York Factory. We had heard from Mr. Stuart that Fort Chepewyan was too much im-

now given the separate name of Dipper Lake.

26. Hood wrote '29' in error, but this was changed by someone else, perhaps Franklin, in pencil.

27. By the Mudjatik River. *Matchattik* in Cree means 'a bad tree'. Very few have travelled the difficult passage upstream and thence by portage to Cree Lake and down the Cree River to Black Lake, as J. B. Tyrrell did in July, 1892.

28. The present Indian settlement of Patuanak is near these Shagwenaw Rapids.

29. The many McLeods are most confusing. The North West Company had a John McLeod as clerk on the Churchill in 1816 and clerk at Ile-à-la-Crosse at amalgamation in 1821. The Hudson's Bay Company manager at Ile-à-la-Crosse from 1819 to 1821 was John McLeod of Ross, first hired as a writer in 1811.

poverished to supply the wants of the expedition, and we found Ile-à-la-Crosse in the same condition; which indeed, we might have foreseen, from the exhausted state of Cumberland House, but could not have provided against. We never had heard before our departure from York, that the posts in the interior only received annually, the stores necessary for the consumption of a single year. It was fortunate for us, that Mr. Franklin had desired 10 bags of pemmican, to be sent from the Saskashawan across the plains to Ile-à-la-Crosse, for our use.[30] This resource was untouched; but we could not embark more than five pieces in our own canoes. However, Mr. McLeod agreed to send a canoe after us to the Methye Portage, with the pemmican, and we calculated that the diminution of our provision would there enable us to receive it.

The latitude of the Forts, is 55°26'45" N., and longitude 107°52'55" W. The whole distance travelled from Cumberland House, is 448 statute miles. The breadth of the lake increases from one to ten miles, and its length is 31. The Beaver River enters it on the southeast side, and another river which has not been named [Canoe], on the southwest. Both these rivers are branches of the Missinnippi, as it is the only outlet from the lake. The banks appeared to be rocky, and the beach in many places sandy, but its waters are yellow and muddy. It produces a variety of fish, among which its whitefish are esteemed the best in the country. The only birds visible at this season, are common to every part of the Missinnippi; gulls, ducks, pigeons, goatsuckers [nighthawks], and the raven; the geese and swans pay a momentary visit in passing to the north and returning.

There was little in the forts, differing from the establishments that we had before seen. The ground on which they are erected is sandy, and favourable to cultivation. Curiosity, however, was satisfied by the first experiment; and utility alone has been unable to extend it. Ile-à-la-Crosse is frequented by the Crees, and the Chepewyans.[31] It is

30. This had been arranged with Dugald Cameron of the North West Company at Green Lake, when Franklin stopped there in February 1820 on his winter overland journey from Fort Carlton to Ile-à-la-Crosse.

31. Indeed, it marks the boundary between these two tribes to this day. The modern spelling is Ile-à-la-Crosse. (In most instances, Hood's journal gives the gender incorrectly, 'le Crosse' instead of 'la Crosse'.) The first trading post here was built by Thomas Frobisher in 1776. It is not 'the island of the cross', as the Catholic mission was not established until 1846; it is the island—or really a peninsula whose base is sometimes flooded—where the Indians played the game of lacrosse. Hood's calculation of both latitude and longitude is correct to the nearest minute.

not the dread of the Indians, but of one another that has brought the rival companies so close together at every trading post; each party seeking to prevent the other from engaging the affections of the Indians, and monopolizing the trade. Wherever a settlement is made by the one, the other immediately follows, without considering the eligibility of the place; for it may injure its opponent, though it cannot benefit itself, which is the first object of all other commercial bodies, but the second of the fur traders.

On the evening of the 30th, we embarked and entered a wide channel [Aubichon Arm] to the northward of the forts, and extending towards the northwest. It gradually decreased in breadth till it became a river [McBeth Channel], which is the third fork of the Missinnippi, and its current being almost insensible, we entered the Clear [Churchill] Lake at 10 a.m. on the first of July. Of this lake, which is very large, no part is known except the south border, but its extent would lead us to conclude that its evaporation must be supplied by another river to the northward, especially as the small channel [Kisis] that communicates with Buffalo Lake is motionless.[32] The existence of such a river is asserted by the Indians, and a shorter passage might be found by it, across the height of land, to the Clearwater River, than the portage from the Methye Lake.

In Buffalo [Peter Pond] Lake,[33] the wind was too strong for us to proceed, and we therefore encamped upon a gravel beach thrown up by the waves. At 3 a.m., July 2nd, we embarked, and at 4 p.m., entered the mouth of the Methye [La Loche] River. The lake is 34 miles in length and 14 in breadth. It is probably very deep, for we saw no islands in this wide expanse, except at the borders. On the southwest side were two forts,[34] belonging to the Companies, and near them, a solitary hill 700 or 800 feet high. At 8 p.m., we encamped in the Methye River at the confluence of the River Pembina [Kimowin River]. A route has been explored by it, to the Red Willow [Christina] River, across the height of land, but the difficulties of it were so great that the ordinary route is preferred.

On the 3rd [July], we passed through the Methye River, and en-

32. Kisis Channel is now the site of the village of Buffalo Narrows.

33. Now named for the famous trader who was at Ile-à-la-Crosse in the winter of

1782–83. In 1778, Pond was the first fur trader to reach the rich Athabasca region.

34. Probably Dillon, on the south shore at the mouth of the Dillon River.

camped on the borders of the Methye Lake [Lac la Loche].[35] The soil from Ile-à-la-Crosse to this place is sandy, with some portion of clay, and the trees numerous; but the Methye River is rocky and so shallow that, to lighten the canoes, we made two portages of five and two miles. The paths were overflowed with cold spring water, and barricadoed by fallen trees. We should have been contented to immerse ourselves wholly had the puddle been sufficiently deep, for the mosquitoes devoured every part that was exposed to them.

On the 4th, we crossed the Methye Lake, and landed at the portage on the northwest side, in one of the sources of the Missinnippi. The lake is 17 miles in length, with a large island in the middle. We proceeded to the north side of the portage with two men, carrying a tent and some instruments, leaving the canoes and cargoes to be transported by daily journeys of two or three miles. The distance is 14 statute miles, and there are two small lakes about five miles from the north side.[36] Several species of fish are found in them, though they have no known communication with any other body of water, being situated on the elevation of the height. The road was a gentle ascent, miry from the late rainy weather, and shaded by pines [spruce], poplars, birches, and cypresses [jack-pine], which terminated our view.[37] On the north side, we discovered through an opening in the trees, that we were on a hill 800 or 900 feet high and at the edge of a steep descent.[38] We were prepared to expect an extensive prospect, but the magnificent scene before us was so superior to what the nature of the country had promised, that it banished even our sense of suffering from the mosquitoes which hovered in clouds about our heads. Two parallel chains of hills extended towards the setting sun, their various projecting outlines exhibiting the several gradations of distance, and the opposite bases

35. *Methy*, spelled *miyey* by Lacombe, was the Cree name and *la loche* the French name for the burbot, a small edible freshwater fish found in large deep lakes. The large Chipewyan settlement of La Loche is now about six miles north of the river mouth.

36. The trail went between these two small lakes, along the south shore of the appropriately named Rendezvous Lake. Use of this trail by fur traders began with Peter Pond in 1778. For a recent description, see Henry T. Epp and Tim Jones, 'The Methy Portage—Proposal for a Saskatchewan Historic and Nature Trail', *Blue Jay* 27 (1969), 101–7.

37. To complete the confusion, Hood used the voyageurs' term, 'cypres' for pine. The jack-pine is the commonest conifer on this portage.

38. The Clearwater River is here about 1,000 feet, and the hills over 1,500 feet above sea level. The English name is a translation from the Cree *wasagamew*, from *was*, 'clear' or 'brilliant' and *gamiw*, 'water'.

closing at the horizon. On the nearest eminence, the objects were clearly defined by their dark shadows; the yellow rays blended their softening hues with brilliant green on the next, and beyond it, all distinction melted into grey and purple. In the long valley between, the smooth and colourless Clearwater River wound its spiral course, broken and scattered by encroaching woods. An exuberance of rich herbage covered the soil, and lofty trees climbed the precipice at our feet, hiding its brink with their summits. Impatient as we were, and blinded with pain, we paid a tribute of admiration which this beautiful landscape is capable of exciting, unaided by the borrowed charms of a calm atmosphere glowing with the vivid tints of evening.

We descended to the banks of the Clearwater River, and having encamped, the two men returned to assist their companions. We had sometimes before procured a little rest, by closing the tent and burning wood, or flashing gun powder within, the smoke driving the mosquitoes into the crannies of the ground. But this remedy was now ineffectual, though we employed it so perseveringly as to incur suffocation. They swarmed under our blankets, goring us with their envenomed trunks, and steeping our clothes in blood. We rose at daylight in a fever, and our misery was unmitigated during our whole stay.

The mosquitoes of America resemble in shape those of Africa and Europe, but differ essentially in size, and in other particulars. There are two distinct species, the largest of which is brown, and the smallest, black.[39] Where they are bred, cannot easily be determined, for they are numerous in every soil. They make their first appearance in May and the cold destroys them in September. In July, they are most voracious, and fortunately for the traders, the journeys from the trading posts to the factories are generally concluded at that period. The food of the mosquito is blood, which it can extract by penetrating the hide of a buffalo, and if it is not disturbed, it gorges itself so as to swell its body into a transparent globe. The wound does not swell, like that of the African mosquito, but it is infinitely more painful, and when multiplied an hundred fold, and continued for as many successive days, it becomes an evil of such magnitude, that cold, famine, and every other

39. Well over thirty species of mosquito occur in any one part of Saskatchewan or Alberta. The males feed on nectar and only the females partake of blood. The six mouth parts are like little needles, and form two main channels through the victim's skin: one to secrete saliva containing anti-clotting protein and the other to suck the victim's blood.

concomitant of an inhospitable climate, must yield the pre-eminence to it. It chases the buffalo to the plains, irritating him to madness, and the reindeer to the sea shore, from which they do not return till the scourge has ceased.

On the 6th [July], the thermometer was 106° in the sun and on the 7th, 110°. The mosquitoes sought the shade, in the heat of the day, which we felt no inclination to contend with them. It was some satisfaction to us to see the havoc made among them, by a large and beautiful species of dragonfly, called the mosquito hawk, which wheeled through their retreats with great velocity, swallowing its prey without a momentary diminution of its speed;[40] but the temporary relief that we had hoped for, was only an exchange of tormentors. Our new assailant, the horsefly, or bulldog, ranged in the hottest glare of the sun, and carried off a portion of flesh at each attack.[41] Another noxious insect, the smallest, but not the least formidable, was the sandfly, known in Canada by the name of the Brulot.[42] To such annoyance all travellers must submit, and it would be unworthy to complain of that grievance in the pursuit of knowledge, which is endured for the sake of profit. This detail of it has only been made as an excuse for the scantiness of our observations on the most interesting part of the country through which we passed.

The north side of the Methye Portage is in Latitude 56°41'40" N. and Longitude 109°52'0" W. It is, by our course, 124 miles from Ile-à-la-Crosse, and considered as a branch of the Missinnippi, 592 miles from the Frog Portage. The Clearwater River, passing through the valley described above, evidently rises not far to the eastward. The height, computed by the same mode as that of the Echiamamis, is 2,467 feet above the level of the sea, admitting it to be 900 feet above the Clearwater River. The country in a line between it and the mouth of Mackenzie's River is a continual descent, although to the eastward of that line, there may be several heights between it and the Arctic Sea. To the eastward, the land descends to Hudson's Bay, and to the westward

40. The dragon-flies are relatively fast insects, but Hood's term 'mosquito hawk' must not be confused with the common name for a bird, the nighthawk. Long bristles on the dragon-fly's front legs are bent slightly to form a basket to catch the mosquitoes.

41. The horse-fly makes a much larger and coarser incision than the mosquito; the mouth parts might be considered as daggers, compared to the 'needles' of the mosquito.

42. The sand-flies are so small that the Indians call them 'no-see-ums'. They have six very fine 'needlets' which cause a bothersome sting.

also, till the Athapescow River cuts through it, from whence it ascends to the Rocky Mountains. Daring was the spirit of enterprise that first led commerce, with her cumbrous train, from the waters of Hudson's Bay to those of the Arctic Sea, across an obstacle to navigation so stupendous as this; and persevering has been the industry which drew riches from a source so remote.[43]

On the 8th, two men arrived, and informed us that they had brought our ten bags of pemmican from Ile-à-la-Crosse, but that they were found to be rotten. Thus were we unexpectedly deprived of the most essential of our stores; for we knew Fort Chepewyan to be destitute of provisions, and that Mr. Franklin depended upon us for a supply, whereas, enough did not remain for our own use. On the 9th, the canoes and cargoes reached the north side of the portage. Our people had selected two bags of pemmican less mouldy than the rest, which they left on the beach. Its decay was caused by some defect in the mode of mixing it.[44]

On the 10th [July], we embarked in the Clearwater River, and proceeded down the current. The hills, the banks, and bed of the river were composed of fine yellow sand, with some lime and claystone rocks. The surface soil was alluvial. At 8 a.m. we passed a portage on which the limestone rocks were singularly scattered through the woods, bearing the appearance of houses and turrets overgrown with moss. The earth emitted a hollow sound, and the river was divided by rocks into narrow crooked channels, every object indicating that some convulsion had disturbed the general order of nature at this place. We had passed a portage above it, and after two long portages below it, we encamped. Near the last was a small stream so strongly impregnated with sulphur as to taint the air to a great distance round it. We saw two brown bears on the hills in the course of the day.

At daylight on the 11th, we embarked. The hills continued on both sides, to the mouth of the river, varying from 600 to 1,000 feet in height. They declined to the banks in long green slopes, diversified by woody mounds and copses. The pines were not here, in thick impenetrable masses, but perched aloft in single groups on the heights, or shrouded

43. During the Hudson's Bay Company's long prosperous period from 1718 to 1778, it paid a 10% annual dividend to its shareholders. These were leaner years as the company was sustaining heavy losses in the new Athabasca region, aggravated by widespread conflicts with the opposing company.

44. Such pemmican decay was almost unknown. The keeping qualities of pemmican were said to be virtually unlimited.

by the livelier hues of the poplar and willow.

We passed the mouth of the Red Willow [Christina] River, on the south bank, flowing through a deep ravine. It is the continuation of the route by the Pembina, before mentioned. At noon we entered the majestic Athapescow, or Elk River. Besides the Clearwater River, another small stream, the Riviere La Biche joins it at this point, which is called the Forks.[45] Its banks were inaccessible cliffs, apparently of clay and stones, about 200 feet high, and its windings in the south were encircled by high mountains. Its breadth exceeded half a mile, and was swelled to a mile in many places, by long muddy islands in the middle, covered with trees. No more portages interrupted our course, but a swift current hurried us towards the quarter in which our anticipated discoveries were to commence. The passing cliffs returned a loud confusion of echoes, to the sprightly canoe song, and the dashing paddles; and the eagles, watching with half-closed eyes on the pine tops, started from their airy rest, and prepared their drowsy pinions for flight.

About 20 miles from the forks are some salt pits and plains, said to be very extensive. The height of the banks was reduced to 20 or 30 feet, and the hills ranged themselves at an increased distance from the banks in the same variety as those of the Clearwater River. At sunset we encamped on a small sandy island, but the next morning made a speedy retreat to the canoes, the water having nearly overflowed our encampment. We passed two deserted settlements of the fur traders on opposite banks, at a place called Pierre au Calumet.[46] Beyond it, the hills disappeared, and the banks were no longer visible above the trees. The river carries away yearly large portions of soil, which increase its breadth and diminish its depth, rendering the water so muddy that it was scarcely drinkable. Whole forests of timber are drifted down the stream, and

45. *La Biche* is the French word for deer. Actually two smaller streams enter near the main forks: the Horse, on the west side of the forks, entering the Athabasca, and the Hangingstone, on the east side of the forks, entering the Clearwater. At the apex of the forks is Fort McMurray, established by the North West Company in 1788.

46. A calumet was a peace pipe. The Hudson's Bay Company post here was founded only the previous year, 1819, during Colin Robertson's expansion program. The first winter, Aulay McAulay was short of food and had to surrender his trade goods to John Stuart of the North West Company in return for subsistence, abandoning the post in December. The more established North West Company post, founded in 1802, was across the river on the east bank, and here Franklin, Back, and Hepburn, on their winter hike from Fort Carlton to Fort Chipewyan, had enjoyed the hospitality of senior partner, John Stuart, from 19 to 22 March that year. The site is 2½ miles north of present Bitumount.

choke up the channels between the islands at its mouth. We observed the traces of herds of [wood] buffaloes where they had crossed the river, the trees being trodden down and strewed, as if by a whirlwind.

At 4 p.m. [July 12], we left the main branch of the Athapescow, entering a small river called the Embarras.[47] It is narrow and muddy, with pines of an enormous size on its banks. Some of them are 200 feet high, and three or four in diameter. At 9 p.m., we landed and encamped, but finding ourselves in a nest of mosquitoes, we continued our journey before daybreak, and at 8 a.m., emerged into the Athapescow Lake. A strong wind agitated this sea of fresh water, which, however, we crossed without any accident, and landed on the north side of it, at Fort Chepewyan, where we had the satisfaction to find our companions in good health, and of experiencing that sympathy in our anxiety, on the state of our affairs, the reality of which was only to be expected from those who were to share our future fortunes.

47. The French word *embarras* means hindrance or difficulty and was used by the voyageurs for debris or tangled driftwood at a river entrance, necessitating a 'carry'.

7

Fort Chipewyan to
Fort Enterprize

Proceedings of the Expedition from
Fort Chepewyan to Fort Enterprize

Our present situation was discouraging, though not hopeless, and the traders had prognosticated that we should pass the winter at Fort Chepewyan. Mr. Franklin had engaged 12 Canadians in the service of the expedition, and caused two strong canoes to be built for him. But the men stipulated to be furnished with clothing, for which our small store was insufficient. The fort could not provide them with food for a single day, and they were scattered about the country, or fishing a scanty and uncertain meal from the lake, disgusted at so unpropitious a commencement of the enterprize. On us, they had relied for an ample relief of every want, and instead of answering these sanguine expectations, our arrival had increased both the number of sufferers, and the difficulty of maintaining them.[1]

But these embarrassments were overlooked in the contemplation of prospects which flattered us with the success of our ultimate objects. Mr. Franklin's original plan was to descend by Mackenzie's River to the Great Bear Lake, which was reported to have a communication by three portages, with the Coppermine River. Considering however that he would thereby be removed too far from the Great Slave Lake to receive the supply of ammunition in the winter, which was absolutely necessary for the prosecution of our journey, and also the Esquimaux in-

1. Early in June, Franklin had engaged thirteen voyageurs, six from the Hudson's Bay Company and seven from the North West Company. The bowsmen and steersmen were offered 1600 Halifax livres [£ 80] per annum, while the *milieux* or middlemen were offered 1200 livres [£ 60], roughly double the usual salary paid to voyageurs by the fur companies prior to 1818. In comparison, the fur company clerks, able to read and write, received 2000 livres [£ 100] per year. [Harold A. Innis, *The Fur Trade in Canada. An Introduction to Canadian Economic History.* (Toronto: University of Toronto Press, 1956), pp. 226 and 239.] Hood and Richardson had eleven men when they left Cumberland House; after Louis St. Jean drowned, they gained a guide and foreman from the last of the Athabasca brigade going east. Perhaps the latter two did not continue all the way, as Franklin gave the number of men arriving at Fort Chipewyan with Hood and Richardson as ten. They then discharged 'those men who were less willing to undertake the journey', the three Orkneymen from Cumberland House, three Canadian voyageurs and one American. One of the canoes built for Franklin at Fort Chipewyan was 32' 6" in length and 4' 10" wide.

terpreter; he fixed upon a height of land near [Little] Marten Lake, for our winter abode. At this time, a gentleman named Wentzel, in the service of the North West Company on the north side of the Slave Lake, who had already procured some Indian hunters for us, and given much information to Mr. Franklin respecting Bear and Marten Lakes, volunteered to accompany the expedition, undertaking the management of the Indian hunters, with whom he was well acquainted. No pecuniary conditions were made with this meritorious offer, which was accepted by Mr. Franklin, and approved by the partners of the North West Company at Fort Chepewyan. Two rivers were mentioned by Mr. Wentzel, rising near the Coppermine River, and running into the Slave Lake, abounding in winter with reindeer, according to the Indian accounts. The hunters secured for us amounted to eight, with a chief named the Gros Pied, all of the Copper or Red Knife Indian tribe.[2] They required guns, ammunition, a little tobacco, and some trifling articles of clothing, which were promised to them; and, in the meantime, they were employed in collecting provisions for us, on the north and south sides of the Slave Lake. Other hunters were appointed to meet us on the Slave River, the banks of which abound with buffaloes and moose deer, and it receives two small rivers, well stocked with fish. Of our English stores, we had preserved two barrels of flour, some chocolate, arrowroot, portable soups, and meats, which we had reserved for the winter. This was sufficient to prevent us from starving, unless detained by any misfortune, even if our other resources failed. Mr. Franklin determined on pushing forward, a resolution to which the Canadians agreed without demur.

Till the 18th [July], we were fully occupied in assembling the people, and satisfying their demands. We made a distribution of all that we could spare, and the gentlemen in charge of the North West and Hudson's Bay Companies' posts contributed what was in their power to assist us. The people, if not contented, were silent, for they saw that solicitation could not produce our compliance, without adding to our store; an uncommon exertion of thought for Canadians. It was neces-

2. The Yellowknife Indians, so named for their tools of native copper. Their original population has been estimated as 430. In 1823, during the interval between the two Franklin expeditions, they were crushed by the Dogribs, and the remnant retreated to the northeast corner of Great Slave Lake and amalgamated with the Chipewyans. In 1934, their estimated population was only 150. [Diamond Jenness, *The Indians of Canada*, Nat. Museum of Canada, Bull. 65, Anthropological Series No. 15, (1934), p. 389.]

sary to discharge six persons from our service, as Mr. Franklin proposed that the expedition should consist of 20 men, besides the officers, including two interpreters, whom we expected to meet at the Slave Lake.[3] In this number, our three Englishmen enrolled themselves, deterred by the dread of famine and fatigue, which they thought we were doomed to encounter.[4] Hepburn still remained, consigned alone to the society of foreigners, whose language he could not speak; but his constancy absolved his country from the disgrace attached to it by the rest.[5]

Fort Chepewyan is in Latitude 58°42'37" N. Longitude 111°18'20" W. by lunars east and west of the moon, the chronometers which we brought up being 4½ miles to the eastward.[6] The Athapescow River, including the Embarras, and the Clearwater River, is 233 statute miles in length, and the distance which we had travelled from Cumberland House, 811½ miles. The lake, which has been well surveyed by Mr. Turner,[7] extends more than 6° to the eastward. Opposite to the Fort, it is only seven miles wide, and full of islands, which with the north shore are rocky, with little soil; the trees are thinly scattered, and the earth abounds with berries. The south shore is low, consisting of alluvial mud brought down by the river. The ranges of hills which we lost sight

3. In fact, the party that left Fort Providence two weeks later consisted of the four officers, Hepburn, Wentzel, seventeen voyageurs, two interpreters, the wives of three voyageurs, and three children, a total of thirty-one. That winter, two Eskimo interpreters arrived from Hudson Bay and were added to the party, while two voyageurs, Belleau and Connoyer or Cournoyee, were discharged. Parent, Gagne, Dumas, and Forcier returned with Wentzel from the mouth of the Coppermine, so that after 19 July 1821, the expedition did consist of twenty men: five Englishmen, two Eskimos, two interpreters and eleven voyageurs. One Eskimo was lost and presumed dead and only two of the eleven voyageurs were to survive.

4. 'This number' refers to the six staying behind. Future events proved that the three who declined to go further, probably all Orkneymen, had assessed the situation very accurately.

5. The distinction between officers and men was maintained, and Hepburn was forced to share quarters with the French-speaking voyageurs.

6. An error of four minutes in the timepiece would cause an error of one degree of longitude, a matter of 36 miles at this latitude. An error of only half a minute in the pocket watch would explain the 4½-mile error here. On this occasion, it was the difficult lunar observations that were slightly in error. Hood placed the fort six miles too far west from its true location of 111°10'. The calculation of longitude based on the chronometers was about 111°11', nearly correct.

7. Philip Turnor, 1752-1800. He was a surveyor, the first specifically engaged in that capacity by the Hudson's Bay Company in 1778. At Cumberland House in 1789, he gave instruction in surveying to David Thompson and Peter Fidler. He surveyed Lake Athabasca in 1790-92 and Arrowsmith's map of 1795 embodied his discoveries.

of below Pierre au Calumet, diverge from the river, about 20 miles to the northward of it, in a north-northeast and north-northwest direction. The end of the former was in sight, EbN, from the mouth of the Embarras, five or six leagues, and the latter terminates at a lake to the westward [Lake Claire], in the parallel of Fort Chepewyan. We were informed that the country, from Pierre au Calumet in a direct line to the Methye Portage, is covered by hills of the same magnitude. Near Pierre au Calumet, on the west bank of the river, is an extensive hill, about 2000 feet high with a lake on its summit. It is called Birch Hill.[8]

Fort Chepewyan is a handsome, capacious, wooden building, with turrets and bastions to defend its flanks. It is the chief, and was for many years the only, establishment of the North West Company in the Athapescow country;[9] the canoes from Mackenzie's River receiving their supplies here, as the distance to Lake Superior is too great to admit of their voyage thither and return, the same year. The Hudson's Bay Company fort is on an island, one mile from Fort Chepewyan.[10] They carried their trade across the Methye Portage in 1815, and settled themselves at Ile-à-la-Crosse, Lake Athapescow and the Peace River, where they brought opposition to the gates of their rivals. This measure was thought injudicious by many of their own party, and it was attended by the most disastrous consequences in the first winter, eighteen persons perishing in the Peace River, where no previous arrangements had been made to supply them with provisions.[11] The Hudson's Bay Company have since maintained their position, and the only gainers in the contest are the Indians, who have, however, lost what industry and

8. The Birch Mountains, elevation 2,646 feet, or about 1,900 feet above river level.

9. An earlier post of the same name was begun in 1788 by Mackenzie at what is now 'Old Fort Point' on the south shore. In 1804 the post was moved to the present site on a rocky northshore peninsula. In 1820, George Keith was in charge of the North West Company post, assisted by Simon McGillivray, the half-breed son of William McGillivray.

10. On Potato Island, previously known as Coal Island. Here Fort Wedderburn [named for Andrew Wedderburn, later Andrew W. Colvile, a dominant member of the H. B. C. Committee in London] was founded by John Clarke in 1815. George

Simpson was to arrive here on 20 September 1820. Fort Wedderburn was abandoned in favour of the mainshore establishment of the North West Company when the two companies merged in 1821.

11. After founding Fort Chipewyan, Clarke founded four other posts before pushing, without adequate provisions, into the Peace River country. In that first winter of 1815-16, three men died before Clarke's assistant, George McDougald, gave up his eighty pieces of trading goods to William McIntosh of the rival company in return for food. Thirteen other men, one woman, and a child perished in an unsuccessful attempt to reach Fort Wedderburn. The north is unforgiving to the unprepared.

principle they before possessed, which have become superfluous to them by the present mode of obtaining profit. The Chepewyans, meeting with encouragement from one party, in proportion to their treachery to the other, have amassed stores of ammunition and tobacco, which render them independent; and the distresses which their seducers incur in the want of subsistence, if not a just, cannot be considered an unexpected return.

We embarked at noon on the 18th in three canoes, that which was damaged at the Otter Portage being unserviceable. A moose had been killed before our departure and we received one day's provision.[12] At 2 p.m., we entered the Stoney River [Rivière des Rochers] which, and another river on the west side [Chenal des Quatre Fourches], are the discharges of the Athapescow into the Slave River. At 4 p.m., we entered the Slave River, called the Peace River, above the junction of the Stoney River. It is twice as broad as the Athapescow, but more shallow and exceedingly rapid.[13] Its banks are low and woody; our speed was too great to ascertain the nature of the soil, or any other particular, the current rushing in a thousand eddies among the islands, and whirling the canoes in various directions; at one moment retrograding them, and the next precipitating them with sidelong sweep far clear of dangers which appeared inevitable. This violent agitation of the river continued for ten miles and was occasioned by banks of alluvial soil traversing its descent at the bottom. At 7 p.m., a storm of wind, rain and thunder, drove us on shore where we encamped in a swamp. The tents, however, were soon blown over and the fires extinguished by the rain; but not before we had boiled some provisions, and dispatched our meat, sitting in the mire. Swarms of mosquitoes succeeded the storm, and despairing to obtain repose, we reimbarked at midnight.

12. 'Seventy pounds of moosemeat and a little barley were all that our kind friend Mr. Smith was enabled to give us,' said Richardson. This was Edward Smith, then a partner of the North West Company and later a chief factor of the Mackenzie River Department of the amalgamated company. Smith was host at Fort Chipewyan when George Back returned from his explorations in April and May 1835.

13. The Slave River begins where the Riviere des Rochers meets the Peace River. This was the productive Peace River delta, which provided much of the livelihood of nearby Indians until completion of the Bennett Dam, upriver in British Columbia, in 1967. Since then, the area of nine delta lakes has shrunk from 638 to 456 square miles and Lake Claire is so shallow that it can no longer support fish during winter. Muskrat habitat has been destroyed and waterfowl breeding areas reduced. The west bank of the Slave River, for most of its length, is now the eastern boundary of Wood Buffalo Park, the only known breeding area of the Whooping Crane.

The river ran in abrupt windings till 6 a.m., when its course became perfectly straight for ten miles, and we perceived rocks on the banks, projecting through the soil. At 10 a.m., we landed at the mouth of the Dog River, on the east bank and set the nets.[14] In the evening they were taken up, and produced only two red suckers, so that we were necessitated to consume part of our preserved meats and portable soups. We derived one benefit from our delay, which was wholesome water, that of the Slave River being a muddy puddle.

At daylight on the 20th [July], we embarked, and in the Dog Rapid, two of the canoes were dashed against each other so violently, that the end of one was broken off from the gunwales. We were fortunately close to the shore, or the disabled canoe would have sunk. In three hours, it was in a condition to proceed, and we entered a narrow sluice, between a large island, and the east bank, in which we crossed four portages. The river outside is impassable from falls and rapids. At 1 p.m., we crossed the Mountain Portage, over a steep peninsula, extending into the main river, which was a mile wide, and broken by a ledge of rocks, crossing it from one bank to the other. The long uninterrupted perspective, the large trees encountering the rocks with noisy crush, and throwing volumes of spray in the air; the pelicans sailing down the rapid in pursuit of fish, and the green islets which seemed to float on its brink, rendered it a view of imposing grandeur, unparalleled in the whole course of our journey.

Having passed the Pelican Portage,[15] near the last, we continued six miles in the open river and encamped at the Portage of the Drowned.[16] It is so called from an accident, which several years ago proved fatal to the crews of two canoes. A guide had been sent across to ascertain whether the rapid might be descended in safety, and he was desired to signify the affirmative by firing a gun. A person who was with

14. Almost opposite, on the west bank, is the present settlement of Fitzgerald, originally named Smith Landing.

15. Note that modern maps show Mountain Rapids downstream (north) of the Pelican Rapids, the reversal of the order given by Mackenzie, Hood, and Franklin. As evidence that modern maps are incorrect on this subject, pelicans in 1967 nested on an island next to the rapids named 'Pelican' by the explorers. The 16 miles of rapids between Fitzgerald and Fort Smith form the only impediment to water transportation between Fort McMurray, Alberta, and the Arctic Ocean at the mouth of the Mackenzie.

16. The site of Fort Smith, founded in 1870-74. It was the administrative centre for the district of Mackenzie in the Northwest Territories from 1953 until 1 April 1968 when the new territorial government in Yellowknife assumed full responsibility for the Mackenzie district.

him, inconsiderately discharged his piece at a bird, and the canoes, immediately entering the rapid, were dashed to pieces, and the people perished.

On the 21st [July], at daylight we embarked. The portages had included 12 miles of the river, in which the descent was not less than 40 feet. Below them, the rocks ceased, and from hence to the mouth of the river the soil is alluvial mud. The channel of the river was evidently deeper, for its breadth was the same and the strength of the current greatly diminished. At 8 a.m., we landed at the mouth of the Salt River, in which we set the nets, and went up the river with a single canoe, to explore some salt springs at its source. It was about 20 miles in length, exceedingly crooked, and its banks were sandy, with pines, poplars, and several species of willows. Ten miles from its source, the water was as salt as the ocean. We encamped upon a large plain of sand and clay, bounded by hills, and walked three miles towards the principal spring, but the mosquitoes compelled us to give up our project. The springs had apparently overflowed the plain, and the salt was left in heaps by the evaporation of the water. It was very fine and white, and we filled some casks with it.[17]

On the 22nd, we embarked on our return. While turning round a point, a large [wood] buffalo rushed into the water before us, and was ascending the opposite bank, when, receiving two balls in the head, he wheeled, and presented his front to the canoe. We stationed ourselves out of his reach, and eager to secure so desirable a prize, fired upon him till he fell, which was not before he had been struck by 14 balls. The carcass was dragged on the bank, and the canoe loaded with meat. At 4 p.m., we arrived at the mouth of the river. Our nets had not produced a single meal, but that was no longer of any importance to us. A fish peculiar to the northern rivers, was caught here, called by the Canadians, the *Poisson Inconnu*. It is an excellent species of the Salmon Trout.

At 7 p.m., we had a storm of wind and snow from southwest with the thermometer at 70°.[18] On the 23rd [July], at 2 a.m., we embarked. For twelve hours we made head against waves which threatened to

17. George Back paid another visit on 5 August 1833. As late as 1916, four tons of pure sodium chloride were collected here annually.

18. A subconscious slip by Hood; snow at

70° F. is not credible. Franklin said '... a violent thunder-storm came on with heavy rain; thermometer 70°.'[*Journey 1819-22*, p. 197.]

founder the canoes, steering close to the shore to obtain the shelter of the bank from the wind. Not daring to venture across, when a turn of the river deprived us of it, we encamped on a small island. On the 24th, we made more progress, notwithstanding the continuation of the wind. The course of the Slave River is remarkably winding, making in one place a circuit of seven or eight miles round a peninsula, which is joined to the west bank by an isthmus 20 yards wide. Fourteen miles from the Slave Lake, the river separates into two large branches, which are subdivided by many smaller streams, like the mouth of the Ganges. We passed through one of the small streams [Nagle Channel] and landed, on the 25th, at Moose Deer Island, in the Great Slave Lake.

We found that Mr. Wentzel was at Fort Providence, on the north side of the lake, with the Gros Pied and his band, who were growing very impatient for our arrival. The two forts supplied us with a quantity of dried meat, but as their hunters were absent, and daily expected to return with some more, our departure was postponed for them. At this place, we were joined by one of our interpreters for the Copper Indians, a Bois brulée, named Pierre St. Germain.

The Forts are in Latitude 61°11'8" N., Longitude 113°51'35" W. and 260 statute miles from Fort Chepewyan, by the course of the Slave and Stoney Rivers. They are situated on an ascent in front of the lake, and the wind from that quarter in winter drifts the snow above the stockades, which are 16 feet high. The Hudson's Bay Company fort is the northernmost of their establishments in America.[19] Two small branches of the Slave River, divide Moose Deer Island from the main. The land is low and sandy, as far as we could discern it, and the woods thin. But the driftwood from the river affords abundance of fuel. It is piled on the beach, and the low islands forming natural piers, extending several hundred yards into the water. When it becomes saturated, it sinks, and shoals of it are found at the bottom in many parts of the lake. The Indians frequenting the Forts are Chepewyans and Red Knives,

19. Fort Resolution, then on Moose Deer Island, is now on the mainland at the northern extremity of Resolution Bay, just south of the delta. In 1820-21, the manager was Robert McVicar. He and his beautiful Scottish wife provided hospitality to both Franklin expeditions. McVicar was reprimanded by George Simpson for jeopardizing his fur trade by being overly generous to the expedition and Back corroborates that 'in many articles, he gave me the whole he had in his possession'. Between the two Franklin expeditions and long afterwards, McVicar corresponded with Franklin, Richardson, and Back. ['Some Unpublished Letters of Sir John Franklin, Sir John Richardson and others,' *Trans. Women's Can. Hist. Soc. of Toronto,* 17 (1917-18), 12-36.]

who cross from the north side of the lake. The ordinary provisions are buffaloes, moose deer, and reindeer in winter. The dogs are of a different species from the wolfish breed at Cumberland House, which is probably owing to their intermixture with European dogs, brought from Hudson's Bay. They have long hanging ears, short tails, and heads like those of an English foxhound.

On the evening of the 26th, the hunters arrived and we received a small additional supply [450 lbs.] of dried moose meat. On the 27th, we embarked, and passed the channels between several large islands and the main at the mouths of the Slave River. From Moose Deer Island, the south coast of the lake extends 23 miles* NEbN and then turns to the eastward; at this point, is a small island [Stony Island] on which a fishery is established. As the weather was fine, and the lake smooth, we paddled across to a cluster called the Reindeer Islands [Iles du Goulet, the southernmost of the Iles du Large], 11 miles NbE^1/$_2$E, and encamped. The land was visible from north to EbS, but whether the main or large islands, we could not determine. On the 28th we sailed with a strong gale to an island NbE^1/$_4$E, near Sir Alexander Mackenzie's cape, which appears to be the western extremity of an island [Wilson Island]. The wind abating, we continued our way NWbW, across the mouths of two deep bays on the right, divided by a promontory, or perhaps Mackenzie's Big Island.[20] At the mouth of the first of these, the temperature of the water sunk from 59° to 48°, indicating the discharge of some great river from the northward. The depth was 40 fathoms. The main is 16 miles NWbN of Mackenzie's Cape, and from thence, an arm of the lake penetrates northwest to an unknown distance. We coasted the east side of it, and the opposite shore was always visible. It is filled with dangerous breakers and rocky islands. Twenty one miles from the entrance of it is Fort Providence, at which we landed on the morning of the 29th.[21]

*"All the distances hitherto inserted, are statute miles. For the future they are geographical, unless specified as statute" [Robert Hood].

20. The promontory is the western tip of the Caribou Islands. They then crossed to the mainland at Gros Cap (Big Cape).

21. In 1820, Wentzel's Fort Providence was on the north shore, 16 miles south-south-east of the present site of Yellowknife. It may have been initiated by Peter Pond in 1786 as an outpost of the

North West Company fort at Moose Deer Island, and was activated in 1789 by Laurent LeRoux, Mackenzie's assistant. In the 1790s it was an important provision depot with up to ten men, but by 1822 it had only two men. In July, 1823, the council of the Hudson's Bay Company voted to abandon it. It is not to be confused with the

Mr. Wentzel had long been anxiously expecting us, and the Gros Pied with his party were fishing on the lake for their support. Messengers were dispatched to them, and the chief sent an Indian for some tobacco, according to their custom with strangers. As we were informed that external appearances made lasting impressions on the Indians, we prepared for the occasion by pitching the tents, and decorating ourselves with remnants of our European apparel. A small silken ensign was hoisted on a pole before the camp. The next day, the Gros Pied arrived with his hunters and two guides. On landing, they were presented with medals, and conducted into the Fort, where the Indians seated themselves on the floor, and the chief took possession of a chair. When the preliminaries of lighting their pipes were concluded, Mr. Franklin commenced the conference by acquainting the chief, through the interpreters, that we were war chiefs, the subjects of a great king beyond the ocean, who was the sovereign also of the trading companies in this country.[22] That we had been sent by him, not for the purpose of traffic, in which war chiefs did not concern themselves, but to examine the seas situated on the northern shore, to ascertain if it was possible for large ships to be brought there with merchandise for the natives, and to enquire into the nature of all the productions of the land. That we desired the assistance of the Indians, in guiding us and providing us with food; and that it was the wish of the great chief our master, that hostilities should cease throughout the country, especially with the Esquimaux, whom he considered his children, in common with the other natives. Finally, that we had now little more than was necessary for ourselves, having travelled a great distance; but that if the Indians performed their engagement with us, they should be remunerated with cloth, ammunition, and tobacco, on our arrival at Churchill.

The chief replied, that he would attend us with his young men, to the end of our journey; that the white people had always been friendly to the Indians, who, before the connection now existing was established, had lived by snaring, and shooting deer with arrows, which means of obtaining food and clothing were not to be depended upon.

---

present Fort Providence, on the Mackenzie River, many miles to the west, nor with an intermediate location at Deep Bay, where the Mackenzie River takes origin from Great Slave Lake. [Dale Perry and W. Dean Clark, *Musk-ox* 8 (1971), 1-13.]

22. Unknown to Hood, George IV, who had been Prince Regent since his father became permanently insane in 1811, had been king in his own right since the death of George III on 29 January 1820. This news reached the expedition in the packet delivered on 6 December.

That their distress had often been great, till the white people brought them guns and cloth. That it was true, the Copper Indians had long since made war upon the Esquimaux at the sea,[23] but that peace was desired by his tribe more than war. He added, that the Esquimaux had never met a stranger whom they did not find an enemy, and that they would probably regard us as such, at first. He then asked if we had not a medicine chief, who could prevent any person from dying, while he remained on their lands. This was a report which had obtained general circulation respecting Dr. Richardson, which must have originated among the Canadians. A proper explanation was given to the chief, which policy would have prompted if truth had not; for when these northern nations detect a falsehood in the dealings of the traders, they make it an eternal subject of reproach, and their confidence is irrecoverably lost.

The guides were desired to give an account of the best route to the Coppermine River, upon which they drew with charcoal on the floor a chain of 25 small lakes, extending towards the northeast and connected by a river, the mouth of which was to the northward of Fort Providence. Near the northeasternmost lake, one of the guides, named Kescarrah, drew the Coppermine River, running in a westerly direction towards the Great Bear Lake, and then northerly to the sea, which we judged to be in 70° N. or 71° N., by the height of the sun at midnight in July.[24] The other guide drew the river in a straight line to the sea, about NbW, from the above mentioned place, but after some dispute, admitted the correctness of the first delineation. This man was the chief's brother, and he said that he had accompanied Mr. Hearne in his journey;[25] that though he was then very young, he remembered that the white man was on the Coppermine River, near the sea, which he did not however actually reach. None of the Indians could give any information with respect to the coast to the eastward of the mouth of the river. To the westward, they had crossed a large peninsula on their war excursions, and they observed some islands in the sea covered with trees.[26] Messrs.

23. For example, the massacre of the occupants of seven tents near the Bloody Falls at the mouth of the Coppermine on 17 July 1771, described in all its gory detail by Samuel Hearne, [Journey 1769-1772, pp. 153-162.]

24. It proved to be at 67°48′ N, not 71°54′ as Hearne had estimated.

25. Forty-nine years previously; apparently this brother was Annoethai-yazzeh.

26. Perhaps they were covered with driftwood or possibly, low shrubs. This is north of the tree line. The gentle promontory has no name but its tip is Cape Krusenstern.

Franklin and Back conversed with several Chepewyans at the Athapescow Lake, who described a similar promontory to the eastward, which they supposed to be the northeastern termination of America. It is more probably the entrance of a gulf, like Chesterfield's Inlet, extending towards the south; for the Indians who were with Mr. Hearne, reported to him that many rivers which they crossed in their journey, entered the sea at a short distance to the eastward.[27]

The route proposed to us had not been traversed by the Indians in canoes, and they were unable to enumerate the portages; but they thought we might reach the source of the river in ten days. At this place, the woods ceased, and the lake at which we were to winter was three days journey to the northward of it. On its borders were trees fit for building a house, and from thence to the Coppermine River, was a portage, across which the Indians travel in four days. All the lakes abounded in fish, and in the middle of August, the reindeer return in great numbers from the seashore. Such was the substance of their information upon which the following plan was formed; to proceed with all possible expedition to the lake above mentioned, and having collected some provisions, to leave men employed in building a winter abode while we descended the Coppermine River, in two canoes, to the sea; after which we were to return, leaving the canoes in a secure place on the north side of the long portage. And this we hoped to accomplish before the commencement of winter.

We gave guns, ammunition, tobacco, blankets and cloth, to the Indians. Our remaining stores were a few unserviceable guns, eight pistols, 24 broad daggers, two barrels of powder, and balls for 2/3 of that quantity, nails and fastenings for a boat, some knives, chisels, files, axes, and a hand saw; six nets, with meshes of different sizes; some cloth, needles, looking glasses, blankets, and beads. Our provision was two barrels of flour, two cases of chocolate, two canisters of tea, 200 dried reindeer tongues, and portable soups, arrowroot, and dried moose meat for ten days. The expedition consisted of 28 persons, including five officers, two interpreters and three Bois brulée women, who were engaged to make shoes and clothes at the winter establishment.[28]

In the evening, we divided a few gallons of rum between the

27. Bathurst Inlet forms the major part of the 675 miles of coastline the expedition explored the next summer.

28. Jean Baptiste Adam, the second interpreter, now joined them at Fort Providence. Three children were not counted.

Canadians and Indians, and the night was passed in mirth and revelry. The Canadians amused themselves by singing and dancing, imitating the gestures of a particular person, who placed himself in ludicrous postures, and performed extraordinary feats of activity. The gravity of the chief gave way to violent bursts of laughter, and indeed, the confusion of languages, dresses, and unartificial character, had something in it more entertaining than a common masquerade. In return, he desired his young men to exhibit the slave dance; and ranging themselves in a circle, with their legs widely separated, they began to jump simultaneously sideways. Their bodies were bent, their hands placed on their hips, and they uttered forcibly the interjection Ha! at each jump. Devoid as were their gestures of grace, and their notes of harmony, this vigorous exercise had irresistible charms for them; some whom the potent effects of the spirits had stretched on the floor, rose from their besotted sleep and joined the circle; bouncing with uncouth alacrity, but out of time, to the great discomfiture of their sober companions. Our amusement was interrupted by an untoward accident, Mr. Franklin's tent having taken fire from some embers which had been placed in it, to expel the mosquitoes. Hepburn was asleep with several powder horns near his head, and did not awake, till the tent poles fell upon him, when he escaped without hurt. The tent, part of the flag, some cloaks and bedding were burnt; an inconsiderable loss, but we dreaded its consequences upon the superstitious and fickle dispositions of the Indians and did not communicate it to them. The chief, however, was informed of it by one of his people, and expressed his desire that no future misfortunes should be concealed from him.

On the 1st of August, we prevailed upon the Indians to set out in their canoes, retaining one guide.

Fort Providence is in Lat. 62°17'24" N., Long. 114°9'34" W., distant 67 miles in a direct line from Moose Deer Island.[29] It is the northernmost establishment of the North West Company, except those on Mackenzie's River. The people subsist on reindeer and moose deer, which are brought by the Copper and Dogrib Indians.[30] Very few furs

29. About 77 statute miles. Since the footnote to this effect, Hood is now using geographical or nautical miles of 6,080 feet per mile. 62°17' is correct and the longitude given by Hood is only three minutes in error; the true reading is 114°06'.

30. Dogrib Indians, another

Athapaskan-dialect tribe, living west of the Yellowknife or Copper Indians, between Great Slave Lake and Great Bear Lake. In pre-European times they may have numbered 1250. [James Mooney, 'The Aboriginal Population of America North of

are collected, but the superabundance of provision enables Fort Providence to supply the post at Moose Deer Island. The fish common to every part of the lake, are *Poisson Inconnu*, trouts, pikes, carps [suckers] and whitefish.

The whole north border and the islands are granite rocks, with no other soil than the roots of moss. The trees are stunted pines, poplars and birches, with rose and red currant bushes. Very little is known of the limits of the lake, except the south border, between Moose Deer Island and the mouth of Mackenzie's River. The outline of the whole was laid down by Mr. Arrowsmith, on Sir Alexander Mackenzie's authority, who is the only person that has attempted to survey it. But a very striking difference will be seen between his map, and ours, in the breadth of the lake from the fishing island to the north main shore, the distance being a degree less than he has made it. To the westward of the wide channel which we entered, is another communicating by a river with Marten Lake, in which was once established a post of the North West Company.[31] The Indians report the extent of the Slave Lake to the eastward to be so great that they have descended a river from it to the sea in three days.[32] The Chepewyans allege that this river does not flow from the lake, but passes near it, in its course to the sea. In the former case, the lake is placed in a singular situation; the rivers on the north and south sides, immediately opposite to each other, flowing into it, and those on the east and west ends, flowing out of it; which however, is a natural result, admitting the land to rise from the surface of the water, on the north and south sides, and to decline on the east and west. If even the above mentioned river passes close to the end of the lake, instead of flowing from it, the singularity of its position is the same.

It is seldom entirely frozen before the 1st of December, owing to its great depth, and the ice, which is seven feet thick, breaks up in the middle of June, one month after that of the Slave River. In winter, it often cracks with prodigious noise, for 60 or 70 miles along the edge,

Mexico', (ed. J. R. Swanton), Smithsonian Misc. Collections 80, No. 7 (1928), p. 26.]

31. Here Hood refers to the larger Marten lake, Lac la Martre, which drains southeast by R. la Martre into Marian Lake, the extension of the upper arm of Great Slave Lake, north of the present settlement of Rae. The Snare River which drains Winter Lake and, in turn, Little Marten Lake, joins

Marian Lake at Rae.

32. Of course there is no outlet from Great Slave Lake to the eastward. Even after crossing the height of land, it is not a short journey to the Arctic Ocean. In 1834 Back took 52 days travelling down the Great Fish River or Back River. To descend the Thelon to Chesterfield Inlet on Hudson Bay would be less difficult.

from the unequal flow of the rivers running into it.[33]

On the evening of the 2nd of August, we embarked, having in addition to our three canoes, a small one carrying the women. The same rocky labyrinth continued, till we landed at the mouth of a channel [Yellowknife Bay], eight miles NWbN of Fort Providence. The entrance of it was four miles wide, and the arm of the lake verged out of sight towards the northwest, the opposite shore being still visible. This channel penetrated into its eastern border. At 4 a.m. the next morning we proceeded to the head of the channel,[34] where we found the Gros Pied and his party. We were soon surrounded by a little fleet of canoes, containing the Indians, their wives and children, and in company with them we entered a river 150 yards wide, with banks well covered by pines and poplars, but the naked hills behind them betrayed the barrenness of the country. We named it the Yellowknife River.

We crossed a short portage, at which was a fall of five feet over slate rocks and a lake to the northward of it, six miles in length.[35] Our attendants spread over its surface, and the expedition appeared increased to an interesting bulk; but not more unwieldy from this accession; for the multitude was directed to one point, and sped its way with undiminished velocity, vacating the wide space which it occupied, before the eye could rest upon its numbers.

We found a portage of nearly a mile, to the northward of the lake, and three falls in the river.[36] The Indians went before us across it, cutting away the trees to make a passage for our large canoes. They had so much the advantage of us at the portages, that we soon perceived they had overcalculated our speed in supposing it possible for us to reach the source of the river in ten days. The men carried their small canoes; and, the women and children, the clothes and provisions, and at the end of a portage they were ready to embark; while it was necessary for our people to return four times before they could transport the whole of the weighty cargo with which we were burthened. After another portage we encamped, well satisfied with our first day's progress in discovery, and with more reason than we imagined; for we could

33. This happens in a lake without water flowing in or out. The ice contracts in cold weather.

34. Near the present site of Yellowknife, since 18 September, 1967 the capital of the Northwest Territories.

35. Lake Prosperous. See plate 20.

36. Greyling Falls, called by Franklin the Bow String Portage. There is now a power plant here.

by no means equal it during the remainder of our journey, this year. We were 30 miles NbW½W of Fort Providence.

The men and officers were divided into watches for the night, to inspire the Indians with confidence, by showing them a habit of vigilance, and the chief, who suffered nothing to escape his observation, remarked that he should sleep without anxiety among the Esquimaux, for he perceived that no enemy could surprise us. Our camp was pitched upon uneven, rocky ground, and the straggling tents, the dark, busy figures flitting before the fires, and the cloudless sky, might have represented a wandering arab horde in the stony desert, but it was a scene which will not often disturb the repose of this peaceful waste.

On the 4th [August], we crossed a small lake [Quyta Lake] and four portages including five falls of the river. We then left it, to avoid some dangerous rapids, and making three portages between grassy ponds, rejoined it at the fourth, and encamped. On the 5th, we crossed five portages and another lake [Rocky Lake], bordered by rocks so irregular, that they appeared to be piles heaped upon one another as if they had fallen from the clouds. The pines and poplars gradually diminished in size, though not in number, except where the birch and larch predominated. A sixth portage of half a mile put a period to our labours on this day. The dried meats were exhausted, and nothing remained but the portable soups and a few pounds of preserved meats. Our men were, however, still vigorous, and the Indians assured us that we should soon meet with reindeer, and lakes abounding in fish.

The Gros Pied exercised an authority over his band, to which no chief among the Crees has any pretensions. He directed them to assist us at the portages, and they cheerfully complied, notwithstanding the natural repugnance of the Indians to labour. He preserved as much distance from them as a savage state will admit, occupying a canvas tent with his two wives, and carefully avoiding all manual labour. In his canoe, he was paddled by his son, and a young Dogrib Indian, whom he had adopted as his servant, performing for him such offices as an Indian expects from his son. He narrowly watched all our motions and made rational enquiries on subjects that excited his curiosity. He received a share of our meals, and ate many things which may have been disagreeable to his palate; but he deemed it a breach of civility to refuse what was offered with the intention of pleasing him. He used a knife and fork when it was presented to him, though evidently much to his inconvenience.

The wives and children of the Indians constituted almost half our numbers, some of the canoes containing women only. The canoes are constructed in the same manner as those of the Crees, except that the heads and sterns are not circular, but cut off from the gunwales so as to form right angles with the sterns. One of them was a Dogrib canoe, and it resembled the Esquimaux canoes, being sharp at both extremities. The Indians sit on the bottom, and if there are two persons in a canoe, they paddle together on the same side, and lift their paddles to the other, to recover the direction of their course. This mode is similar to that of the Crees, and of the Chepewyans.

On the 6th [August], we crossed three portages, including two miles, and entered a narrow lake [Fishing Lake]. The hills became higher and more rugged, and the portages more frequent, as we advanced to the northward, ledges of rocks crossing the river at every mile, so that we were glad of the relief afforded by the lake, though only eight miles in length. We encamped in the middle of it, and set the nets, but the few whitefish and red suckers which we caught did not answer the accounts we had received of lakes abounding in fish. The Indians themselves began to be distressed by want of provision, and the Gros Pied sent his hunters forward to look for reindeer. On the 7th we crossed a portage of 2,500 yards into a small lake, and rejoined the river by another. The former of these was a hill of sand, upon which the trees were of larger growth than usual. After two more portages, our guides advised us to leave the river on the right, and proceed through a chain of portages and lakes, extending to the northeast, which was the best route.[37] We had already much reason to doubt the correctness of their intelligence with regard to the portages, but however, we complied. In the portage to the first lake, was a valley covered by an enormous mass of ice eight or nine feet in depth. Beneath it, the stones appeared to have been the bed of a river or of some inundation from it. We could obtain no account of its formation, but the Indians alleged that they had always seen it. It was partially shaded from the sun by a high hill near it. The Latitude of the portage is 63°22'15" N. and Longitude 114°25'30" W.[38]

On the 8th [August] when the men were at the north side, with their burthens, the moss and fallen trees round the canoes took fire, and

37. The Nine Lakes, parallel to, but on the *west* side of the Yellowknife. (i.e., they left the river by going left).

38. Icy Portage. The longitude given by Hood is about eight miles too far west.

they were rescued from the flames with much difficulty by the people, who fortunately returned for another load in time to aid the exertions of two persons who were present.[39] It was painful to reflect upon the frequent risks to which our expedition was exposed by accidents of such trivial import in any other circumstances.

We did not reach the river again till the 9th, having crossed nine small lakes, including ten miles, of which distance the portages occupied one-third. The weight of the canoes and cargoes was four tons, and the continued fatigue of our men had reduced their strength and spirits to the lowest ebb. Our fishing was never successful, and we had no other provision for them than arrowroot, mixed with portable soup; a food too unsubstantial to sustain their vigour in this exhausting labour, and they clamoured incessantly for a greater quantity than we thought it advisable to give them, as we knew not when to expect our promised supplies. We crossed a portage of half a mile in the river, and then entered a lake ten miles in length [Lower Carp Lake], where we remained till the 11th, endeavouring to catch some fish; but chiefly to recruit our people, three of whom were lame.

The Gros Pied went forward to join the hunters, and promised to make a large fire as a signal to us when he met with reindeer. Our whole Indian party had left us, to seek those animals in the barren country to the northward of us. Having taken about 20 carp, whitefish, and trout, we embarked, and at noon on the 12th, arrived at the place where the Indians usually leave their canoes, considering themselves upon their hunting lands. We had crossed three lakes since the 9th, separated by portages in the river; the two first were each ten miles in length and we named them the Carp Lakes; the third, which we named the Reindeer Lake, was eight miles long.

We ascended a hill on the north side of it, where we found the Gros Pied, who pointed out several columns of smoke at a great distance to the northeast. At the south end of the lake, the woods discontinued,[40]

39. Franklin gives a different version of this episode, the surrounding moss catching fire during the night at the camp.

40. The tree line. Modern maps show the limit of trees now to be just south of Sandy and Grizzlebear lakes, about 17 miles from the south shore of Dissension Lake. This slow northward extension over the last 150 years has been noted in other areas and has been ascribed to a slight amelioration in climate during the 20th century. From about 5000 to 1500 B.C., however, forests extended up to 200 miles further north, as indicated by fossil forest soils. [W. N. Irving, 'Prehistory of Hudson Bay, Part II–The Barren Grounds', in Science, History and Hudson Bay, ed. C. S. Beals and D. A. Shenstone, (Ottawa: Queen's Printer, 1968), I, 26-54.]

and the rest of the country was a naked desert of coarse brown sand, diversified by small rocky hills and lakes. We could not trace the river beyond the next lake, except by small brooks, and the guide informed us that our future journey would be from lake to lake for six days. The length of the Yellowknife River is 156 statute miles, the latitude of its source 64°1′30″ N. and longitude 113°36′ W.

On the 13th [August], we caught 21 carp [suckers], and then crossed seven lakes and portages. Notwithstanding that we were rapidly approaching the columns of smoke seen on the 12th, our people gave up all hope of relief. They imagined that the Indians were cajoling us, and that in leading them into an inhospitable country, we were incurring dangers of which we were ignorant, but determined to obtain experience by sacrificing them. In the morning, their discontents broke forth into threats of desertion, which Mr. Franklin silenced by denouncing the heaviest punishment against the ringleaders. Few could have borne such hardships without murmuring; but the complaints of our people were very ill timed. We had scarcely encamped before four hunters arrived, bringing the flesh of two reindeer, and after this period we suffered no more from deficiency of provisions, nor were we again censured for temerity: the Canadians never exercising reflection unless they are hungry.[41]

On the 14th, we sent St. Germain with the hunters for meat, and by the direction of the guide, changed our course from NNE to NEbE, which he said was a longer but less difficult route than the other. As all the visible routes were equally beset by portages, we thought it better to depend upon him, than upon chance; accordingly, we crossed three lakes and portages, and encamped. On the borders of the first lake was a grove of stunted pines, an object now become the most agreeable to us that the prospect could afford. Our only fuel was the roots of decayed pines, of which we could not often collect a sufficient quantity. There was some relief from absolute barrenness on the face of the country, in the dwarf birch bushes, the reindeer moss, and a variety of excellent berries.

On the 16th we crossed two lakes [Orkney and Sandy Lakes] and portages into a lake ten miles long. We were alarmed at the second lake to find one of the barrels of powder missing, and supposing it to have

41. These events resulted in the present name of Dissension Lake, for the lake where they had camped the previous night.

The dissension occurred at breakfast, before their day of travel through seven lakes.

been left at a portage on the 15th, we sent back the small canoe for it, with three men and encamped to await their return, at the portage on the north side of the third lake, which we named the Grizzle Bear Lake. At 9 p.m. they arrived, bringing with them the cask of powder; and the next morning the hunters gave us notice that they had killed several deer. Our men brought the carcasses of nine, and we employed the day in smoking them over a slow fire. The small canoe went forward to secure four more. On the 17th, the Gros Pied joined us and asked permission to absent himself for ten days, to provide clothing for his family, as the skin of the reindeer is unfit for that purpose after the month of September.[42] We could not refuse to grant so reasonable a request, but caused St. Germain to accompany him, that his absence might not exceed the appointed time.

This portage had a sandy beach, and we caught some fine whitefish and trout on the north border of it. The magnitude of the hills greatly increased, and the few valleys not filled by lakes were mossy swamps. The Indians warned us to be upon our guard against bears, which, they said, were numerous in this country. They called them grizzle bears, and described them to be of a white colour; but they are probably a peculiar species, for the grizzle bear is grey and the white sea bear has never been found at such a distance from the coast.

On the 17th [August], we met the small canoe with four deer, and on the 18th, encamped on the north side of a large irregular lake [Aurora], near a small grove of pines, having crossed six lakes and portages from Grizzle Bear Lake. We had, at length, penetrated into the native haunts of the reindeer, whose antlers were moving forests on the ridges of the hills, where they assembled to graze in security. On the 19th, after two long portages, we fell upon a little river, running towards the northwest, which brought us to the lake chosen by the Gros Pied for our winter residence.[43] It was surrounded by thin woods of stunted pine which we judged to be too small for the erection of a house. Dr. Richardson and Mr. Wentzel had set out on foot in the morning, and not appearing when we encamped, we were under some anxiety for their safety. On the 20th, we went to the western extremity of the lake

42. It is true that by September, the hair has grown so long and thick that the hides are no longer in prime condition for clothing. [A. W. F. Banfield, *Preliminary Investigation of the Barren Ground Caribou* (Ottawa: Canadian Wildlife Service, 1954), II, 64.]

43. Appropriately named for their site of winter residence, Winter Lake is about 12 miles long.

which was about five miles in length, extending east-northeast and west-southwest. Here we found a river [Snare River] 50 yards wide, running to the southwest. At the discharge of the lake was a strong rapid, near which were our companions, who had passed the night at the foot of a tree. Half a mile below it, we landed on the north bank of the river, at the most eligible place which offered itself for our abode.

8

Fort Enterprize to Point Lake

Building of a Winter Residence.

On examination, we soon perceived our mistake with regard to the trees, many of which, though not more than 30 or 40 feet high, were two feet in diameter at the root. We fixed upon the top of the bank, which was flat and sandy, for the construction of our habitation. The beauty of the situation far exceeded our most sanguine expectations. Behind us, the ascent of the bank closed our view, but sheltered us from the northern winds. To the eastward was the lake which we had left, and to the westward, at the distance of three miles, appeared another [Roundrock Lake], the river winding between them, bounded by sloping woods of pine and birch, and flat, sandy, eminences decked with a rich carpet of the light green reindeer moss. The sole remaining characteristic of the country we had lately traversed, was a gloomy barrier of sterile hills in front, parallel to the river, which only served to heighten the enjoyment of our retreat, by reminding us of the misery which we had escaped.

On the 21st [August], we divided the people into two parties, sending one to cut wood for the buildings, and the other to bring meat, which we dried for our voyage on the Coppermine River. To give the Gros Pied information of our arrival, we set fire to some bushes on the south side of the river [August 20], but the wind rising from the southeast, it spread with extraordinary noise through the whole wood, burning furiously for three days and enveloping us in the smoke; the flames stretching almost across the river. On the fourth day [August 23] it was extinguished by heavy rain, but our fine prospect was metamorphosed into a hideous waste, bristled over with naked black poles.

The buildings were formed in the shape of three sides of a square; that on the left was intended for a storehouse, the middle building for the officers, and that on the right for the Canadians. The only tools made use of were hatchets, yet the storehouse was finished in five days, and the stores were immediately lodged in it.

We named the lake to the eastward, Winter Lake, and the river, Winter [Snare] River. It discharges itself into the Slave Lake to the northward of the Yellowknife River, and its navigation is said to be more interrupted by portages. It enters Winter Lake on the north side, between which and the Coppermine River, it rises.[1] The place of our abode we called Fort Enterprize. It is in Latitude 64°28'30" N., Longitude by chronometers 113°4'45" W. and distance across the barren country 29½ statute miles.[2] The canoes and cargoes were carried, in the whole journey from Fort Providence 21½ statute miles, so that our men, traversing each portage eight times, had, besides the fatigue of paddling, walked 172 miles, on rocky or swampy ground, and half that distance with burthens of 200 Tlb., on their shoulders.[3]

The soil in the neighbourhood of Fort Enterprize is sandy, and the rocks chiefly granite. Besides the pine it produces the dwarf birch, and some birch trees; the *Jackashapucca,* and the *Maskago,* or Indian tea plant, are also numerous. But the most valuable and general productions are the berries, some of which are, I believe, well known in Canada. The cloudberry, the magpie-eye berry [arctic bearberry], the crowberry, and the cranberry, are creeping shrubs, and the blueberry grows upon a small bush. It is called by the Indians, the Indian berry, for its superior excellence. All these, except the cloudberry, flourish vigorously even to the summits of the most barren hills, affording a plentiful repast to many species of animals and birds. They are particularly the food of the bears, whose path may be traced by their devastations.

The birds remaining at our arrival were partridges, ravens, whiskey jacks, gulls, stock ducks [mallards] and teals. We set two nets below the rapid and they furnished us daily with 50 or 60 fish, which were trouts, whitefish, pikes and carp [suckers]. Some of the trouts were large, but the whitefish were small and inferior to those of the Slave Lake.

On the 24th [August], the small pools of water were frozen in the night, and the next day a flock of geese were seen flying to the southward. We could scarcely credit the evidence of our senses on these tokens of departing summer. On the 26th the Gros Pied arrived, with St. Germain and his party. He desired a conference, and acquainted us that some Copper Indians who with their chief, had been stationed by Mr. Wentzel at some distance on the Coppermine River, to prepare

1. This is actually a tributary, Winter River, draining a string of lakes from Little Marten Lake. The Snare River proper enters at the southeast corner of Winter Lake.

2. See Hood's painting of the fort nearing completion [plate 22]. The latitude given is

correct; the longitude is only two miles too far east.

3. Franklin says 180 pounds; 200 troy pounds would be 166 pounds avoirdupois. Each man carried two 'pieces' of 80 to 90 pounds each.

provisions for us, were gone to the Great Bear Lake, supposing that we had given up our project of visiting the sea. This was a prelude to intelligence still more mortifying. He said that winter was about to commence, that the leaves were falling, and the geese returning from the sea; that we should be 40 days going down the Coppermine River, and that we might be blocked by the ice in the next moon. He added that there was no wood within many days' journey, and that the reindeer had left the river to pass the winter in the woods. In answer, we told him that we had instruments by which we could ascertain the state of the air and of the water, and that we knew the winter not to be so near as he imagined. We reminded him of his former accounts of the river, and asked why he had then disguised the truth. He replied, that he had been ignorant of our slow mode of travelling; that every other difference in his descriptions, arose from the advance of winter; and that if we departed against his advice, he would permit his young men to accompany us, but that from the moment they quitted him, he should lament them as dead. We continued to press him with several arguments, such as the swiftness of our canoes, where the portages were few, and the possibility of carrying provisions to the river; upon which, he sullenly declared, that he would take his young men from us; that he had always believed us to be wise and experienced chiefs; instead of which, he was convinced by our obstinacy and rashness, that we resembled all other white people.

We were at a loss to determine whether his conduct proceeded from caprice, or a real interest in our welfare. It was, however, impossible for us to subsist without hunters. One fact which corroborated with his statement, according to Mr. Wentzel, was that the Red Knives generally visited Fort Providence by the ice in the Yellowknife River, in the latter end of September. Our scheme, therefore, with all its advantages, was relinquished. It was possible that we might perish at Fort Enterprize during the winter, without having even determined the great question of the true situation of the sea at the mouth of the river. We had hoped to open a communication with the Esquimaux, from whom we might have ascertained whether our route on the coast was to be performed by land or by water. Or, if they had manifested hostile inclinations we should have learned the necessary precautions for our future defence, and have fully provided ourselves from the Slave Lake, with what experience had taught us was necessary. Whereas we were now again consigned to ten months of anxious suspense and vague conjecture, less endurable than incessant action, and more dreadful than an endless array of perils; for the spirit which braves the last, will be broken by the first, and if this undertaking can claim no other preeminence, it is at least distinguished by the most tedious and vexatious delays that have been incurred in the whole progress of discovery. Mr. Franklin having desired the opinions of the officers, on the feasibility of the original plan, it was decided to be impracticable. All agreed that the distance to the Coppermine River should be determined, but the majority did not think it advisable to attempt any further discovery this year. Mr. Franklin accordingly directed that Mr. Back and I should proceed with one canoe to the river, to find the shortest route thither. He desired that our absence might not exceed ten days, and that we would bring the canoe back to Fort Enterprize.

An affair of still greater importance absorbed all our present consideration. Hepburn had set out to hunt before sunrise on the 24th [August], and the weather having since been rainy and foggy, we concluded from his long absence that the poor man had wandered out of the track, or become the prey of some ferocious animal. On the 26th, two hunters were sent in search of him, but at sunset, they returned without success. On the 27th, seven hunters set out on the same mission. In the evening, several vollies from them announced his safety. He was haggard, and worn with the fatigue of walking day and night, while bewildered by the fog; but the hunters found him directing his way towards the fort. Although he had killed several deer [caribou], such was the perturbation of his mind, that he could not eat, and his only sustenance was a partridge and some berries. His health was reestablished the next day.[4]

On the 28th, we gave the chief and his hunters some ammunition and clothing, and dispatched them to collect the fat of the deer, as a store for the pemmican which we intended to make in spring. We did not choose to acquaint the chief with the measure we had taken, till after its execution.[5] Two hunters were retained to provide for the fort.

On the 29th [August], we embarked, with St. Germain, eight Canadians, and one Indian, who undertook to guide us. We had dried

4. Franklin gives a slightly different version: Hepburn was lost for one day less and shot a caribou but ate only its tongue; he was found by three hunters and a boy.

5. I interpret this to mean that this exploratory journey to the Coppermine was carried out without the knowledge of the Gros Pied; this contradicts Franklin's account.

meat for eight days' provisions, two small tents, and a few instruments. Three miles from the rapid, we entered Winter River, on the north side of the lake, and crossed five portages into a large, singularly shaped lake [Little Marten Lake], where we encamped. Between the two first of these portages, was a small lake, on the borders of which we saw some groves of pine and birch trees; but nothing remained beyond it, except the dwarf birch, so that we found difficulty in cooking our provisions. There is a large mass of rock, on the west bank at the third portage, about 400 feet high, called by the Indians, the Slave Rock. The Dogribs, or Slaves,[6] frequent this part of the country in autumn, in pursuit of the deer and often embark on the Coppermine River. Our guide pointed out their track, which is marked by large stones on the hills.

On the 30th [August], the guide told us, to our infinite surprise, that he was totally ignorant of the route to the Coppermine River, having been there only once with other Copper Indians, who had set out from a different place. We despaired of finding the mouth of the Winter River, on the north side of the lake; for it resembled a polypus, from the number of channels into which it was divided by long promontories running towards the center. The Indian discovered it to be the Lesser Marten Lake, and we proceeded to the northern extremity of one of the channels, and from the top of a hill, saw the Winter River running into a channel to the westward. It was too shallow for the canoe, and we could perceive no large lakes to the northward, to afford us a respite to the labour of carrying; nor did our time admit of it, as we were enjoined to bring the canoe back. We therefore left it in the bushes, and St. Germain drew upon it a man and house, with charcoal, that if the Slaves found it, they might recognize it to be the property of white people.

We commenced our march with the tents, a few blankets and part of the dried meat. After fording the Winter River, we directed our course NbE where the Indian had shown us a range of hills, from which he thought the Coppermine River would be visible. We killed two reindeer about three miles to the northward of Marten Lake, and buried them under stones as a resource on our return. At sunset we encamped among some dwarf birches near a small lake. The next day at noon, we ascended the hills which we had seen from Marten Lake, but could not discern the river. There were several lakes three or four miles in length,

6. Franklin estimated that there were 200 Dogrib men and boys between the west end of Great Slave Lake and Great Bear Lake. The Slave Indians were an adjacent and related tribe, along the Upper Mackenzie and Slave rivers.

with brooks running out of them to the northeast. This was the last height of land between the Slave Lake and the Coppermine River, and allowing ten feet of descent from the source of the Yellowknife River to Winter Lake, it is 1,689 feet above the level of the sea.[7] In the former calculations for the heights, one foot has been allowed for each mile of the lakes, but in this, the Slave Lake is excluded.

These hills were about 500 feet high, rocky, with some sand, and the valleys between, heaps of large bare stones, which had been the beds of temporary inundations, and mossy swamps, through which our march was disagreeable and fatiguing. We were forced to make many circuits, to avoid the lakes, and rambled late in search of bushes for our fire, but without being successful. On the 1st of September we continued our march to the northward surrounded by herds of reindeer, gambolling about us, and darting over the rocks at full speed, on any alarm. It was easy to shoot them, by crouching behind a stone, when they advanced before the wind; and we killed several, disposing of them in holes covered with stones, and replenishing the store which we carried. In the evening, the Indian told us that we should see the river from the summit of a chain of hills on the right; accordingly, he led us three miles to the eastward, and we then perceived it at the distance of three miles, north-northwest; so that he had unnecessarily carried us out of the nearest way in which we were proceeding towards it. We encamped half a mile from the bank, on a rivulet, where the dwarf birches were of a larger size than usual.

During the night, the tents were overthrown by a storm of wind and snow from northwest. It continued with such violence the next day that we did not deem it prudent to march. We were, however, well satisfied with the discovery of the river; the first fruit of our labours, which was worthy of the expedition, and which we had scarcely dared to expect; for after the detection of so many fallacies, we might reasonably have doubted the existence of any river in this quarter.

The gale brought with it, from their northern haunts, long flights of [snow] geese, stretching like white clouds from the northern to the southern horizon, and mingling their ceaseless screams with the uproar of the wind among the hills. They are of that description, called Wavy's in this country, being white, with yellow feet and some black feathers on each wing.

7. Winter Lake is only 1,191 feet, Little Marten Lake 1,310 feet, and the surrounding hills 1,500 to 1,600 feet above sea level.

On the 3rd [September], we went to the edge of the river, which is, by computation, in Latitude 65°12′ N. and Longitude 112°40′ W., distant from Fort Enterprize, 45 miles NbE. This distance is doubled in walking it, by the necessity of making large circuits round the lakes, and by the succession of rocky hills which occupy the whole way. The river was one mile wide, and bordered by lofty hills on each side, in many places precipitous at the water's edge.[8] Their barren deformity was now concealed by the snow, but we saw several patches of stunted pines on small brooks in the valleys. We traced the river four miles, round a mountainous promontory to the westward, and perceiving its course extending five or six miles west-northwest, we encamped near some pines, and once more enjoyed the luxury of a comfortable fire. The temperature of the river was 35, and the thermometer fell to 20° in the air during the night. As our sole object was to determine whether the river approached nearer to Fort Enterprize, than where we had fallen upon it, we returned on the banks to the eastward, being satisfied by the appearance of the mountains between south and west, that no further examination was necessary in that direction. On the evening of the 4th, the river apparently divided into two branches, one of which was visible east-northeast for five miles, and the other extended to the southeast. It was full of rocky islands, and deeply indented by bays, which rendered it in some places three miles wide. We coasted the southeast branch till the 6th, when we ascertained it to be nothing more than a channel or bay, receiving a small stream from the southward.[9] We then determined to return, but encamped to observe an eclipse which was to take place on the 7th.

The part of the river which we left, extending east-northeast, was in Latitude by computation 65°12′30″ N., Longitude 112°26′ W. The cloudiness of the weather prevented us from obtaining a single observation during this journey; but the long practice of estimating distances by the eye, had rendered that mode of computation tolerably correct. There was no current distinguishable near the bank, although we judged by a ripple in the middle that the stream ran to the westward. It may therefore be presumed that this was a lake through which the river

8. Point Lake is a lengthy widening of the Coppermine River.

9. This channel from the south-east carried the waters of the Coppermine River into Point Lake. Only 15 miles upstream (south) was Obstruction Rapids where, just over 12 months later, a serious delay resulted for the weakened, hungry men returning to Winter Lake after exploration of 675 miles of arctic coastline.

runs. It might have been expected, from the height of its surface above the level of the sea, greater than that of the Slave Lake,[10] that its current would be very rapid, much broken by falls, or its course exceedingly crooked. From the nature of its banks, it is certainly deep, and the ice formed upon it, probably remains till late in the year. We concluded it to be the southwestern extremity of the grand western inflexion described by the guides. Its waters were clear, and no object whatever was floating on the surface; but the season for driftwood is the breaking up of the ice, and if the Coppermine River carries any, it must be deposited in the lakes farther to the eastward.[11] The hills along the banks are round, and broken in many parts into huge fragments, which are scattered below the precipices. We saw numerous herds of reindeer, some groundhogs,[12] alpine [arctic] hares, and partridges. In our march, we broke the ice on the surface of the swamps at every step, and several of the people were lamed by wounding their ankles against its edges.

On the 7th [September], a southeast wind with snow obscured our view of the eclipse, and we commenced our return, directing ourselves towards Marten Lake by the compass. The Indian, however, insisted that we should alter our course more to the westward, alleging that no bushes were to be found by the route which we had chosen. We complied, but did not obtain any advantage by yielding this point, for we encamped in the snow, when the light failed us, without finding any bushes. On the 8th we fell upon our former track, and encamped near the place where we slept on the 31st of August. We now perceived the true motive of our guide, for having conducted us to our former track. He had left the skins of the reindeer which he had killed, in different places, supposing that we should return after having seen the river, and he employed this subterfuge to recover them, when he saw our intention of proceeding by a different route.

On the 9th, we encamped within three miles of Marten Lake, where we found the reindeer's meat rotten, and our whole party made their repast upon three geese. The reindeer had disappeared, but the southerly wind had tempted the geese to alight and feed on the berries.

10. Point Lake is 1,229 feet, but Great Slave Lake only 518 feet above sea level.

11. The upper reaches of the Coppermine are indeed north of the tree line, but downstream from Point Lake a projection of tree line follows the Coppermine River valley for many miles.

12. The arctic ground squirrel, a large tundra species easily confused with a woodchuck or marmot except for its lack of black feet. This was a species new to science, later named by Richardson in honour of Edward Parry. It abounded at Fort Enterprize.

The blueberries and cloudberries were destroyed by the snow, but the crowberry received an additional flavour, and its juice became a strong purple dye. The cranberry does not decay till the year after it has been produced.

On the morning of the 10th we reached Marten Lake and immediately embarked, as the dried meat which we had left was rendered unfit for use by wet. The shores swarmed with deer which we did not molest but proceeded so expeditiously, that at 8 p.m. we arrived at Fort Enterprize, where we had sufficient employment for the night, in removing a troublesome species of filth [lice] which we had contracted by admitting too close a contact with our Indian guide.

Mr. Franklin and Dr. Richardson had set out on the 9th with two men, and Kescarrah, the old guide, in search of the Coppermine River.[13] They were unprovided with tents and we feared that they would suffer much from the inclemency of the weather.

Under Mr. Wentzel's superintendence, our house had made rapid progress, and the fishery was established in the lake. The tents were sheltered by inclosures of pines, leaving large spaces for fires; a contrivance which completely excluded the cold.

On the 13th [September], another storm of snow summoned the geese from their pasture, and they finally quitted the country on the 14th. On the evening of the 15th, Messrs. Franklin and Richardson arrived. They had found the river in Latitude by observation 65°13′and Longitude 112°56′ W. and returned immediately, after having distinctly ascertained a slight current to the westward. This place must have been the extreme point to the west-northwest, which we saw. It appeared that their track had furnished more wood than ours, and Mr. Franklin fixed upon it, as the future route for the canoes.

The whole distance travelled by the expedition in the year 1820, was 1,516 statute miles.

---

13. With Hood and Back having failed to return by the twelfth day, and the eclipse past, Franklin may have become impatient. He and Richardson, with Kescarrah, Hepburn, and Samandre, made a return trip to the Coppermine, totalling over 120 miles, in seven days.

N.B. I beg leave to offer, as some apology for the illegibility of many parts of this narrative, that the pressure of other duties has compelled me to write it, from notes, within the last fortnight.

ROBERT HOOD

Fort Enterprize
April 16, 1821

S
7

Sacred to the Memory of
LIEUTENANTS ROBERT and GEORGE HOOD, R.N.
SONS of the REV^D RICHARD HOOD, L.L.D. of this Town!

The former of whom, while engaged in the overland Arctic Expedition,
Under the command of CAPTAIN FRANKLIN, R.N.
After having, with unshaken fortitude, endured
unparralleled dangers and privations,
AND, BY HIS SKILL IN SCIENCE,
Essentially contributed to the utility of the enterprise,
Was ASSASSINATED. by an IROQUOIS, October 20. 1821.
Thus terminating, At the early age of four and twenty,
A short but brilliant career,
Distinguished by varied talent and steady determination,
Which were rapidly opening a path to the highest honours of his profession
THE LATTER, UNDER CAPTAIN OWEN, R.N.
Employed also in the cause of science, on the Eastern Coast of Africa,
perished by a Fever, February. 6th 1823, Being also 24 Years of age.
If his services were less distinguished,
or his fate attracted less of public sympathy,
Than that of his lamented brother,
He required only a more prominent situation
For the display of his uncommon talents and acquirements.

As a tribute of sincere respect
For
the merit of their Fellow Townsmen
This Monument was erected
By
some of the Inhabitants
of Bury.

MEMORIAL TABLET TO HOOD, ST. MARY'S CHURCH, BURY, LANCASHIRE

EPILOGUE

The Death of Hood

Hood's formal journal, compiled from his diary and from memory, was completed at Fort Enterprize 16 April 1821, but actually covers the activities of the expedition only to 15 September 1820.

Unfortunately we do not have Hood's account of the long, tedious, cold winter at Fort Enterprize. To complete the final chapter of Hood's activities we must draw from Franklin's account. We know that their indoor thermometer once registered 15 degrees below zero, at a distance of 16 feet from the fire. Two chronometers, placed beneath the pillows to keep them warm, stopped when the bedroom temperature reached 40 degrees below zero.

Hood was kept busy with his maps and paintings, writing up his formal journal that is published here, and making observations on the aurora and the variations of the magnetic needle.

The winter seemed unbelievably long. On 21 April the ice on the Snare River below the fort still measured five feet in thickness. By 7 May bare ground appeared on the hills and the next day the sight of a simple house-fly brought cheerfulness to the whole residence. A merganser, two gulls and some loons were seen on 9 May and numbers of ducks and geese and a robin on 14 May. The latter made spring official as the natives considered it the infallible precursor of warm weather.

On 4 June 1821, a party of fifteen voyageurs and eight Copper Indians, led by Dr. Richardson, set off from Fort Enterprize for the mouth of the Coppermine. Franklin, Back, Hood, Hepburn, and Wentzel left ten days later, accompanied by some of the voyageurs who had returned to aid them, two Eskimos, and two interpreters. They joined Richardson's party on the shores of Point Lake, an expansion of the Coppermine River where the ice was still six or seven feet thick on 21 June. Here Dr. Richardson found the first recorded nest of the Eskimo Curlew. They travelled with difficulty over melting ice and finally, on 1 and 2 July, reached some stretches of open water in the river that allowed them to paddle their birchbark canoes, a relief after 117 miles of dragging them along on sledges. Further travel of about 217 miles downstream brought them on 18 July to the Arctic Ocean, seen here previously by only one white man, Samuel Hearne.

Mr. Wentzel, the Copper Indians, and four voyageurs now returned to Fort Enterprize and thence to Fort Providence. The expedition remaining consisted of twenty men: Franklin, Richardson, Back and Hood, the English seaman Hepburn, two Eskimos, two interpreters, and eleven voyageurs.

From 20 July to 17 August they carefully mapped about 675 statute miles of coastline never before seen by white men. They carried with them food for fifteen days; but, in spite of killing some geese, swans, and cranes, a seal, a fox, a muskox, four bears, and thirteen caribou, after one month they had provisions for only three days. They were forced to travel on one handful of pemmican per man per day, in place of the usual daily ration of one and a half pounds.

The expedition's return from Point Turnagain across the mouth of Bathurst Inlet to the mouth of the Hood River took five days, beginning on 22 August. They then spent three days converting their large canoes to two smaller ones and set off southwards on foot on 31 August. The voyageurs took turns leading the way, with Hood always in second position, to renew the bearings and keep the day's leader on course.

On 9 September they crossed the Burnside River just east of Kathawachaga Lake, one voyageur ferrying one passenger at a time in the small canoe. It was not a pleasant ride, for each passenger was required to lie on his back in the leaky canoe, which became partly filled with cold water before the south shore was reached.

On 11 September, drifting snow and a temperature of 20° forced them to stay within their tents. It was their seventh day without adequate food and they ate only once that day. The following day, after trudging eleven miles through deep snow in a snowstorm, they consumed their last provisions of meat.

On 13 September, their way was barred by Contwoyto Lake, which forced them to make an exhausting detour up steep hills to the northwest. Their only food was a single ptarmigan and some *tripe de roche*; this unpalatable lichen was nauseous to all, but also caused some diarrhea, Hood being the greatest sufferer. The same day they learned that the voyageurs had destroyed the three fishing nets some time after leaving Hood's River. Because the men were getting noticeably weaker each day, most of the instruments were left behind. Hood loaned his gun to Michel, the Iroquois – a significant gesture in the light of later events.

On 14 September, Perrault, one of the voyageurs, magnanimously presented each of the officers with a small piece of meat he had saved from his allowance. This act of self-denial and kindness filled their eyes with tears. That day they killed two caribou and reached the Contwoyto River flowing north between Contwoyto Lake (the Rum Lake of Samuel Hearne) and Kathawachaga Lake. Pierre St. Germain, their best hunter and interpreter, the voyageur Solomon Belanger (otherwise known as Belanger *le gros*, to differentiate him from J. B. Belanger *le rouge*), and Franklin attempted to cross the river. The canoe upset in the middle of the rapid; the hefty Belanger steadied it and prevented it from being swept downstream while St. Germain placed Franklin in it and then re-embarked himself. After the canoe capsized once more, Franklin was deposited on the west shore and St. Germain was swept down the rapids away from Belanger, finally reaching the east shore. All were immobilized by the frigid water. The exhausted Belanger, in waist-deep water, cried piteously for relief, but only on the fourth rescue attempt was the canoe able to reach him with a small cord and drag him perfectly senseless through the rapid. Under Dr. Richardson's orders, Belanger was stripped of his icy clothing and rolled up in blankets with two naked voyageurs, while a fire was built. Meanwhile Franklin's position was desperate – alone on the opposite side of the river, in icy clothing, with no means of obtaining food or making a fire. The loss of his summer's journal was an additional source of grief. Several others were ferried across to join Franklin that day and the remainder the next morning. These rapids are appropriately named Belanger Rapids on modern maps.

On 15 September, they killed one caribou, and then ascended the steep, craggy, snow-covered Willingham Hills. Large stones badly galled their feet, but, with meat to sustain them, they covered nearly twenty-three miles in the next two days by Franklin's reckoning and then ten miles a day after that on nearly empty stomachs. Even allowing a fairly straight course, measurements on a modern map disclose that Franklin underestimated the distances by at least one-third in terms of statute miles. This was a remarkable achievement for a band of starving men.

Each night, their blankets were inadequate to keep them warm. If a fire could be made, they thawed their moccasins, and put on the dry pair they carried; some nights with insufficient fire, they dared not remove their footgear as they would be frozen by morning. Each officer wrote his daily notes and read prayers before he ate his meagre supper, often part of a ptarmigan and some brew of lichens, in the dark before falling shivering asleep. By 20 September, the country became more hilly and laborious, eroding the strength of the stoutest members. This day Hood was particularly weak and had to relinquish his position as second in line, Dr. Richardson taking his place. The next day, Richardson was finally forced to discard his summer's scientific collection of rocks and plants, including many new species which were thus destined to remain undescribed for years to come. The next five days were spent on a circuitous route around Eda Lake and then northwest along Lake Providence. At times the officers had to fall behind with the debilitated Hood. On 23 September the last canoe, severely damaged by rough treatment, was abandoned by the voyageurs. On the twenty-fifth they killed five small caribou and rested for the day, eating two substantial meals after eight days of famine; the voyageurs consumed in one sitting about a third of their portions, including the contents of the caribou stomachs.

On 26 September, they reached the rushing, icy waters of the Coppermine River – but now had no canoe in which to cross. They spent two days searching for trees large enough to construct a raft, without success, since they were north of the tree line. On 29 September, in desperation, they bound willows into eight large faggots to make a flimsy raft-like structure. The men stood waist-deep in the icy waters, battling the current and a strong breeze from the opposite shore, but Dr. Richardson's single paddle was insufficient to propel the clumsy makeshift, and they had no poles long enough to touch bottom. Richardson set out to swim across with a line around his waist but with his first steps stepped on a dagger, cutting his foot to the bone. When his arms became numb and useless, he turned on his back and almost gained the opposite bank, only to become powerless from the cold. When he sank, the men pulled on the line; the surgeon came again to the surface and they pulled him back to shore in an almost lifeless state. He was rolled in blankets before the fire and in a few hours was able to converse, but the skin of his whole left side was without sensation all that winter. The voyageurs gasped when they saw his debilitated frame, a mere skeleton, and they exclaimed 'Ah que nous sommes maigres!'

On 1 October, they found the spine of a deer which had been killed that summer and they divided the putrid marrow among them. In vain they searched for some pitch or gum with which to join some of the tent canvas into a canoe. By 2 October, the snow was eighteen inches deep, and they despaired of reaching Fort Enterprize alive, though it was only forty miles distant and the Indians had promised to have it well stocked with provisions. The faithful Hepburn each day collected enough *tripe de roche* for the entire party. Richardson was lame from his injured foot, Back so weak he could not walk without a stick, and Hood reduced to a perfect shadow from the diarrhea which the *tripe de roche* never failed to give him. A ptarmigan which was reserved for poor Hood was treacherously stolen by one of the men.

St. Germain spent three days making tent canvas into a little cockleshell canoe, and on 4 October, after a wait of nearly nine days, he succeeded in crossing the Coppermine River. The craft was brought back and forth by a rope, so that each man in turn crossed, though on later trips it almost filled with frigid water, soaking their clothing and bedding – and there was insufficient material to build a fire on the far side. Back immediately set out for Fort Enterprize with the strongest men, St. Germain, Solomon Belanger, and Beauparlant, to seek help.

By 5 October the remaining members of the party were exhausted by a walk of eight miles, and on the next day, Credit and Vaillant, weakened by diarrhea, fell irretrievably behind and perished. Richardson and the seaman Hepburn volunteered to stay behind with the weakened Hood, camping on 7 October in a thicket of willows near a supply of *tripe de roche*. The other men, relieved of the burdens of one tent and the supply of ammunition, went on with Franklin. On 8 October J. B. Belanger and Michel, and later Perrault and Fontano, too weak to carry on, turned back towards Richardson's tent, but only Michel reached them next day – having Perrault's gun and forty-eight balls, with which he killed a hare and a ptarmigan. On 11 October Michel brought them so-called 'wolf meat' which they consumed, only later realizing that it was probably a portion of either Perrault or J. B. Belanger, who may have been murdered by Michel. The expected relief party from Fort Enterprize had not appeared, and Hood began to experience giddiness and dimness of sight. By 18 October, Hood was unable to eat more than one or two spoonfuls of *tripe de roche*, because of the crampy diarrhea it produced. He was now so weak that he could scarcely sit up; he felt thoroughly chilled all night, even though Dr. Richardson slept close beside him. Michel became moody. Circumstantial evidence suggests that Michel, on 20 October, after a loud argument with Hood, shot Hood through the back of the head, even as he was reading *Bickersteth's Scripture Help*. Michel protested subsequently that he was incapable of such an act, but carefully avoided leaving Richardson and Hepburn together. In this atmosphere of distrust, the three remaining men passed a restless night, each on his guard. On 21 October they boiled and ate Hood's buffalo robe after singeing the hair off it, and in the afternoon Michel killed several ptarmigan which he shared with them.

Storm-stayed on 22 October, the party set out next day for the previous winter's fort and again Michel's behaviour became so suspicious that Richardson feared he was readying his gun in order to attack them. Richardson now could discuss for the first time privately with Hepburn the circumstantial evidence against Michel and reached the decision of his guilt. When the Iroquois rejoined them, Richardson shot him through the head. At dusk on 29 October Richardson and Hepburn finally reached the tomb-like Fort Enterprize, to encounter the 'ghostly countenances, dilated eye-balls and sepulchral voices' of Mr. Franklin and his companions.

Franklin and his remaining men (Peltier, Samandre, Adam, and Benoit) had reached deserted and empty Fort Enterprize on 11 October. From the ashes and refuse heap of the previous winter, they gathered several caribou skins and bones for soup, and tore up the wooden flooring of adjacent rooms for firewood. Back and his three companions had arrived two days earlier and had left only that morning for Round Rock Lake to search for the Indians. On 14 October, Solomon Belanger returned, covered with ice and almost speechless after falling into the rapid, and reported that Back had not yet located the Indians. On 18 October Belanger left again to rejoin Back.

Still without provisions on 20 October, Franklin with Augustus and Benoit set out for Fort Providence, leaving Peltier and Samandre to care for Adam, whose tissues were swollen from nutritional deficiency. The next day Franklin broke his snowshoes and finding himself very weak, returned to camp, leaving Augustus and Benoit to go ahead. Peltier and Samandre meanwhile became even weaker and more dispirited than Adam. Premonition of death haunted Peltier who repeatedly stated that if help did not arrive by 1 November, he would die

— and both he and Samandre passed away that very night. The starving survivors, in contrast to their sunken faces, had bloated abdomens and legs swollen by fluid; they urinated up to ten times nightly.

Meanwhile Back had camped less than a day's march from the fort from 14 to 30 October, having difficulty persuading his men to move on, particularly after Beauparlant's death on 17 October. On 3 November, Back encountered fresh tracks of Indians and with this hope of succour at last, sent St. Germain on to the site of the Indians' winter camp, which was reached also by Benoit and Augustus on their way to Fort Providence. On 7 November three Indians brought relief to Franklin and Richardson at Fort Enterprize with the first small supply of dried caribou meat, some fat, and a few tongues; this resulted in painful diarrhea from over-indulgence.

The next day the bodies of Peltier and Samandre were laboriously dragged out and covered with snow by Richardson and Hepburn. The Indians brought firewood and cleaned the dirt and bone fragments from the building. The beards of Richardson and Hepburn were particularly offensive to the Indians and they were prevailed upon to shave off their beards of nearly three months' growth. November 9 provided a feast of four large trout which Crooked-Foot caught in the lake. A larger party of Indians, with Benoit, arrived with more food on 15 November. The next day they left their camp and after ten days' slow travelling reached Akaitcho's camp. They set out for Fort Providence on 1 December and on the sixth were met by Belanger with two trains of dogs, carrying rum, tobacco, tea, sugar, fresh clothing, and letters from home. They were able to change their clothing for the first time in 102 days.

At this time they opened the packet and learned the news of the promotions of Back and Hood from midshipman to lieutenant, and of Franklin's promotion from lieutenant to commander, the latter retroactive to 1 January 1821. Thus Hood had been dead for forty-seven days before news of his promotion reached the party.

The messages also told of Parry's success by sea much farther north, wintering on Melville Island in 1819-20 and then pushing west to longitude 113° in August 1820. This was one year before the Franklin expedition explored the arctic coast from 115° West to 109°20′ West, leaving not an east-west gap but an unexplored north-south gap of over four hundred miles (occupied as we now know mainly by inhospitable Victoria Island).

The party arrived at Fort Providence on 11 December and a week later reached Moose Deer Island at the south shore of Great Slave Lake. By the end of February their nutrition was restored and the swelling of their limbs had subsided. They left on 26 May, reached Fort Chipewyan on 2 June, Norway House on 4 July, and York Factory on 14 July 1822.

The expedition had covered 5550 miles and had under adverse conditions, been the first to traverse a portion of the arctic coastline of mainland North America.

The accuracy of their observations and completeness of their studies far excelled those of their predecessors, Hearne and Mackenzie. Important advances resulted in the fields of geography, terrestrial magnetism, climatology, geology, ichthyology, ornithology, mammalogy, and botany. Their observations of the aurora borealis were more complete and detailed than any others to be reported in the next hundred years. All these achievements had been aided in full measure by Robert Hood during two strenuous, productive years.

To the credit of Franklin, Richardson and Back, we must acknowledge that they learned from their mistakes. Lesser men, after their horrendous experiences, would have retired from exploration. Yet all three officers returned in 1825 on a well-organized, well-planned expedition to survey for the first time another 1237 miles of arctic coastline, without serious difficulty and, apart from an accident on the return journey, without loss of life. Their studies of natural history alone occupied six volumes.

LICHENS OF THE BARREN GROUNDS
(September and October, 1821).

This [*Gyrophora Muhlenbergii*] and the three preceding species [*Gyrophora proboscidea, Gyrophora hyperborea* & *Gyrophora pensyl-vanica*] were found in greater or less abundance in all rocky places throughout our journey. We used them all four as articles of food, but not having the means of extracting the bitter principle from them, they proved noxious to several of the party, producing severe bowel complaints. The Indians use the *G. Muhlenbergii*, rejecting the others, and when boiled along with fish-roe or other animal matter, it is agreeable and nutritious. On the Barren Grounds this lichen is scarce, and we were obliged to resort to the other three, which served the purpose of allaying the appetite, but were very inefficient in recruiting our strength.

Dr. John Richardson,
Botanical Appendix
in Franklin, *Journey 1819-22,* p. 759.

COMMENTARY

Hood's Paintings

Much as we appreciate the work of Hood's pen, we are even more appreciative of the delicate sensitivity of his brush. He and George Back were the first artists to visit the Saskatchewan River, twenty-seven years before Paul Kane. Hood's artistic ability must have influenced, and may have been the deciding factor in, his appointment to the first Franklin expedition. Prior to the invention of photography, an artist, especially one whose landscapes were almost photographic in their reproduction of detail, was considered essential to the success of any major scientific expedition. Paintings also added to the interest and saleability of the journals produced on the expedition's return.

L. H. Neatby (*In Quest of the North West Passage*, p. 57) has rated Hood's sketches as 'the first and among the best of the Canadian northland, but marked by a tender melancholy which distinguishes them from the robust and vigorous drawings of Back'. Hood's drawings reveal an appreciation of composition and proportion, although they are sometimes primitive in their lack of perspective.

To appreciate them fully, we must understand the handicaps under which many of these paintings were created. At Cumberland House in midwinter, seated near the fire in a makeshift log building 'rather too airy for this climate', Hood tells how 'our pens and brushes were frozen to the paper and we felt, at the same time, the extremes of cold and heat at each side of our persons'. Dr. Richardson also described this setting: 'The miserable log houses in which we dwell are scarcely to be distinguished, in their winter dress, from the fallen trees with which the woods abound.'

Hood's paintings of wildlife are in some ways his most interesting studies, and as the first attempts of a young artist to portray these difficult subjects they exhibit remarkable talent. They are best appreciated in relation to the standards of his time. In the early 1800s, the art of bird painting had been mastered by few men; even the work of the best of these early artists now appears stodgy and lifeless. Hood did not live to see or participate in the advances in the art that became evident when John James Audubon began publication in 1827, followed by John Edward Gray in 1830 and John Gould in 1832.

William Swainson later used the bird skins from the second Franklin expedition as models. He illustrated and co-authored with John Richardson the volume on the birds of North America. Seventy-five years later, Alfred Newton in his authoritative history of ornithology, *A Dictionary of Birds* (London, 1896, pp. 23, 28), spoke of the artists of this time as copying 'the distortions of the "bird-stuffer"...quite unable to vivify the preserved specimens contained in Museums', yet he rated as an exception Swainson, 'who as an ornithological artist had no rival in his time'. Hood seems to have drawn many of his subjects from life, and it is my opinion that his paintings of the canvasback and magpie are of better quality than the best work of Swainson. Few would disagree that Hood's paintings are much superior to the contemporary American bird paintings of the famous Alexander Wilson.

To the naturalist, a number of Hood's paintings have major scientific and historical importance, particularly those of the magpie, black-backed three-toed woodpecker, yellow-headed blackbird, hoary redpoll, red-necked grebe, evening grosbeak, wood duck, Eskimo curlew, and round whitefish.

To the ethnologist and etymologist, the Cree names given for various birds and animals by Hood and Richardson should be of considerable interest. The Cree Indians, living a nomadic life of hunting and trapping, evidently recognized more species of birds and animals than is apparent from any of the Cree dictionaries, and probably more species than they recognize now in their more settled mode of life. The published Cree dictionaries have failed to include most of these terms, probably because the lexicographers, Father Lacombe and the Reverend E. A. Watkins, had little knowledge of natural history. Of course, unwritten language among a widely dispersed population would be particularly subject to local names. One need only think of the number of different folk names given to birds by English-speaking settlers. Further, one suspects that on a few occasions the helpful Indians may have invented names to satisfy the curiosity of Hood or Richardson.

In the following descriptions of individual paintings, I have given Richardson's versions of the Cree names for the birds and animals depicted by Hood, with such variants as are to be found in Lacombe and Watkins and in Richard Faries, *A Dictionary of the Cree Language* (Toronto: Church of England, 1938). I am indebted to Robert Gallernault, specialist in Saulteaux and Cree languages and local history, for modern versions.

Eight paintings by Hood served as models for the engraver of illustrations in the journal of the first Franklin expedition. In addition, Hood's representation of the White Wolf (plate 12) was superimposed by the engraver on a background of the Dogrib Rock by George Back. Only three other of these previously published scenes have been reproduced here (plates 19, 20, and 21). A comparison of these plates, reproduced from the original watercolours, with the engravings in the Franklin journal show how much could be lost when the engraver 'tidied up' the original.

The other twenty paintings reproduced here are published for the first time. Hood's colours were accurate, especially considering the materials available to him, and after 150 years they are remarkably well preserved.

The following notes explain the significance and circumstances of each painting. Since Hood assisted Dr. Richardson in his natural history observations and collections, relevant quotations from Richardson concerning species painted by Hood are included.

1. A View of Stromness   July 1819

Taken from the Holms opposite to it. A revenue brig lying in the harbour and kelp burning in the foreground.

2. The Hudson's Bay Company Fleet   31 July 1819

Prince of Wales, Eddystone and *Wear*. The three ships are passing through a large field of ice during a thick fog west of Cape Farewell, latitude 59°28'N, longitude 49°22'W. In other words, they were nearly 200 miles west of the southern tip of Greenland.

3. Likenesses of Esquimaux   August 1819

These portraits of three of the Esquimaux who came out to meet the ships off the Savage Islands were no doubt based on hurried sketches at the time of the brief encounter. The infant within its mother's parka is portrayed as having an unrealistically small head. Hood no doubt painted the infant from memory, unaware that even at birth, each dimension of the infant's cranium is already more than half the corresponding measurement of that of an adult, while the infant's face is proportionately smaller.

4. Likenesses of Bois Brûlés   February 1820

Quatoo, Atatoo, and Sasasis, obviously dressed in their best to pose for Hood, represent his most successful portraits. They lived at Cumberland House, and, in spite of their Cree names, their clothing, if correctly depicted, suggests that they may have been living with their Scottish fathers.

Hood subtitled this, 'The Children of Europeans by Indian Women'. The term *bois brûlés*, literally 'burned woods', implying dusky or smoky skin, referred to halfbreeds of either Scottish or French parentage. Hood's journal suggests some prejudice against the French-Indian hybrids or Métis; he considered the Scottish-Indian halfbreeds superior. Perhaps more of the latter had the advantage of being raised in company posts and had some instruction from their fathers.

5. Wolverene   Cumberland House   2 February 1820

Gulo luscus. Hood's title reads 'Wolverene pulling upon himself a trap formed of heavy trees, length 4 ft.' This is the deadfall trap described by Hood in chapter 4. The painting gives a distorted, elongated view of this thick-set animal, and its lateral stripe is not visible in the dark shade. The sombre darkness of the forest floor is well conveyed, even though the animal itself is not. Richardson described it as a cunning animal of great strength, much hated by the hunters because of the mischief it did their traps.

Hood gave its Cree name as *okeekoohawgees*, though Richardson added two more versions, *ommeethatsees* and *okeecoohagew,* the latter closest to the modern Cree pronunciation. Lacombe gave no name for the 'carcajou', while Watkins gave the Cree name as *kwekwuakao,* and Faries as *kwekwuhakao.*

6. Lynx   Cumberland House   April 1820

Lynx canadensis. This animal has just killed a Snowshoe Hare, *Lepus americanus.* Richardson listed the lynx as 'not uncommon in the woody districts of the interior, since seven to nine thousand are annually procured by the Hudson's Bay Company'. It is still quite common throughout the wooded parts of Saskatchewan. Richardson was perhaps the first to note that its numbers varied cyclically, reaching a peak when the hare, its chief prey, was also at its peak numerically.

Hood gave the Cree name as *peeshoo,* while Lacombe spelled it *pisiw* and Watkins *pisew.* The Snowshoe or Varying Hare, locally known as 'bush rabbit', was *wawpoos,* spelled by Lacombe *wapus* and by Faries *wapoos.*

7. Fisher   Cumberland House   April 1820

Martes pennanti. Here the fisher is shown on the edge of a clearing near the Cumberland House post on Pine Island, leaving its normal forest habitat to chase a frog. Richardson described it as the largest and strongest of the weasels, preying principally on mice but also on frogs in summer. A common furbearing animal at the time, it was later virtually extirpated from Saskatchewan.

Hood gave its Cree name as *otchoek*, spelled *otchek* by Lacombe, *oochak* or *wuchak* by Watkins, and *ochak* by Faries.

8. Buffalo Bull   May 1820

Bison bison. Hood's subtitle reads 'Indian hunters attacking a herd in the plains bordering on the Saskashawan'. Hood perhaps saw a few plains bison on his visit to the north edge of the Pasquia Hills in late March and early April of 1820. However, this fine painting of a buffalo hunt on more open plains in summer must have been based on descriptions of such hunts by those who had taken part in them. This painting antedates by twenty-six years similar scenes by Paul Kane.

Richardson reported that bison were then 'extremely numerous on the plains of the Saskatchewan. . . . The flesh of a bison in good condition is very juicy and well flavoured, much resembling that of a well-fed beef. The tongue is reckoned a delicacy, and may be cured so as to surpass the tongue of an English cow. The hump of flesh covering the long spinous processes of the first dorsal vertebrae is much esteemed. It is named bos by the Canadian voyagers . . . has a fine grain, and when salted and cut tranversely it is almost as rich and tender as the tongue.

The fine wool which clothes the bison renders its skin when properly dressed an excellent blanket; and they are valued so highly, that a good one sells for three or four pounds in Canada, where they are used as wrappers by those who travel over the snow in carioles.'

The Cree name was *moostoosh* according to Richardson, spelled *mustus* by Lacombe. It was sometimes called *muscotay-moostoos* or 'prairie buffalo'.

9. **Doe Moose**   Pasquia Hills   3 April 1820

Alces alces. The female moose sketched feeding on the tops of willows is the one described at some length by Hood in chapter 3. The moose is still a common game animal in the area.

Richardson gave the Cree name as *moosoa*, pronounced nasally, Lacombe as *moswa*, and some later authorities as *mooswa* and *mooswu*.

10. **Otter**   Cumberland House   3 March 1820

Lutra canadensis. The specimen shown here was killed at Cumberland House and measured 3 ft. 11 in. in length. Richardson made the following comment: 'In the winter season, it frequents rapids and falls, to have the advantage of open water; and when its usual haunts are frozen over, it will travel to a great distance through the snow, in search of a rapid that has resisted the severity of the weather. If seen, and pursued by hunters on these journies, it will throw itself forward on its belly, and slide through the snow for several yards, leaving a deep furrow behind it. This movement is repeated with so much rapidity, that even a swift runner on snow-shoes has much trouble in overtaking it.'

At that time otters were common, and Sabine recorded that 7,300 were sent to England by the Hudson's Bay Company in 1822. Later trapping reduced their numbers quite markedly in the present province of Saskatchewan.

The Cree name given by Richardson was *neekeek,* while Lacombe and Faries spelled this *nikik.* and Watkins, *nekik.*

11. Ermine   Cumberland House   1820

Mustela erminea richardsonii. This specimen measured 14½ inches in length and was probably a male; this largest subspecies may reach 15½ inches. It is pictured here in the officers' makeshift winter quarters at Cumberland House in the winter of 1819-20. The black tip of its tail is largely obscured by shadow in the drawing. Richardson noted: 'It is a bold animal and often domesticates itself in the habitations of the fur traders, where it may be heard the livelong night pursuing the white-footed mouse.' Bonaparte in 1838 named this subspecies for John Richardson, based on the specimen collected at Great Bear Lake on the second Franklin expedition.

The Cree names given by Richardson were *seegoos* and *shacooshew,* while Lacombe renders this as *sikkus,* Watkins as *sekoosew,* and Faries as *sikosew.*

12. White Wolf near Fort Enterprize   March 1821

Canis lupus. This very large wolf was killed near Fort Enterprize. Hood's legend tells us that its length from nose to insertion of tail, was 4 ft. 3 in. Richardson confirmed this figure and gave the length of the tail as 19 inches, for a total length of 71 inches! Hood gave the height of the fore shoulder as 2 ft. 11 in., the length of the fore foot as 1 ft. 8 in. and the length of the head as 11¼ in.

Hood's painting was superimposed by the engraver on George Back's painting of Dog Rib Rock in Franklin's journal. The gray or timber wolf *Canis lupus,* varies in colour from nearly black to nearly white, the latter animals usually occurring in the far north.

Richardson gave the Cree name for all colour phases as *mahaygan,* spelled *mahigan* by Lacombe.

13. Winter Birds at Cumberland House No. 1   1820

Hood completed this and the following painting at Cumberland House in 1820. These were the first winter birds painted in northern North America. Here the individual paintings of seven species are represented on a background of trees and branches.

White-winged Crossbill, *Loxia leucoptera.* Hood's legend named these 'Young Cross bill, length 5 inches' and 'Cross bill, length 7 inches.' They are a young bird and an adult male. Richardson reported that 'this Crossbill inhabits the dense white-spruce forests of the fur-countries, feeding principally on the seeds of the cones . . . in September it collects in small flocks, which fly from tree to tree making a chattering noise.'

The Cree name was given by Richardson as *pemmoo-koo-chae-shees* from *pemu,* twisted, and *koot* or *kootay,* nose.

Sharp-tailed Grouse, *Pedioecetes phasianellus.* Hood's legend used the fur-trader's usual name of 'pheasant' for this fine game bird and gave its length as 1 foot, 9 inches. Richardson said that 'it abounds on the outskirts of the Saskatchewan plains and is found throughout the woody districts of the fur-countries.' Richardson described how the grouse dances wore the grass quite bare in a circle of fifteen to twenty feet in diameter. In 1890, Ernest E. Thompson [Seton] was to remark that 'the whole performance reminds one so strongly of a Cree dance as to suggest the possibility of its being the prototype of the Indian exercise'.

Hearne and Richardson gave the Cree name as *aw-kis-cow.*

Yellow-headed Blackbird, *Xanthocephalus xanthocephalus.* This was the only summer resident included by Hood in this painting of winter birds. The specimens collected by Hood and Richardson, including the male depicted here, were an undescribed species. The specimens were carried to York Factory by the fur company canoes, with all the portages that trip entails, and shipped to London. Unfortunately, as Richardson complained, 'they were irrecoverably lost after their arrival in London; and were not, therefore, described by Mr. Sabine in the narrative of Sir John Franklin's first Journey.' The chance to publish the first description of this new species in 1823 was thereby lost as well.

The priority of scientific description of the yellow-headed blackbird thus passed to another specimen, also collected in May of 1820, by the expedition of Major Stephen H. Long in what is now Nebraska.

Long's Rocky Mountain Expedition, with Thomas Say as zoologist, was sent to ascertain the nature of the western borders of the Louisiana Purchase, acquired from France in 1803. Their specimen of the yellow-headed blackbird was described by C. L. Bonaparte in 1825 and 1826 and thus became the scientific 'type specimen', usurping that honour from the specimen here painted by Hood.

Richardson reported that the 'Saffron-headed Maizebird' arrived on the Saskatchewan River about 20 May and was more numerous than its associate, the red-winged blackbird (the reverse of the modern situation), committing 'even greater havoc in the corn-fields'. No doubt the small plot of perhaps just a few acres of wheat or barley was most vulnerable to the depredations of these birds.

The Cree name for blackbird was given by Richardson as *chuck-chuck-kaioo* and by Faries as *chuckukuyoo*. R. Gallernault says that this name applies to all species of blackbirds, including even the cowbird.

Black-backed Three-toed Woodpecker, *Picoides arcticus*. Hood's legend simply said 'woodpecker, length 1 ft. 1 in.' This was another undescribed species, but again, unfortunately, it was not described by Sabine in the appendix to the journal of the first Franklin expedition. Perhaps this specimen, too, was lost.

Thomas Drummond, Richardson's assistant naturalist on the second Franklin expedition, journeyed to the headwaters of the Athabasca River near Jasper and collected a male of this species sometime between the fall of 1825 and the spring of 1827. This second specimen was then described by Swainson and Richardson in *Volume Two, The Birds*, of *Fauna Boreali-Americana*. The type locality is the Athabasca headwaters—not Cumberland House, Saskatchewan, as would have been the case had someone published a description based on the first painting by Hood.

The Cree name for the smaller woodpeckers is *paupastuow*, as given for the downy woodpecker by Richardson, spelled *papastao* by Faries. It means 'spotted' or 'speckled', referring to the white spots and bars on the otherwise black downy and hairy woodpeckers.

Black-capped Chickadee, *Parus atricapillus*. Hood called this a 'Reed Sparrow, length five inches'. Richardson pointed out its close similarity to the tits of Britain and noted that 'its loose plumage, like that of the Canadian Jay, is well qualified for its protection in the severe arctic winters'. He found that it was 'one of the most common birds in the fur-countries, a small family inhabiting almost every thicket'.

Richardson gave its Cree name as *peecheh-keeskaeshees*, which R. Gallernault translates loosely as 'a small being inside of a body'. This name was rendered by Faries as *kichekanases*. Further south, the Crees render its name, derived from its call, as *chikomeses* (Faries) and tell a long, involved legend where by the chickadees tell Wiskejak that he is eating his scab: *omicimeechow*, the chickadee seems to be saying in Cree.

Snow Bunting, *Plectrophenax nivalis*. Hood called this the Snowbird and gave its length as 6³/₄ inches. Richardson stated that they 'winter within the limits of the fur-countries...in large flocks'...[and linger] 'about the Forts and open places, picking up grass-seeds, until the snow becomes deep; and it is only during the months of December and January that it retires to the southward of the Saskatchewan'.

Richardson gave the Cree name as *sheegun-peetheesees*. This might be derived from *see-kwun* 'spring' and *peyases* or *peethaysees* 'little bird', suggesting that its first return in large flocks was the very first promise of spring.

Hoary Redpoll, *Acanthis hornemanni*. This chickadee-sized, red-capped and rather pale little bird was also called 'snowbird' by Hood; it is obviously a redpoll. The large amount of white at its rump is good evidence that it is a hoary redpoll, depicted some twenty-three years before the Danish naturalist, C. Holboell, described a Greenland specimen as a new species separate from the common redpoll. Birds of this size, collected by the blunderbusses of the day, were often largely demolished by the shot, leaving only an ill-assorted collection of feathers for the artist to portray.

14. Winter Birds at Cumberland House No. 2   January 1820

Individual paintings have been cut out and pasted on a background of dull grey. The following five species are represented:

Black-billed Magpie, *Pica pica*. A male and female magpie were caught in traps at Cumberland House on 10 November 1819. When their skins reached England, Joseph Sabine realized that they were somewhat different from the magpies in Europe. He described them in the Zoological Appendix to Franklin's *Journey 1819-22* (pp. 671-72) as '*Corvus hudsonius*, Hudson's Bay Magpie. A new and hitherto undescribed species'. The Cumberland magpies had a smaller body but longer tail, with a loose tuft of greyish and white feathers on the back. Later naturalists considered the North American bird to represent only a subspecies, now called *Pica pica hudsonia* (Sabine), and the specimen pictured here by Hood is thus recognized as the type specimen for this North American subspecies, with Cumberland House its type locality. Richardson said, 'It does not entirely quit the banks of the Saskatchewan even in winter.'

The Cree name as given by Richardson was *ootaw-kee-askee*, rendered by Lacombe as *apistikakakis (apisti* 'small' and *kakakiw* 'crow'; *kakakiw* in turn is derived from the 'caw caw' call of the crow).

Evening Grosbeak, *Hesperiphona vespertina*. Hood depicts a female which he calls 'Grey Grosbeak', and a male, 'Yellow Grosbeak'. This species was much more uncommon and restricted in the 1820s than it is today. Indeed, Hood's painting represents the first authentic record of this species anywhere.

In her article on the evening grosbeak in A. C. Bent's authoritative *Life Histories of North American Birds* (U.S. Nat. Mus. Bull. 237, I, 206-56), Doris Huestis Speirs states that it was first described by William Cooper in 1825, from a specimen shot 7 April 1823, by an Indian boy with a bow and arrow at Sault Ste. Marie, Michigan. Hood's record antedates this by three years; had a study skin been set back to England in 1820, Cumberland House would have claimed the priority as the type locality in place of Sault Ste. Marie. It is of interest that by the end of the nineteenth century, no evening grosbeak nest had yet been found, nor were there any summer sightings east of Manitoba. Since settlement, with maples, elms, and ash trees planted in cities and villages and on farmsteads, this species has increased in numbers and now wanders more widely. It has extended its range far to the east across Ontario and even into the forests of New Brunswick.

These specimens from the first Franklin expedition evidently failed to reach England, and on the second Franklin expedition Richardson was unable to obtain a specimen of the evening grosbeak. At his special request, J. P. Pruden, the Hudson's Bay Company factor at

Carlton House, finally obtained a male in 1829 and sent it to England. Swainson's watercolour of this specimen, the first published, appeared as figure 68 in *Fauna Boreali Americana*, volume 2, published in February 1832.

The Crees called it the *seesebasquit-pethaysish* or 'sugar-bird' because it frequented the maple groves along the North Saskatchewan. Lacombe gives 'maple sugar' as *sisipaskwat* and 'little bird' as *piyesis*. R. Gallernault indicates that *y* sounds of the plains Cree were often rendered as *th* by the woods Cree further north, hence *piyesis = petheesis*.

Robin, *Turdus migratorius*. This species was not actually a winter visitor, but was noted by Hood as one of the earliest residents to arrive in the spring. Widely distributed in early times, it was listed as 'very common' by Richardson. It has thrived with settlement, and is now more numerous in farmyards, towns, and cities than it is or was in the untouched forests.

Richardson gave its Cree name as *peepeechew*, spelled *pipitchiw* by Lacombe, *pipechao* by Watkins, and *pipichew* by Faries. This name is still used by the Crees today; it is one of relatively few songbirds to be singled out for a special name.

Willow Ptarmigan, *Lagopus lagopus*. Together with the ruffed grouse and the spruce grouse, the ptarmigan was included in the term 'partridge' by Hood. In 1819, ptarmigan appeared on 15 November at Cumberland House, where, according to Franklin, they were considered the infallible harbingers of severe weather. Members of the grouse family are not particularly strong fliers and the nearest ptarmigan nesting areas are on the barren lands of the Northwest Territories, 400 miles to the north. In most years of the 1800s, they came as far south as Carlton, Prince Albert, and Nipawin but they now reach the settled areas of Saskatchewan quite irregularly. The last big influx in the Nipawin area was in 1931-32, when they arrived 6 November. At Cumberland House, they still appear almost every winter, but often are not seen until January or even February. Three were sighted by the writer on an Audubon Christmas Bird Count at Cumberland House on 2 January 1971.

Richardson gave the Cree name as *wawpeethaeo* and Lacombe as *wabipihyew. (wapi* or *wapay* = white and R. Gallernault tells me that grouse (plural) is *peeyawouk* or *peethawouk).* Faries gives the name of *wapiyao.*

Pine Grosbeak, *Pinicola enucleator.* This winter wanderer, now fairly common, has also increased in numbers since the 1820s when Richardson listed it as 'scarce' and 'seldom seen'. It nests far to the north in the extreme northeast corner of Saskatchewan and in the Northwest Territories. The showy rosy males are very much in the minority in any flock, with the majority females and juveniles in drab plumage.

Richardson gave its Cree name as *wuskuneethow,* which R. Gallernault tells me means 'he goes around in circles', or 'he is here all the time'.

15. Waterfowl at Cumberland House No. 1   May 1820

Hood's two paintings of the waterfowl at Cumberland House are the first such habitat scenes from the western half of this continent.

Bufflehead, *Bucephala albeola.* The 'butterball' of the sportsman was 'extremely common' in the 1820s, though by the 1960s it was much less common than its close relative the Common Goldeneye. The bufflehead nests in hollow trees, which in many localities are less available now than they were in Hood's time. Where artificial nest-boxes are provided, the bufflehead will often use them. It was originally named 'buffalo-head' because of its disproportionately large head. A small duck, it is a swift flier and a deep diver. It is relatively unpalatable, not considered worth the expenditure of shot by an Indian or fur trader.

Hood reported its Cree name as *wappanowsheep* or 'conjuring duck', and in the legend to the painting gave its length as 1 ft. 2 in. *Sesep* or *sisib* was Cree for duck, while *wapanow* meant a kind of magician who made charms. Perhaps its resemblance to a magician, with its natty black-and-white dress, and its habit of rapid appearance and disappearance while diving, was an observation of the Europeans. On the other hand, it might be more logical to translate this as 'white-cheeked duck', from *wapi* 'white', *manaway* 'cheek', and *sisib* 'duck', since it is a duck with white cheeks.

Canvasback, *Aythya valisineria.* Richardson reported this duck to be common throughout the fur countries. After the advent of settlement, it decreased greatly in numbers, particularly as marshes were drained for agriculture. It is the most coveted American game bird and now sustains heavy hunting pressure, especially in the southern states where its wild rice diet improves its flavour.

Hood gave its Cree name as *missequyowawesheep* or 'long-necked duck', and its length as 2 ft. 3 in. Lacombe gives *misi* 'much', *kikweyaw*, 'his neck', and *sisib* 'duck'. R. Gallernault tells me it is now called the *takwokesip* or 'autumn duck' *(takwakin* = autumn).

Ruddy Duck, *Oxyura jamaicensis*. This unique little duck 'frequents the small lakes of the interior up to the 58th parallel' and was 'not uncommon' in the 1820s, according to Richardson. A sprightly, comical bird, with its white cheek patch, bright bill, and erect tail, it lays enormous eggs in relation to its size. Though a good table bird, it is not sought by many hunters.

Hood gave its Cree name as *sheham*, but gave no English equivalent. He said that its length was 18 inches.

Lesser Scaup, *Aythya affinis*. This is Hood's poorest representation, almost unrecognizable, with the head and neck disproportionately small. It was as common in the 1820s as it is today. Hood called this the *maskagosheep* or Marsh Duck and gave its length as 19 inches. Lacombe gives 'marsh' as *maskek* and 'duck' as *sisib*, while Watkins gives 'swamp duck' as *muskagoosip*, and Faries as *muskakosip*.

Pintail, *Anas acuta*. Hearne found this species with the mallard in 'vast multitudes' at Cumberland House when he founded the post in 1774. Richardson in the 1820s was much less impressed by its numbers and rated it below most of the other species of waterfowl, with the modest notation, 'not rare'. Since then it has learned to live in close proximity to man. In the past twenty years or so, increasing numbers have accompanied the mallards into the grain fields to feed.

Richardson gave its Indian name as *keeneego yaway-sheep*, but incorrectly attributed it to the Chipewyan rather than Cree Indians. The Cree name today is given by Faries as *kinikwuyoowawisip*, or 'long-necked duck'.

Shoveler, *Spatula clypeata*. Richardson found this duck, now often called 'spoonbill' by hunters, to be very common, especially near the Saskatchewan River in spring and fall. Its numbers have probably changed little since that time. It sieves small organisms from the mud, but due to the consequent flavour ranks low as a game bird.

Hood gave its Cree name as *athaguscowcoutayou* or 'broad-billed duck', and its length as 1 ft. 8 in. Watkins gave its Cree name as *ayukuskikootawisip*, and Faries as *uyukuskikotawisip*. *Ayakask* in Cree means 'very large' and *kootaw* or *coutayou* means 'nose', though this word is not given in Lacombe or Watkins. Richardson gave the shoveler's Cree name as *mimenick*, and Lacombe gives *miminik* as 'a type of duck'.

Red-breasted Merganser, *Mergus serrator*. This species, common on the lakes and rivers in the 1820s, is still relatively common today. It eats small fish but nowhere constitutes a threat to the fisherman. Its fishy taste makes it undesirable as a table bird.

Hood gave its Cree name as *oseeke* and Richardson gave its Saulteaux name as *kanwan-seek*. Faries gives *usik* for 'merganser'. Hood gave its English name as 'merganser' and its length as 1 ft. 10 in.

16. Waterfowl at Cumberland House No. 2   May 1820

Blue-winged Teal, *Anas discors*. This species was common north to the 58th parallel in the 1820s and in the 1960s was the most abundant of the surface-feeding ducks on the marshes south of Cumberland House. Further south, half of its breeding habitat, like that of the other dabbling ducks, has been destroyed by agriculture. It is a small but delicious table bird.

Hood gave its Cree name as *apistesheepiss*, from *apisti* 'small' and *sisib* 'duck'. The suffix *iss*, or correctly *sis*, also means 'small' or 'diminutive'. Richardson gave its Cree name as *cheesteh-qua-nan-weeshep* or 'Shoestring Duck', while Watkins gave its Cree name as *cheschisip*, and Faries as *upichisip*. Faries gives *chestinakoonayape* for 'shoestring'. Hood gave its length as 1 ft. 11 in.

Red-necked Grebe, *Podiceps grisegena*. Richardson listed this species as 'not common' in the 1820s, perhaps because the canoeists did not venture much into the marshy areas. A second specimen was collected by Richardson prior to his departure from Great Slave Lake on 26 May

1822, but none were collected by Richardson or Drummond on the second Franklin expedition in 1825-27. Since it was not included in Wilson's *American Ornithology* of 1808-14, Sabine presumed these specimens to be the first records of this species for North America. Today it is a fairly common, regularly distributed, but rather solitary species along bulrush shores. It has a wailing, loon-like cry.

Hood gave the Cree name as *sekepe* and gave its length as 1 ft. 11 in. Richardson spelled this name as *seekeep* and Lacombe as *sikkip*. The term appeared to encompass all species of grebes or 'hell-divers' and the coot or 'mud-hen', and Lacombe used it for *poule d'eau*, as well as the *sarcelle* or teal.

Mallard, *Anas platyrhynchos*. Hood called this simply the 'stock duck' as it was known in England, the bird from which domestic ducks originated. Hearne found it in 'vast multitudes' in 1774 and Richardson listed it as 'common' in the 1820s, while Roderick Ross MacFarlane listed it as 'very abundant' at Cumberland House in the 1890s. It is still one of the most common and widely distributed ducks in the area and the most sought-after game bird in Saskatchewan.

Hood gave no Cree name, but Richardson called it *ethin-neesew-sheesheep*, whereas Watkins called it *eyinesip*. *Eyinew* meant 'one of the human race', but this is not the connotation of 'human's duck' or 'domestic duck'. Instead it means 'man duck' or 'drake' in the sense of a well-dressed or well-plumed man; the Crees give this species name to both the drake and hen mallard.

Wood Duck, *Aix sponsa*. Richardson listed this species as rare, present only south of latitude 54°. Sabine, in preparing the Zoological Appendix to Franklin's first *Journey*, included it on the basis of Hood's drawing, which he evidently had seen. Another specimen was collected by Richardson at Cumberland House in May 1827. It remains rare to this day at Cumberland House and some thirty miles south of there on the Carrot River, the only localities in Saskatchewan where it may occasionally be seen in summer. Chief Factor Roderick Ross MacFarlane found a nest with one egg in a hollow tree near Cumberland House in early June, 1890, and forwarded it to the Smithsonian Institution in Washington, D. C., one of only two Saskatchewan nesting records.

Hood gave its Cree name as *nosesesheep*, but Lacombe gives *noses* as 'female' and *nosesib* as 'female duck'. Faries spells this *noosasip*.

Hood gave its length as 1 ft. 5^{1}/$_{2}$ in.

17. Prince of Wales striking against the Rocks   7 August 1819

The becalmed ship is being towed clear of the promontory by its small boat, after being carried by the ebb tide against the rocky shore and intervening ice floes.

18. Prince of Wales and Eddystone trading with Esquimaux   13 August 1819

Hood describes this episode of trading with the Esquimaux people from the Upper Savage Islands in Hudson Straits in chapter 1 of his journal. The Eskimos have come miles from land in their small kayaks and large umiaks on this calm day.

19. Trout Falls and Portage   September 1819

Here the men were dragging the heavy York boat up the sixteen-foot-high rocky incline. This original painting by Hood portrays realistically the men's already shabby clothing. Unfortunately when Edward Finden prepared the engraving of this painting for publication in Franklin's journal, he saw fit to 'improve' the appearance by adding neat and tidy coats or vests.

20. Expedition crossing Lake Prosperous   3 August 1820

This painting by Hood was published in Franklin's *Journey to the Shores of the Polar Sea 1819-22*. However, the engraver made a number of changes in the published version. These have detracted from the authenticity that pervades the original, depicted here, where the rock dominates imposingly, the trees are more realistically irregular, and the motley group of birchbark canoes and their rather untidily dressed occupants are more prominent in the foreground.

21. An Evening View of [Little] Marten Lake.   29-30 August 1820

Again, the engraver made some changes in this view of Little Marten Lake. The barren foreground, the foggy shoreline merging with the clouds in the background, the stance of the caribou, and the nondescript clothing of the men all combine to make the original painting seem more genuine than the stylized version published by the engraver.

22. Fort Enterprize   September 1820

This painting by Hood appears to look down the valley of the Snare River. Thus it gives a very different vista from Back's painting from the foot of Winter Lake, with the fort on the hill at a distance, which was published in Franklin's journal. Back's was painted about eight months later, when the snows were beginning to melt, on 13 May 1821. Hood's painting shows the log buildings and an associated tent-like structure to excellent advantage.

23. Birds at Fort Enterprize   1821

These, the last-known completed works by Robert Hood, were painted in the winter of 1820-21. They are part of a single flight scene, evidently painted on a single large sheet.

Canada Goose, *Branta canadensis.* This specimen had a length of 2 ft. 5 in. and a wingspread of 5 ft. 2 in. Neither this nor any other example of this species was brought home by the first Franklin expedition, no doubt simply because it was so common and well known. At Cumberland House in 1820, Hood first observed geese on 10-12 April and at Fort Enterprize in 1821, on 12-14 May. The name Hood gave for this species was that used throughout the Northwest, 'bustard', from the French *outarde.* When settlers first arrived in New France, this large goose reminded them of the great bustard of Europe, even though they are quite dissimilar.

The Cree name given by Richardson was *neescah* or *mistehay-neescah. Mistahi* means much or many, here used in the sense of 'large' or 'big'—'the big goose'. Lacombe and Watkins spelled this *niska* and Faries, *nisku.*

Old-Squaw Duck, *Clangula hyemalis.* Richardson, following the usage of Pennant, called this the 'Long-tailed Duck', while the Hudson's Bay residents called it 'Old Wife' or 'Swallow-tailed Duck'.

Richardson wrote of the old-squaw as follows: 'The long-tailed duck is one of the most clamorous of the tribe, and is celebrated in the songs of the Canadian voyageurs, by the name of *caccawee* . . . [it] feeds principally on the sea; they pass over the interior of the continent, however, in their migrations, occasionally lighting upon the rivers and lakes to feed upon insects. In 1821, they passed Fort Enterprize in latitude 64°30′ on their way to the shores of the Arctic sea, in small numbers, on the 24th and 25th of May.'

Hood gave the Copper Indians' name for this species as *hankghallay*.

Common Scoter, *Oidemia nigra*. This is the only scoter without a white patch on its wing or head. Hood gave the length of this specimen as 1 ft. 5 in. and its wingspread as 2 ft. 5½ in. It is a subarctic bird and is to be expected at Fort Enterprize, although its breeding range is unmapped since there are definite nesting records for only three Canadian localities.

Hood said it was 'called by the Copper Indians, *touettannatjinny*'. Richardson gave the Cree name for scoter as *cuscusitatum*.

Snow Goose, *Chen caerulescens*. Hood's specimen was 2 ft. 3 in. in length and had a wingspan of 5 ft. 0 in. Hood used the French name of *Oie de neige*, quite as appropriate as the modern French name of *L'Oie blanche*. Richardson found that it bred in great numbers on the barren grounds and he preserved a male killed at Fort Enterprize on 1 June 1821. Hood's painting of Marten Lake, 29-30 August 1820, shows a flock of this species taking wing up a shaft of sunlight breaking through the clouds (pl. 21).

The blue goose, formerly considered to be a separate species, has been shown by recent studies to be merely a colour phase of the snow goose.

The Cree name was *waewae-oo* or *wapaw-waeoo*, according to Richardson, or *wehwew*, according to Lacombe—imitations of the call of the bird. Other Indian tribes arrived at similar names in the same manner, including the Ojibway *wewe* and the Chinook *wawa*; this is also the origin of the modern sportsman's name of 'wavey'.

Eskimo Curlew, *Numenius borealis*. Hood gave this its French name of *Les Courlis*; his specimen measured 1 ft. 2½ in. in length with a wingspan of 2 ft. 3 in. On 13 June 1821, on the journey to the Arctic Ocean from Fort Enterprize, Richardson discovered one of these curlews 'hatching on three eggs on the shore of Point Lake'. When he approached the nest, 'she ran a short distance, crouching close to the ground, and then stopped to observe the fate of the object of her cares'. This was the first nest ever recorded for this species, then abundant in migration through the Mississippi and Atlantic flyways.

Later, between 1862 and 1866, Chief Factor Roderick Ross MacFarlane found them breeding abundantly on the barren grounds east of the Anderson River. He collected thirty sets of eggs and commented: 'Among the many joyous bird notes which greet one while crossing these [barren] grounds, especially on a fine sunshiny morning, none seemed more familiar or pleasanter than the prolonged mellow whistle of the Esquimaux Curlew.' The Copper Indians, according to Richardson, believed that this species betrayed the approach of strangers and thus foiled some of their stealthy attacks on their Eskimo neighbours. Prior to 1900, the Eskimo curlew suffered a very marked decline, probably due to excessive shooting in migration. From 1945 to 1959, they were thought to be extinct, but a very few individuals have since been sighted in migration.

Richardson gave the Cree name as *weekee-meneesew*; this word means 'sweet grass' in Cree, according to R. Gallernault.

Common Loon, *Gavia immer*. The length of this specimen was 2 ft. 3 in. and its wingspan 4 ft; it is evidently depicted diving under water. Richardson mentioned his experiences as follows: 'They breed on the shores of small lakes, laying two eggs at a time. Their cry is loud, has a peculiarly hollow and melancholy tone, and when often repeated is said to portend rain. The Canadian voyageurs never fail to make a loud hooting noise when this bird passes, for the purpose of rendering it, as they say, foolish. It is certain that it is thus frequently induced to fly in circles round the canoe, and often attracted within gun-shot. In water, they are watchful, and dive so instantaneously, that it is difficult to shoot them....They arrive in that season when the ice of the lakes continues entire, except, perhaps, a small basin of open water where a rivulet happens to flow in, or where the discharge of the lake takes place. When the birds are observed to alight in these places, the hunter runs to the margin of the ice, they instantly dive, but are obliged after a time to come to the surface to breathe, when he has an opportunity of shooting them. In this way, upwards of twenty were killed at Fort Enterprize in the spring of 1821, in a piece of water only a few yards square.' One of these birds was no doubt the one drawn by Hood.

The Cree name was given by Richardson as *eithinnew-moqua*, by Watkins as *moak* or *moakwa* and by Lacombe as *makwa*. (See Mallard for a discussion of *ethinew*).

24. Canadian Fish   Fort Enterprise   1821

These meticulous drawings, almost photographic in detail, are a fine example of Hood's skill as an artist. They are from top to bottom:

Lake Trout. *Salvelinus namaycush.* This fish, drawn at the scale of half an inch to a foot, was caught in the Snare River as it left Winter Lake at Fort Enterprize, in May 1822. Richardson considered this conspecific with the English Common Trout, *Salmo fario,* and stated that specimens weighed up to 40 or even 60 pounds. 'The Canadian voyageurs are fond of eating it raw, in a frozen state, after scorching it for a second or two over a quick fire, until the scales can be easily detached, but not continuing the application of the heat long enough to thaw the interior. The stomach when boiled is a favourite morsel with the same people.' It normally inhabits only lakes with a depth greater than fifty feet, but Hood mentioned it as occurring at Rock House on the Hayes River in spawning time in September and October.

The Crees gave it the name of *nammecoos* or *namaycush,* hence the unique use of a Cree word as a scientific Latin name. This was spelled *namekus* by Lacombe and *numakoos* by Watkins.

Whitefish, *Coregonus clupeaformis.* Richardson described in detail a specimen taken at Pine Island Lake (Cumberland Lake), Cumberland House in 1819-20, together with the following notes:

'Several Indian hordes mainly subsist upon it, and it forms the principal food at many of the fur posts, for eight or nine months of the year,–the supply of other articles of the diet being scanty and casual. Though it is a rich, fat fish instead of producing satiety it becomes daily more agreeable to the palate; and I know, from experience, that though deprived of bread and vegetables, one may live wholly upon this fish for months, or even years, without tiring . . . . The mode of cooking the *Attihawmeg* is generally by boiling . . . . The Copper Indians strike the fish through holes cut in the ice, using a very ingenious fish-gig, constructed of rein-deer horns.'

Hood gave the Cree name as *attickameg*, Richardson as *attihaw-meg*, Lacombe as *atikkamek*, Watkins as *utikoomak*, and Faries as *utikumak*.

Round Whitefish, *Prosopium cylindraceum quadrilaterale*. Called the Round Fish by Hood, it was found by the expedition in Winter Lake and off the mouth of the Coppermine River. It is also illustrated opposite page 204 in Volume III of *Fauna Boreali-Americana*. A new form, not previously described, Richardson gave it the scientific name of *quadrilaterale* because its body was less compressed than that of the lake whitefish of the genus *Coregonus*, mentioned above. This is probably the type specimen that was drawn by Hood, and the type locality is Fort Enterprize.

1. A VIEW OF STROMNESS JULY 1819

2. THE HUDSON'S BAY COMPANY FLEET 31 JULY 1819

3. LIKENESSES OF ESQUIMAUX AUGUST 1819

Atatoo

Sasasis

Quatoo

4. LIKENESSES OF BOIS BRÛLÉS FEBRUARY 1820

5. WOLVERENE CUMBERLAND HOUSE 2 FEBRUARY 1820

6. LYNX CUMBERLAND HOUSE APRIL 1820

7 FISHER CUMBERLAND HOUSE APRIL 1820

S. BUFFALO BULL MAY 1820

9. DOE MOOSE PASQUIA HILLS 3 APRIL 1820

10. OTTER CUMBERLAND HOUSE 3 MARCH 1820

11. ERMINE   CUMBERLAND HOUSE 1820

12. WHITE WOLF NEAR FORT ENTERPRIZE MARCH 1821

13. WINTER BIRDS AT CUMBERLAND HOUSE NO. 1 1820

White-winged Crossbill   White-winged Crossbill   Sharp-tailed Grouse

Yellow-headed Blackbird   White-winged Crossbill   Snow Bunting

Black-backed Three-toed Woodpecker   Black-capped Chickadee   Hoary Redpoll

14. WINTER BIRDS AT CUMBERLAND HOUSE NO. 2 JANUARY 1820

Black-billed Magpie

Willow Ptarmigan

Evening Grosbeak (female)

Robin

Pine Grosbeak (male)

Evening Grosbeak (male)

15. WATERFOWL AT CUMBERLAND HOUSE NO. 1 MAY 1820

Bufflehead

Canvasback

Red-breasted Merganser

Pintail

Shoveler

Lesser Scaup

Ruddy Duck

18. WATERFOWL AT CUMBERLAND HOUSE NO. 2 MAY 1820

Red-necked Grebe   Mallard   Wood Duck

Blue-winged Teal

17. PRINCE OF WALES STRIKING AGAINST THE ROCKS 7 AUGUST 1819

18. PRINCE OF WALES AND EDDYSTONE TRADING WITH THE ESQUIMAUX 13 AUGUST 1819

19. TROUT FALLS AND PORTAGE SEPTEMBER 1819

20. EXPEDITION CROSSING LAKE PROSPEROUS 3 AUGUST 1820

21. AN EVENING VIEW OF MARTEN LAKE 29·30 AUGUST 1820

22. FORT ENTERPRIZE SEPTEMBER 1820

Common Scoter

Common Loon

Old-Squaw Duck

Eskimo Curlew

Canada Goose

Snow Goose

23. BIRDS AT FORT ENTERPRIZE 1821

Lake Trout

Whitefish

Round Whitefish　24. CANADIAN FISH　FORT ENTERPRIZE　MARCH 1821

The Men of The First Franklin Expedition

JOHN FRANKLIN, Lieutenant. Born 16 April 1786, at Spilsby, Lincolnshire. Six weeks before his fourteenth birthday Franklin entered the Navy and only three weeks later participated in the naval battle of Copenhagen on 2 April 1800, 'the greatest victory ever gained' by Nelson. He had his first taste of exploration when he served from 1801 to 1803 as midshipman under his cousin Captain Matthew Flinders, on a second exploration of the coastline of Australia. The attendant hazards of such explorations are of interest in comparison with later expeditions under Franklin's command. Of the eighty officers and men, eight drowned when their boat capsized and nine others died of scurvy just as they completed their trip. Many others were invalided and a few elected to remain in Australia, so, when their ship, the *Investigator*, was pronounced unseaworthy, only twenty-two officers and men took passage for England on the *Porpoise*. She and her sister ship were then wrecked on an unknown reef in the Torres Strait between Australia and New Guinea, and the surviving crew camped on a sandy reef. They were saved by Flinders and twelve men who travelled 759 miles in a lifeboat to Port Jackson (Sydney) to obtain help.

On his return to England with a squadron of East India merchantmen from Canton, Franklin next joined the *Bellerophon*. He participated in the Battle of Trafalgar on 21 October 1805, when the *Bellerophon* sustained the loss of 28 killed and 127 wounded. Other

JOHN FRANKLIN

experiences during the Napoleonic wars included blockade duty between Portugal and Brazil and two battles with Americans at the mouth of the Mississippi in 1814-15. In 1818, Franklin commanded the *Trent*, under Commander Buchan in the *Dorothea*, in an attempt to sail north from Spitzbergen to the pole, but they were turned back by pack ice at 80°34′.

In 1819-22, Franklin was in command of the overland arctic expedition that has been the subject of this book. During it he was promoted to commander and after it, to captain. In 1825-27 he commanded a second expedition of the same nature, and his party explored 350 miles of new arctic coastline west of the Mackenzie River.

For his achievements he received the Paris Geographical Society's gold medal, was knighted on 29 April 1829, and received the honorary degree of D.C.L. from Oxford on 1 July 1829.

From 1830 to 1833 Franklin served in the Mediterranean in command of the *Rainbow*. He was governor of Van Diemen's Land

(Tasmania) from 1837 to 1843. Next he was appointed to the command of the famous but ill-fated attempt to complete the Northwest Passage by ship, from east to west. The *Erebus* and *Terror* sailed from England 19 May 1845 and were last seen 26 July. Franklin died 11 June 1847, his ships frozen in the ice north of King William Island. His men before they died did in fact complete the Northwest Passage by foot; in Richardson's famous words, 'They forged the last link with their lives.'

JOHN RICHARDSON, Surgeon and naturalist. Born 5 November 1787 at Dumfries, Scotland. Two days before his thirteenth birthday, Richardson was apprenticed for three years to his uncle, James Mundell and then to his successor, Samuel Shortridge, both surgeons in Dumfries. His winters were spent attending classes in medicine, Greek, chemistry, and natural history at the University of Edinburgh.

JOHN RICHARDSON

His fifth and sixth years of medical training were spent as house surgeon or intern at the Dumfries and Galloway Infirmary, and the seventh and final year was spent in Edinburgh. On 7 February 1807, at only 19 years of age, he passed his examination for the surgeon's diploma and then went to London where he passed the examinations of the Royal College of Surgeons of London. He was promptly appointed assistant surgeon to the *Nymphe* and his successive appointments were as acting surgeon and then surgeon, off the Denmark coast and in the blockade of Portugal, followed by a voyage to Africa and another to Quebec and then two years in the Mediterranean in the blockade of Toulon. In 1814 his duties brought him again to Halifax and Montreal as surgeon to the first battalion of Royal Marines who in early 1815 occupied an island off the coast of southern Georgia.

In peacetime, unsatisfied with his ordinary medical degree, Richardson studied another two years and wrote a thesis for the higher degree of Doctor of Medicine, which he received in 1817. On 3 April 1819, he was appointed as surgeon and naturalist to the first Franklin expedition, the subject of this book.

In 1825-27, he held the same position on the second Franklin expedition and led the party that explored over five hundred miles of arctic coastline between the Mackenzie and the Coppermine. His natural history contributions resulted in the publication of the *Flora Boreali-Americana* and four volumes of the *Fauna Boreali-Americana.*

In 1828, Richardson returned to his post as surgeon to the marines at Chatham and became chief medical officer of the new Melville Hospital. Early in 1838 he became physician to the Royal Naval Hospital at Haslar and in August 1840 was promoted to the rank of Inspector of Hospitals.

In 1848, Richardson and Dr. John Rae travelled from New York to Sault Ste. Marie by steamer and then in the fastest canoe travel on record, to the mouth of the Mackenzie in one summer, as one of the search parties for the missing Franklin expedition.

Richardson was knighted in 1846, made Companion of the Bath in 1850, received the Royal Medal of the Royal Society of London in 1856 and the degree of LL.D. from Trinity College, Dublin, in 1857. He died 5 June 1865.

GEORGE BACK. Midshipman. Born at Stockport in Cheshire in 1796. He entered the Navy as a midshipman on the *Arethusa* in 1808 and took part in the destruction of the batteries at Lequeitio in northern Spain. In 1809 he was taken prisoner by the French at Deba and at age thirteen was still small enough to be carried in one of the panniers of a sumpter mule across the Pyrenees. While a prisoner at Verdun, he studied mathematics, French, and drawing. In the winter of 1813-14, after Napoleon had lost the battle of Leipzig and the Duke of Wellington was advancing on Paris from the south, Back travelled on foot through France and reached England. He then served as a mid-

GEORGE BACK

shipman with the American coastal blockade. In 1817, he was appointed admiralty mate of the *Bulwark,* and the next year he served under John Franklin on the *Trent* in the arctic voyage north of Spitzbergen.

In 1819-22 he served on the first Franklin expedition. He became a lieutenant during this journey. After service in the West Indies in 1823 he then rejoined Franklin for the second expedition, accompanying him on his journey west of the Mackenzie.

In 1827 Back was promoted to the rank of commander. In 1833, he was placed in command of an expedition in search of the missing northwest passage expedition of John Ross; he left Montreal in late April 1833, wintered at the east end of Great Slave Lake and in 1834 was the first white man to descend the Great Fish River, now called the Back River, to the Arctic Ocean. On his return to England he received the Geographical Society's gold medal, and was promoted to the rank of captain, by order-in-council, an honour which only William IV had previously received.

In 1836 he commanded the *Terror* on a naval expedition to Repulse Bay, with the hope of completing the survey of the arctic coastline to the Back River and on to Cape Turnagain. Before it reached Repulse Bay, his ship became imprisoned in the ice and for ten months drifted back down the east shore of Southampton Island.

He retired as a semi-invalid on half-pay, but was knighted in 1839. He was a Fellow of the Royal Society and Vice-President of the Geographical Society, and also received a D.C.L. degree. He was promoted to the rank of admiral in 1857. He died 23 June 1878.

ROBERT HOOD. Midshipman†* The subject of this book.

JOHN HEPBURN. Seaman (1789-?). During the Napoleonic wars, Hepburn had been taken prisoner by an American privateer, which transferred him to a French trading vessel. He was one of only two ordinary seamen assigned to the first Franklin expedition.

Richardson felt he owed his life to this faithful, steady, reliable seaman on the gruelling trek back from the Arctic in 1821. At the most difficult times, the indefatigable Hepburn could be counted on to cut firewood and gather lichens. On 11 October, only Hepburn had the strength to make an extra trip to bring the tent forward to Richardson's new campsite. On 28 October he repeatedly assisted Richardson, who fell down no less than twenty times in a few hundred yards' struggle over large stones. The ptarmigan he shot on 29 October was the first flesh Franklin had tasted in thirty-one days.

Franklin acknowledged this as follows: 'And here I must be per-

* † = deceased during this journey.

JOHN HEPBURN

mitted to pay the tribute, which is due to the fidelity, exertion and uniform good conduct in the most trying situations, of John Hepburn, an English seaman, and our only attendant, to whom in the latter part of our journey we owe, under Divine Providence, the preservation of the lives of some of our party.'

At the conclusion of the expedition, John Hepburn was 'deservedly rewarded with a permanent situation in one of the dockyards', later described as a 'comfortable situation'. He did not accompany the second Franklin expedition in 1825-27, but when Richardson proposed a search expedition for John Ross in 1832, he had plans to take John Hepburn to care for the winter house.

At the age of sixty-two, probably for sentimental reasons, Hepburn was taken with Lieut. René Bellot in his search for Franklin in 1851-52. Bellot's journal contains a number of interesting stories told him by this gossipy old sailor. Hepburn told Bellot about the wolves at Cumberland House, gave a first-hand account of starvation on the barrens, and told how a Miss Macaulay at Athabasca was a better shot than he, 'whose address Sir John Franklin extols.'

An island, a lake and a river have been named for Hepburn.

SAMUEL WILKS. British seaman. Wilks accompanied the expedition from York Factory as far as Cumberland House. 'Unequal to the fatigue of the journey', he was discharged at Cumberland House in the spring of 1820 and returned to England.

THREE ORKNEYMEN hired at Stromness and one hired at York Factory accompanied the expedition only to Cumberland House. They were then sent back to York Factory to obtain more provisions for Cumberland House.

FOUR 'ENGLISHMEN', at least three of whom were Orkneymen and one perhaps an American, hired at Cumberland House, accompanied the expedition as far as Fort Chipewyan.

WILLARD-FERDINAND WENTZEL. Clerk in charge of the North West Company post at Fort Providence.

Wentzel was probably the son of Adam Wentzel, a Norwegian merchant in Montreal, and Endemia Grout, who were married in Montreal in 1779. He entered the North West Company service in 1799. He then served on the Mackenzie River and at Great Bear Lake. His published letters reveal him to be a literate and intelligent man, and Franklin rated him 'an excellent musician'.

Wentzel said that he had 'so far succeeded as to have collected the choicest hunters of the Red Knife tribe, as well as the most powerful leaders and knowing men amongst them', to aid the Franklin expedition. He later supervised the construction of Fort Enterprize, accompanied George Back as far as Fort Providence on his winter hike of more than 1100 miles to Fort Chipewyan, and in 1821 accompanied the expedition on their 668-mile journey to the mouth of the Coppermine.

On the return from the Coppermine, with the Indians and four voyageurs, Wentzel's party went eleven days without food. Humpy, Akaitcho's brother, failed to keep his promised rendezvous with them at Point Lake. When Wentzel finally encountered Humpy, the Indian hunters were already without ammunition, starving and forced to convert old axes into ball. Wentzel promised to send them ammunition from Fort Providence, but found the fort destitute and could send nothing. Next, three of Humpy's hunters drowned in Lac la Martre and the remainder were literally incapacitated by grief.

Wentzel carried on slowly southward with the official dispatches. He did not reach Fort Chipewyan until 25 October and he then remained there for the winter. Wentzel did not meet the expectations of the expedition in making sure the Indians had provisions ready at Fort Enterprize for their return in the fall of 1821. For this he was rather bitterly criticized. Since Wentzel was then on the defensive, it is hard to assess how much truth there was in his later allegations concerning the 'errors and want of conduct' of the officers. Wentzel spent more than a year in the service of the expedition, without specific promise of recompense, but in March 1823 Franklin ordered that £600 be paid to him.

Wentzel later served the amalgamated Hudson's Bay Company at Fort Simpson, 1822-24; Fort Chipewyan, 1824-25; and Mingan, Montreal department, 1827-29, and then retired. He died of cholera in 1832.

THE INTERPRETERS

PIERRE ST. GERMAIN. Interpreter for the Copper Indians.

Hired at Fort Resolution 24 July 1820, St. Germain proved to be the best hunter and the most intelligent interpreter, and had the most influence with the Indians. He accompanied Back and Hood to the Coppermine River (Point Lake) 29 August–10 September 1820. When supplies arrived at Fort Providence, he led eight voyageurs to get them, leaving 28 November 1820. Seven of them arrived back at Fort Enterprize on 15 January 1821 with two kegs of rum, one barrel of powder, sixty pounds of ball, two rolls of tobacco, and some clothing, each man carrying sixty to ninety pounds; St. Germain returned 27 January, bringing the two Eskimos, Augustus and Junius.

Strong, resourceful, practical, and a man of great stamina, he ferried Franklin across Belanger Rapids on 14 September. The disastrous and dispiriting nine-day delay in crossing the icy Coppermine River finally ended on 4 October 1821 when he completed a little cockleshell canoe out of the fragments of painted canvas in which the officers wrapped their bedding. The next day he was chosen to go with Back, Beauparlant, and Solomon Belanger to obtain the assistance expected at Fort Enterprize. When the Fort was deserted, they went on a further day's travel to Roundrock Lake, where they camped from 14 to 30 October. It was St. Germain who reached Akaitcho's camp on 3 November, sending them with food to the dying men at Fort Enterprize.

JEAN BAPTISTE ADAM. Interpreter for the Copper Indians.
Adam was hired by Mr. Wentzel and was waiting for the expedition on 29 July 1820 at Fort Providence. His hunting ability was second only to that of St. Germain.

On the return journey he travelled with Franklin, reaching Fort Enterprize on 11 October. The next day he was absolutely incapable of rising without assistance and the others had to wait upon him. His extremities were swollen and he was fed a brew of lichens and soup made from the rancid bones of the previous year's rubble. On 30 October Dr. Richardson treated his edema by multiple small incisions in the lower legs, allowing much of the excess water to drain away from the tissues; and the next day he left his bed. On 5 November, Dr. Richardson's incisions again gave relief. By 7 November, Adam became so weak he could hardly speak; the arrival of the Indians that day was just in time to save his life.

THE HUNTERS

The Copper Indians offered peripheral support to the expedition, as their hunters provided essential caribou meat. Their numbers varied and at times more were present in one area than was advisable for efficient hunting; the concentration of expedition men was already too great for optimal 'living off the land'. In anticipation of the northward journey, at Fort Enterprize on 25 May 1821, there were collected no less than thirty hunters, thirty-one women and sixty children.

Their chief was Akaitcho, translated as Big Foot in English and Gros Pied in French, a man of wisdom and compassion. The expedition hired two guides, including old Kescarrah, the father of Greenstockings, and seven or eight hunters. Akaitcho, Kescarrah and five hunters accompanied the expedition to the mouth of the Coppermine, while wives, children and others accompanied them part way. They began their return on the morning of 18 July, a day and a half before Wentzel, who later caught up with them. One Indian, his wife and child, straggled behind on the journey and were presumed to have perished.

On 7 November 1821, it was Boudel-Kell, Crooked-Foot, and the Rat who brought the first relief to the dying men in Fort Enterprize, and the latter two stayed to nurse the men. Franklin acknowledged 'their tender sympathy in our distresses and the assistance they had so cheerfully and promptly rendered'.

THE ESKIMOS

AUGUSTUS, or *TATTANNOEUCK*, 'The Belly'. An Eskimo from the west shore of Hudson Bay, about two hundred miles north of Churchill. When Back arrived at Moose Deer Island fort on Great Slave Lake, on 10 December 1820, Augustus and Junius were living in a snow igloo. Presumably they had been there since freezeup, after being sent from Churchill by Hudson's Bay Company canoes. They arrived at Fort Enterprize on 27 January 1821 with Mr. Wentzel and St. Germain.

After the party crossed the Coppermine on the return journey, Augustus separated from the others yet found his way alone to Fort Enterprize. He left the fort with Benoit on 20 October and reached Akaitcho's camp by 3 November.

When Rev. John West, the first chaplain to the servants of the Hudson's Bay Company, visited Churchill in August 1822, he met John Franklin awaiting a ship home and conversed with Augustus. On West's next visit to Churchill, 21 July–12 August 1823, Augustus was the first to meet him, and acted as his interpreter.

AUGUSTUS

Augustus again served, with his friend Ooligbuk, during the second Franklin expedition, 1825-27, and was in the party that explored west of the Mackenzie. At Pillage Point, Augustus bravely went ashore alone to talk to forty armed Eskimos who had pillaged belongings from the expedition's boats.

In 1830, Augustus was sent on the brig *Montcalm* to Nicol Finlayson's new post at Fort Chimo, Ungava, arriving 13 September. His skills in hunting and fishing were mentioned many times by Finlayson, who acknowledged that he was 'a good interpreter, but a drunken sot.' Augustus was recalled from Fort Chimo at Captain George Back's request in 1833; his name does not appear in Finlayson's Journal after 25 May. He may have been on the brig *Beaver* which left Fort Chimo 30 July but did not arrive at York Factory until 9 September.

He 'expressed his determination to join [Back] and had actually walked from Hudson Bay with that affectionate intention', owing to his 'attachment and generous devotion', said Back. Augustus arrived at Fort Resolution on Great Slave Lake in mid-February 1834, after an extraordinary winter walk of at least 1,200 miles, perhaps accompanying the messenger carrying the 'winter packet' from York Factory. Augustus then set out on the last two hundred miles to Back's wintering place (Fort Reliance) with a Canadian voyageur and an Iroquois. They lost their way and returned to Fort Resolution leaving Augustus, without a gun, to carry on; he later retraced his steps but his body was found about twenty miles from Fort Resolution.

Augustus may be unique among Eskimos in having a species named in his honour. The Brown Elfin butterfly, a new species first collected at Cumberland House, probably by Dr. Richardson in 1827, was named *Callophrys augustinus.*

JUNIUS or *HOEOOTOEROCK*, 'The Ear'† An Eskimo companion of Augustus, who also arrived 27 January 1821 with Mr. Wentzel and St. Germain from Great Slave Lake. On 27 September, one day after the party reached the obstructing icy waters of the Coppermine, Junius strayed away and was not seen again. He was then two hundred miles from the nearest Eskimos and is presumed to have perished, though he was well equipped with ammunition, blankets, knives, and a kettle.

THE VOYAGEURS

LOUIS ST. JEAN†, foreman of one canoe, hired by Richardson at Cumberland House, drowned in Otter Rapids, 19 June 1820.

JEAN BAPTISTE BELLEAU One of the eight men who journeyed from Fort Enterprize on 28 November 1820 for further provisions. He was discharged at Moose Deer Island, Great Slave Lake, on 28 December 1820 by George Back, with Franklin's permission. 'He proved to be too weak to perform the duty of bowman which he had undertaken.'

EMANUEL COURNOYEE OR CONNOYER 'Much tormented by biliary calculi' and unable to work all winter, he was discharged from Fort Enterprize 17 April and sent down to Fort Providence.

JEAN BAPTISTE PARENT, JOSEPH FORCIER, PIERRE DUMAS, and *JOSEPH GAGNE* all accompanied the expedition to the mouth of the Coppermine, returning with W. F. Wentzel. They were eleven days without meat on the 334-mile return journey.

The remaining voyageurs, hired at Fort Chipewyan, some of whom had come from Cumberland House with Richardson and Hood, deserve special mention. They were the ones who accompanied the officers, courageously paddling the birchbark canoes along the unknown arctic shores and later carrying ninety-pound loads on their backs overland on the return journey. The officers carried the scientific instruments and collections, but the tents, ammunition, and even Franklin's blanket, were carried by the men. When we consider that they underwent great exertion, often with little food to sustain them, and that all but two of them gave their lives on an expedition whose purposes were beyond their comprehension, it seems only right to commemorate them, mentioning the few details that we know. Surely they are the unsung, forgotten heroes of this important expedition.

SOLOMON BELANGER, 'Belanger le gros'. Belanger was one of the strongest men with the expedition and one of two voyageurs to survive the full journey. In October 1820, he had accompanied George Back as far as Fort Providence, and returned to Fort Enterprize on 23 November, bearing the mail from England. He had walked continuously for the last thirty-six hours through a storm so severe that the Indians refused to accompany him. 'His locks were matted with snow, and he was incrusted with ice from head to foot.' Again on 17 April 1821, with J. B. Belanger, he took the expedition's mail to Fort Providence. The two men returned 28 April, taking only five days for the return trip, which was even longer than the stated 133 miles.

On 14 September 1821, he was the man immersed so long in the rapids of the Burnside River. On the return journey he accompanied Back, but nearly perished when he fell through the ice of Little Marten Lake on 7 October. They arrived at empty Fort Enterprize 9 October, but left two days later and camped less than a day's march to the southwest. On 14 October, he carried a message to Franklin at Fort Enterprize and then returned to Back on 18 October. It was not until 3 November that Belanger found tracks of Indians in the snow, leading four days later to the relief of the men in the deserted fort.

JOSEPH BENOIT. Franklin speaks of Benoit as the strongest of the voyageurs, yet he does not seem to have been one of his favourites. He tried unsuccessfully to cross the Coppermine 29 September on a makeshift raft of willow faggots. He reached Fort Enterprize in Franklin's party. On 20 October he set out with Augustus for Akaitcho's winter camp, possibly forty miles distant, which they seem not to have reached until 3 November. He was with the second relief party of Akaitcho's Indians that reached Fort Enterprize 15 November. He was the second survivor of the eleven voyageurs who made the difficult return journey from the Arctic.

MATHEW PELONQUIN, nicknamed *CREDIT*† On three occasions in September Credit was missing for a day or two. He next fell behind 6 October 1821, the day after taking his turn carrying the men's tent, exhausted and suffering from diarrhea. Richardson went looking for him, but Credit evidently had retraced his steps towards the previous evening's campfire, and was not seen again. He was probably the first to die.

REGISTE VAILLANT† A trained carpenter and the axeman of the party, Vaillant was the only one to whom the remaining axe could be entrusted after all the others were broken. He was left lying in the snow 6 October. Dr. Richardson went a mile and a half to encourage him, but as he returned from another half mile in search of Credit, Vaillant had progressed only a few yards. J. B. Belanger then went back to help him, but he was lying on his back incapable of being roused, and soon froze to death.

JEAN BAPTISTE BELANGER, 'Belanger le rouge'.† On 7 October, J. B. Belanger and Michel lagged far behind Franklin and appeared very exhausted when they reached the evening encampment after a walk of four and a half miles. On 8 October they told Franklin they would return to the tent of Richardson and Hood. Belanger left the fire two hours ahead of Michel, but failed to arrive.

IGNACE PERRAULT† Perrault impressed the officers with his self denial and kindness on 14 September when he presented each of them with a small piece of meat saved from his allowance. On 8 October, after walking a quarter of a mile in spite of weakness and 'dizzyness', he turned back to join Michel and Belanger. Franklin watched Perrault, carrying a gun and forty-eight balls, walk back until he reached the willows almost at Richardson's fire, from which smoke was still rising. When Michel produced the same gun on 10 October, he claimed to have been given it by Perrault prior to 8 October. Perrault must have perished on that day.

ANTONIO VINCENZA FONTANO† An Italian who had served in the de Meuron regiment of Swiss and German Protestants, Fontano came to Canada in the war of 1812. Lord Selkirk had recruited 140 of these men to convoy his boats to the Red River, in return for grants of land. Fontano was an exception to the rule that voyageurs were either French or Métis.

The second day after the expedition left Fort Enterprize, Fontano became lost; when found on 18 June, he was exhausted with anxiety and hunger. On 8 October, when he was 'seized with a fit of dizzyness and betrayed other symptoms of extreme debility', he spoke to Franklin of his father and begged that, should he survive, Franklin would assist his passage back to Italy. Fontano turned back from Franklin's party that day, about two miles beyond the prevous night's fire. He was walking tolerably well when last seen, but probably collapsed in the snow and perished.

GABRIEL BEAUPARLANT† In 1820-21 Beauparlant was the only voyageur who went all the way back to Fort Chipewyan with George Back, a journey on foot of well over 500 miles each way. This included a record time of ten days and four hours for the 260 to 300 mile leg from Moose Deer Island to Fort Chipewyan. He had been one of the stronger men in the advance party that reached Fort Enterprize on 9 October, leaving again with Back on 11 October. On 16 October while walking to the west end of Round Rock Lake, he complained of weakness and fell behind St. Germain and Back; he collapsed and froze to death in the snow.

MICHEL TEROHAUTE, an Iroquois† Michel left Franklin the morning of 8 October and reached Richardson's camp on 9 October. He carried a note from Franklin saying that he and J. B. Belanger were returning and would show Richardson a clump of spruce a mile further on, that would provide better shelter. Michel produced a hare and a ptarmigan he had shot that morning and Hood offered to share his buffalo robe with him at night. On 10 October, Michel asked the loan of a hatchet and next brought Richardson some meat which he said was from a wolf killed by the stroke of a caribou horn. On 20 October, after Michel and Hood had been arguing by the fire, Hood was found shot through the back of the head. On 23 October, Richardson and Hepburn, alone for the first time, discussed their suspicions and evidence against Michel; when Michel came up, Richardson shot him through the head.

JOSEPH PELTIER† Peltier reached Fort Enterprize with Franklin on 11 October. He nursed the weakest one, J. B. Adam, with the 'tenderest solicitude'. For the rest of the month, he was responsible for getting firewood and pounding the bones gathered from the ashes of the previous year's fires. On 27 October, to gain firewood, he helped tear down the partitions of the buildings twenty yards distant but became so weak he could scarcely lift his hatchet. As early as 20 October, he prophesied that he would die 1 November if help hadn't arrived by then. He called out 'Ah! le monde!' when he heard voices in the neighbouring room on 29 October, but imagine his disappointment when he found the voices were those of Richardson and Hepburn and not those of the hoped-for Indians. He gradually became weaker and died in Fort Enterprize, during the evening of 1 November, three days after the arrival of

Richardson and Hepburn. Franklin praised him for his 'cheerfulness, his unceasing activity and affectionate care and attentions.'

FRANÇOIS SAMANDRE or *SEMANDRE*† Samandre accompanied Franklin and Richardson to Point Lake, 9-15 September, 1820 and acted as cook on the journey from the Arctic. He reached Fort Enterprize with Franklin on 11 October. On 21 October, he would not get up and cried much of the day, but by 26 October he helped Franklin gather lichens and three days later helped carry in some wood. By 1 November, his throat was so sore he could not swallow and he died quietly in the early morning of 2 November.

Modern topographical maps and the official gazeteer of the Northwest Territories commemorate the names of these voyageurs. In addition to the rapids that bear the name of Belanger, lakes near the route of the Franklin expedition have been named for Beauparlant, Belanger, Benoit, Credit, Fontano, Michel, Peltier, Perrault, Samandre, and Vaillant. Other lakes in this area of the Northwest Territories have been named for a number of the Copper Indians, Akaiyessah, Akaitcho, Angelique, Baldhead, Boudelkell, Crooked Foot, Greenstockings, Humpy, Kescarrah, Little Forehead, Long Legs, and Roulante; three of the four voyageurs who returned with Wentzel from the mouth of the Coppermine, Dumas, Forcier, and Gagne; the two Eskimos, Augustus and Junius; the two interpreters, Adam and St. Germain; and Wentzel.

Selected Bibliography

BACK, GEORGE. *Narrative of the Arctic Land Expedition to the mouth of the Great Fish River and along the shores of the Arctic Ocean, in the years 1833, 1834 and 1835*. London: John Murray, 1836.

FRANKLIN, JOHN. *Narrative of a Journey to the Shores of the Polar Sea in the Years 1819, 20, 21 and 22*. London: John Murray, 1823. Reprint, Edmonton: M. G. Hurtig, 1969.

FRANKLIN, JOHN. *Narrative of a Second Expedition to the Shores of the Polar Sea in the Years 1825, 1826 and 1827*. London: John Murray, 1828.

HEARNE, SAMUEL. *A Journey from Prince of Wales's Fort in Hudson's Bay to the Northern Ocean in the Years 1769, 1770, 1771 & 1772*. London: A. Strahan & T. Cadell, 1795.

HEARNE, SAMUEL and PHILIP TURNOR. *Journals of Samuel Hearne and Philip Turnor between the years 1774 and 1792*. Ed. J. B. Tyrrell. Toronto: Champlain Society, 1934.

HOOKER, WILLIAM JACKSON. *Flora Boreali-Americana; or, the Botany of the Northern Parts of British America*. London: Henry G. Bohn, 1840. Reprint, Weinheim: J. Cramer, 1960.

HOUSTON, C. STUART and MAURICE G. STREET. *The Birds of the Saskatchewan River, Carlton to Cumberland*. Regina: Saskatchewan Natural History Society., 1959.

LACOMBE, REV. PÈRE ALBERT, O.M.I. *Dictionnaire de la Langue des Cris*. Montreal: Beauchemin et Valois, 1874.

MACKENZIE, ALEXANDER. *Voyages from Montreal on the River St. Laurence, through the Continent of North America, to the Frozen and Pacific Oceans in the Years 1789 and 1793*. London: T. Cadell, 1801.

MASSON, L. F. R. *Les Bourgeois de la Compagnie du Nord-Ouest, Récits de Voyages, Lettres et Rapports Inédits Relatifs au Nord-Ouest Canadien Publiés avec une Esquisse historique et des Annotations*. 2 vols. Quebec: A. Côté, 1889-90.

MORTON, ARTHUR S. *A History of the Canadian West to 1870-71*. Toronto: Thomas Nelson, 1939.

NEATBY, LESLIE H. *In Quest of the North West Passage*. Toronto: Longmans Green, 1958.

NEATBY, LESLIE H. *The Search for Franklin*. Edmonton: M. G. Hurtig, 1970.

PARRY, WILLIAM EDWARD. *Journal of a Voyage for the Discovery of a North-west Passage from the Atlantic to the Pacific Performed in the Years 1819-20 in His Majesty's Ships Hecla and Griper*. London: John Murray, 1821.

RICH, E. E. *The History of the Hudson's Bay Company 1670-1870*. 2 vols. London: Hudson's Bay Record Society, 1958-59.

RICHARDSON, JOHN. *Fauna Boreali-Americana, or the Zoology of the Northern Parts of British America. Part First, the Mammals*. London: John Murray, 1829.

RICHARDSON, JOHN. *Fauna Boreali-Americana, or the Zoology of the Northern Parts of British America. Part Third, the Fish*. London: Richard Bentley, 1836.

SIMPSON, GEORGE. *Journal of Occurrences in the Athabasca Department by George Simpson, 1820 and 1821 and Report*. Ed. E. E. Rich. Toronto: Champlain Society, 1938.

SWAINSON, WILLIAM and JOHN RICHARDSON. *Fauna Boreali-Americana, or the Zoology of the Northern Parts of British America. Part Second, the Birds*. London: John Murray, 1831 (Feb. 1832).

WATKINS, REV. E. A. *A Dictionary of the Cree Language*. London: Society for Promoting Christian Knowledge, 1865.

Index